Turning Points

Turning Points

Creating Strategic Change in Corporations

Charles J. Fombrun

McGraw-Hill, Inc.

New York   St. Louis   San Francisco   Auckland   Bogotá
Caracas   Lisbon   London   Madrid   Mexico   Milan
Montreal   New Delhi   Paris   San Juan   São Paulo
Singapore   Sydney   Tokyo   Toronto

Library of Congress Cataloging-in-Publication Data

Fombrun, Charles J.
    Turning points : creating strategic change in corporations /
Charles J. Fombrun.
        p.   cm.
    Includes bibliographical references and index.
    ISBN 0–07–021470–0 :
    1. Organizational change.   2. Strategic planning.   I. Title.
HD58.8.F65   1992
658.4′062—dc20   92–5230
                                                                CIP

1 2 3 4 5 6 7 8 9 0   DOC/DOC   9 8 7 6 5 4 3 2

ISBN 0-07-021470-0

*The sponsoring editor for this book was Karen Hansen, the editing supervisor
was Fred Dahl, and the production supervisor was Donald F. Schmidt. It was
set in Baskerville by Inkwell Publishing Services.*

Printed and bound by R. R. Donnelley & Sons Company.

For my parents, Marcel and Odette,
their ideas and ideals,
a continuing source of inspiration.

Contents

Phase 3. Energizing Strategic Change

9. Reshaping Corporate Cultures   **184**

10. Reinventing Structures   **205**

In Conclusion: Creating the Future   **228**

Preface

...current changes are likely to result in a transformation of unprecedented dimensions, a turning point for the planet as a whole.
FRITJOF CAPRA

We live in turbulent times. Rapid technological changes are creating dramatic dislocations in the workplace, altering what people do, the skills they do it with, how prized institutions like schools and unions function, and how business firms compete. At the same time, a political maelstrom is inclining the axis of dialogue away from conflict and toward cooperation, opening up new vistas for increased global integration of financial, product, and labor markets. These and other revolutionary developments are challenging many of our most cherished firms and institutions to rethink how they are organized to deliver quality products, offer valued services, provide satisfying employment, and maintain effective global citizenship. Increasingly, they signify pressure on leaders and managers to execute wrenching revisions of organizations, to carry out strategic change.

Reorientations of this sort are fundamentally creative acts: They require individuals and organizations capable of recognizing the limitations of an existing framework, conceiving alternatives, and mobilizing the necessary support to enact a vision. Like creative work in music, art, and literature, however, these visions do not derive from what came before. Rather, they result when leaders opt to violate the established framework of habits and traditions that inhibits change, and thereby transcend the status quo.

I dedicate this book to those creative spirits struggling to recreate our firms and institutions. Without them, our societal landscape would be littered with the decayed remains of all too many corporate and institutional dinosaurs. As the architects and prime movers of a global transformation—of how work gets done, how products are made, how the core functions of education, communication, and regulation are carried out—they stand guard, like so many St. Peters, at the pearly gates of our collective future. I admire their commitment, their patience, and their drive.

Likely as not, this book would not have been written were it not for many fortuitous events. One such event is my early work with Noel Tichy and Mary Anne Devanna at Columbia University, which led to a book, *Strategic Human Resource Management,* and sparked a continuing interest in how firms implement their strategies. Another resulted from the lively exchanges with Graham Astley and Andy Van de Ven (then at The Wharton School), which inspired a research program that addressed how firms plan and carry out cooperative strategies. Finally, joint research with Eric Abrahamson, Mark Shanley, Ed Zajac, and Stefan Wally provided continuing opportunity to explore and refine some of these ideas.

Writing takes time, however, and I benefited greatly from a sabbatical leave in 1990-1991 that freed me from teaching duties. The Stern School has been my intellectual home since 1984, and I have enjoyed many stimulating discussions with colleagues over the years, especially Bill Starbuck, Ari Ginsberg, and, more recently, Joe Porac, not to mention exposure to many more. A grant from the Salomon Brothers Center for a study of corporate reputations provided welcome respite from financial demands in 1991. Some of the interviews I conducted with prominent executives (to whom I promised confidentiality) certainly informed this book, and I admit to pirating time from that project for this one. The Center was indulgent, and I am grateful to its director Ingo Walter for his understanding.

It is unlikely I would have embarked on this writing project were it not for Ari Ginsberg, the friend and colleague with whom I cotaught an advanced course on Strategic Change in 1988 and 1989. Some of the ideas presented here jelled during lively encounters with various generations of Stern School leaders in training. Actually, Ari and I had intended to write this book together. As so often happens, however, time and other commitments got in the way. Surely we will try again.

I hope to have done justice to what I have learned from the many colleagues, managers, and students I have conversed with over the years. For those of their ideas I have distorted beyond recognition, I apologize, and hasten to point out to readers that I alone am to blame, just as I alone am accountable, of course, for any errors that may remain.

Charles J. Fombrun

Introduction:
Awakenings

All things must change
To something new, to something strange.
HENRY WADSWORTH LONGFELLOW

We are at a turning point. Increasingly we struggle with problems whose roots lie deep within a global matrix of interdependencies that binds together people and nations more closely than ever before. Proximity makes firms and institutions key intermediaries of our social encounters and provokes four sets of concerns about corporate life: the efficiency of our enterprises, their entrepreneurial abilities, the fairness of their actions, and their moral standing. Whether in the board rooms of our corporate behemoths, in the halls of Academe, in school assemblies, in union halls, or in the corridors of Congress; efficiency, entrepreneurship, equity, and ethics—the core components of every firm's performance—command the attention equally and increasingly of employees, managers, CEOs, politicians, regulators, students, and educators.

In recent years, heightened competition brought on by globalization, technological innovation, and the sudden collapse of the Soviet empire has motivated extensive discussion about the declining capabilities of many industries and the need to improve the *efficiency* with which firms produce and distribute goods and services. In companies the world over, this has meant greater interest in probing for new ways of managing employees, deploying resources, relating to suppliers, and organizing production, that can create cost savings and so enhance competitiveness against increasingly aggressive global players. In the United States, many

1

companies, burdened with huge debts incurred during the frenzied 1980s, have begun performing radical surgery on their ailing portfolios.

Simultaneously, rapid changes in technology have provoked firms into a wild scrambling for competitive position. Not long ago managers faced benign environments in which they could survive by making incremental adjustments to their operations. Now radical innovations threaten to wipe out established sources of advantage and force even the mightiest firms to worry about instilling an *entrepreneurial* mind set into their corporate cultures. No firm, large or small, has proven impervious to the far-reaching effects that developments in computerization, communication, and transportation have wrought on offices, factories, and human relationships.

If competition has steadily increased in the last decade, so, too, has the intrusion of the institutional environment on firms' activities taken on greater prominence. Gone are the days of complete managerial discretion. Today, stakeholders demand that managers account for their actions not only to investors and creditors, but also to employees, to local communities, and to special interest groups.[1] Proxy fights are more frequent as top managers face potent challenges to their legitimacy. Where Ralph Nader once sang solos in the wilderness, vocal groups now routinely denounce firms, boycott products, file lawsuits, and initiate legislative proposals in order to bypass lawmakers and appeal directly to voters. Minority groups and their political representatives insist on fair treatment and on equal pay for equal work, forcing managers to show restraint in their traditionally skewed allocation of rewards for corporate performance.

Faced with upheaval, collectively we worry that the burden of change should be borne fairly by all. Within firms, radical changes create personal dislocations. They empower particular departments while others get dissolved. Activist stakeholders demand that their concerns be dealt with justly as strategic decisions emanating from the executive suite lead to plant closures, takeovers, moves, consolidations, de-layerings, and layoffs. We are reminded that even the purest form of market capitalism is at heart a social system, one that ultimately makes value-based choices regarding resource allocations, glorifying winners and chastening losers. Questions of *equity* therefore loom large as a source of controversy in the deployment of resources within firms. Concerns for fairness also declare themselves in sharing national resources across industries, in allocating tax benefits among groups, in setting regulations and tariffs, and in other government interventions designed to influence the dynamics of the economy.

We also are bombarded daily with unsatisfying social outcomes. They result directly from outmoded championing of pure market efficiency as an ideology. Following a decade of laissez-faire rhetoric by Western leaders like Ronald Reagan and Margaret Thatcher, we have recently witnessed a resurgence of interest in the so-called externalities of unbridled rivalry, in the unforeseen impact of corporate activities on the environment.

Consider the thousands of lives lost in Union Carbide's debacle in Bhopal, India in 1984—or the ecological disaster wrought by Exxon's oil spill in Valdez, Alaska in 1989—or the earlier Three Mile Island and Chernobyl nuclear reactor malfunctions. Industrial crises give managers pause to wonder: Was such an accident predictable? If so, would the costs of prevention have been more or less than the cleanup costs? How do you assess the trade-off between economic costs and the social and human hardships a crisis often entails? Who are the true victims when public goods are irreversibly damaged? Dilemmas of this sort appear increasingly probable as firms' activities rely on ever more complex technologies, which are capable of enormous ecological damage and which place larger aggregates of humankind in life-threatening situations.[2] Industrial accidents also become more likely as competition forces firms to cut costs and simultaneously defend and pursue profitability and market share.

After a long hiatus, morality itself has reentered the national consciousness and more frequently animates social debate within firms and among nations. In the United States, placid skies have repeatedly darkened in the last decade as scandal after scandal stormed over prized institutions, whether in Congress, in universities, or on Wall Street. The freewheeling financial manipulations of the 1980s made clear how easily corruptible we all were. Since then, an avalanche of fraudulent actions by bankers in both Japan and the United States have occasioned intense soul searching by the investment communities of Tokyo and Wall Street. Manufacturing industries also reeled as oil spills, exposés, and crises followed each other in dizzying succession. As we call on individuals, firms, and nations to account for these trangressions, an *ethical* wind clearly is sweeping through the board rooms, national councils, governments, and institutions not only of the United States, but also of Japan and Western Europe—a renaissance of moral thinking. Clearly it is not business as usual.

Taken together, efficiency, entrepreneurship, equity, and ethics constitute the motors of change—a set of seemingly irreconcilable forces that today drives strategic change in all our institutions. These criteria represent the central dimensions along which we gauge success and failure. So we chastise schools and universities for wasting resources and for failing to develop critical skills, to prepare students, to instill moral values, to elevate minorities. We scold our unions for selfishly defending their narrow interests and contributing to the decline of once prominent industries. No longer are members of esteemed professional groups like lawyers, accountants, doctors, and scientists beyond reproach as they too are caught bending laws and breaking rules to win financial gain and personal acclaim.

Nowhere is the pressure for strategic change more salient than within profit-seeking firms, the bedrock of the global market economy. Not only do we charge our companies with maintaining their economic performance in increasingly turbulent environments, but we also expect them to demonstrate effectiveness as social institutions. Like other institutions, we ask that they should show efficiency in production, an entrepreneurial ability to adapt, fairness in their dealings with all stakeholders, and adherence to widely accepted moral principles.

Yet many are unprepared.

Therein lies the challenge of effecting radical change. Producing change in an environment that is increasingly global and competitive, pluralistic and activist, calls for significant dexterity. If a new order is to take root, revolutionary restructuring of our business firms and institutions will be required. They, like us, stand at a turning point: Either they allow inertia and momentum to carry them blindly on the downward path to mediocrity and oblivion or they confront outcomes, mobilize attention, brainstorm solutions, and implement choices that enhance their effectiveness and contribute to our social welfare, while still maintaining a solid foundation in competitive processes.

In Outline

Years of research have suggested some conclusions to those of us who study how companies operate. Much of that research is scattered. On the one hand, a growing literature suggests that managers must respond to dramatic change in environmental conditions by artfully redefining their strategies. It offers useful insights into the way competition evolves and how firms can better compete by revising their strategic postures. On the other hand, a large number of studies have examined in detail how managers can alter the internal features of their firms. They offer pragmatic advice on how to implement those changes by manipulating administrative systems, reporting structures, and internal cultures. Despite their obvious complementarity, however, the dialogue between the two literatures has been limited, perhaps largely because their proponents have widely divergent backgrounds: The work on formulation owes its greatest debt to economics, whereas the study of implementation is rooted in sociology.

I bring both sets of these arguments throughout the book in the hope that juxtaposition can generate creativity and will prove useful to leaders of firms and institutions contemplating radical change. In revolutionary periods, guiding firms through turning points requires careful consideration:

1. How we recognize and agree on the need for strategic change.
2. How to revise our firms' competitive postures.
3. How to energize the process of re-creation.

I have therefore broken down the book into parts that mirror these three central phases in the unfolding process of strategic change.

Additionally, two key contentions form the warp and woof of the argument woven throughout *Turning Points.*

First, I emphasize that *strategic change is a subjective process.* Although we aspire to being rational decision makers, as managers most of us are, in fact, impaired: We personalize circumstances and obsessively guard our self-interests. We observe only a limited range of environmental conditions. We screen out unpleasant alternatives. We favor familiar solutions. And we get embroiled in emotional and cognitive traps that thwart our effectiveness.

Subjectivity presents a twofold threat. On the one hand, it induces inertia and momentum, a tendency to carry the past into the future. On the other hand, it encourages tunnel vision, a proclivity to dismiss events that are inconsistent with our assumptions. The failures of many recognizable firms in the auto, steel, and tire industries can be traced to these two sets of blinders worn by managers and stakeholders.

A second theme is that *strategic change is a collective enterprise.* Management writings and the popular press often mislead us into thinking that change is principally engineered and carried out by institutional leaders or top managers. That's wrong. Although top managers do play a key role, the challenge of both conceiving and implementing strategic change of the sort we now need is, in fact, to mobilize support. Like individuals, firms and institutions not only fail to notice, but actively resist conceiving and executing change that they experience as unsettling, disruptive, and bewildering. To overcome the natural inclination everyone has to ignore or actively sabotage strategic change requires extensive debate up, down, and laterally—conversations all too few of us are prepared to carry out in a world raised on individualism, personal gain, hierarchy, power, conflict, and injustice.

A rapidly changing world requires us to develop a new and shared world view within firms and institutions—one that recognizes the merits of generating meaningful participation and developing shared values for unleashing collective energies. If mine is partly an ideological position motivated by respect for the individual, it is also grounded in a growing literature in organization theory, strategic management, and organizational behavior that has elaborated some characteristics of successful processes of radical change.

Personally, I have become convinced that our traditional approach to managing organizations handicaps people. It has created the alienating environment of our large bureaucracies, the paralyzing quagmire of rules and regulations that drains the spirit of even the most enterprising manager. It has also distanced people from their work, separated complementary jobs from one another, and detached top managers from other employees. Written more than 25 years ago, the words of noted management observer Warren Bennis now have the poignant ring of truth: "Bureaucracy," he claimed, "was a monumental discovery for harnessing the muscle power of the Industrial Revolution. In today's world, it is a lifeless crutch that is no longer useful."[3]

The clarion call for more "transformational leaders" appeals to a more empowering form of management, one that recognizes firms' basic capabilities as collective outcomes. It suggests that we need leaders with the vision to chart a strategic course through the political complexities of a divided but connected world, and the resolve to implement that vision. Leaders who do not simply motivate us to comply with directives, but mobilize our creative energies—who do not simply rely on hierarchies to induce conformity to their wishes, but inspire us to climb aboard—who do not imitate what is, but ask us to invent what could be.

Strategic change calls for leaders, surely, but also for run-of-the-mill employees and middle managers who both support the parochial profitability objectives of shareholders and recognize the institutional mission that firms fulfill in a world growing ever more fragmented. Such a collectivist understanding of management perhaps can equip us better to confront the ground swell of ideas and possibilities that challenge our firms and institutions today.

In more detail, here's what readers will find. After presenting an overview of the process of strategic change in Chap. 1, the three chapters in Phase 1 discuss how managers decipher environments. Chapter 2 begins by analyzing the principal external forces that today compel the attention of most executives and oblige them to contemplate strategic change. As firms surface from years of political neglect, careless management, ethical lapses, and financial legerdemain, they face an environment of new capability-destroying technologies and determined global rivals, just when they are overburdened with debt and sluggish from years of heady but false growth. Chapter 3 shows how various features of firms and their environments have built inertia and momentum that retard change and keep many firms moving along their original, albeit suicidal, trajectories.

At the heart of conceiving and making a strategic change lies a cognitive process of interpretation. Managers, like the rest of us, navigate through a fog of information that obscures visibility. Many signals compete for their attention, and, sadly, our crystal balls have little to offer in assessing trends and their likely impact. Simultaneously, political processes and individual biases induce selective filtering and limit our ability to apply ourselves as rationally as we might like to formulating and executing strategies. Chapter 4 dwells on processes that shape interpretations, suggests how we might guard against these biases, and emphasizes the importance of building consensus responses during revolutionary eras.

Having described the current conditions firms face both internally and externally, the three chapters of Phase 2 discuss how upheaval is pushing managers to modify their strategic postures through both competition and cooperation. Chapter 5 describes how converging industries and nation-states force managers to compete more aggressively within business units. Aggressiveness means more carefully deploying resources to improve the timing of strategic actions, their differentiation from the initiatives of competitors, and their segmentation of markets.

Chapter 6 shows how environmental forces compel attention to the underutilized assets that firms have accumulated over the years, which lie dormant beneath corporate umbrellas. Less and less attractive, then, are those financial portfolio views of corporate strategy that described the managers' role as the juggling of assets. If leveraged buyouts and takeovers were themes of the 1980s, then aggressiveness, synergy, and relatedness are likely leitmotifs as companies prepare to compete in the topsy-turvy world of the year 2000.

In Chap. 7, I show that "competing" increasingly means cooperating with rivals to more quickly, efficiently, and effectively build an advantaged position. Such tactics complement other persuasive strategies that firms and their managers rely on to shape environments friendly to their cause. Alliances have proliferated over the last few years as firms faced competitive hurdles difficult to leap over on their own. These collective strategies help managers to overcome inertia and break out of historical trajectories. They also make us aware that competition takes place today less between firms and more between networks. Even traditionally mighty firms are finding it essential to develop stronger allies as competition shifts upward to the level of the collectivity.

The chapters in Phase 3 raise concerns about how managers energize change. To carry out strategic change requires a systematic plan for overcoming inertia, redirecting momentum, and altering trajectories. Chapter 8 points to the vital role played by leaders in mobilizing employees and generating movement. Although much has been written about the act of leadership, our firms continue to be managed more like autocracies and fiefdoms than like inspired hotbeds of innovation. Extant research challenges the widely held command model of change that fails to empower employees. Indeed, a significant challenge facing us as we struggle to reorient our firms lies in the mental models we hold of the corporate structure. Because our personal lexicons consist principally of standard operating procedures, rules, and organization charts, most of us find it difficult to articulate a vision of strategic change. In tomorrow's companies, I argue that the appropriate metaphors are less likely to resemble the military and more so the spiritual as leaders ask of their employees greater commitment to self-actualization, and so try to transform their firms into thinner, more flexible, and more resilient cultures.

As the shamans and witch doctors of their tribes, executives find themselves attending increasingly to the symbols of corporate life, manipulating them to energize employees, shareholders, and other stakeholders. Chapter 9 discusses the cultural consequences of strategic changes that undermine the closed clan-like character of large firms, whose customs and practices evolved slowly over the years. In Chap. 10, I highlight the kinds of formal structures that can help induce these shared values by channeling corporate interactions and molding capabilities. Many cutting-edge firms and institutions are already experimenting with restructurings that encourage the practice of more collective, inclusive, participative management styles. More and more employees work in temporary structures that are better characterized as internal markets or loosely coupled networks than as hierarchies. They force us to recognize the increasingly anachronistic character of our bureaucratic models of organizing.

The final chapter concludes our discussion of the whys and hows of strategic change. As the world's nations and people grow progressively more intertwined, firms and institutions are called on to show their ability as efficient producers of goods and services, as equitable allocators of social and economic benefits, as entrepreneurial vehicles for innovation, and as ethical members of society. To achieve these ends requires visionary leaders—activist executives committed to the task of mobilizing followers within and among organizations. It also calls for a revolutionary transformation, not only of firms, but also of schools, unions, and other key institutions, with an eye to making them more active, more committed, and more involved with their constituents.

If successful, this book should provide insight into how managers can respond to revolutionary changes in environmental conditions. It should therefore help us to engineer more creatively how our companies and institutions pass through strategic turning points in their development.

1

Strategic Change, in a Nutshell

The human mind has first to construct forms independently before we can find them in things.

ALBERT EINSTEIN

These are exhilarating times. Rapidly changing technologies demand that we make ever larger investments in plant and equipment in order to improve aggregate productivity. Falling national barriers make it possible for aggressive global firms to invade traditionally sheltered industries. Regional consolidations in Europe and Asia beckon with large and growing mass markets. With the collapse of the Soviet empire, a new world order is being born that virtually guarantees heightened global interpenetration as Western-style capitalism claims ascendancy over the world's economic affairs. These and other external triggers increasingly require that firms initiate and implement strategic changes designed to improve both their competitive positions and their effectiveness as institutions.

Within companies, the disintegration of paternalistic cultures appears to be well under way, nowhere more visibly perhaps than at AT&T, General Electric, and IBM.

Once the largest company in the world and a well-known parental figure to a million employees, AT&T's transformation has been radical indeed. Following the judicial decree of 1984, the Bell System has rapidly changed from a regulated monopoly to a dynamic and competitive collectivity of eight rival firms—each one a telecommunications powerhouse in its own right and each one actively redefining its mission, exploring new product offerings and technologies, and expanding into foreign markets. To achieve strategic change, however, requires a new mix of skills, a new operating structure, new goals, and a new culture; and, for some time now, the baby Bells and AT&T have been actively redeveloping training programs, revising structures, and invoking new cultural norms in order to increase their competitiveness in the global telecommunications marketplace.[1]

Or take General Electric, the original exemplar of modern management technique. In the postwar era, a team of experts that included Peter Drucker codified managerial wisdom into a "blue book." The eight-volume series delineated the principles of managing as POIM: plan, organize, integrate, measure. These axioms, later augmented by concepts such as "the experience curve" and "strategic business units," ripened from exposure to a generation of management graduates of GE's institute in Crotonville, New York. By the late 1970s, however, they had produced within GE the bloated, layered, hierarchical, fragmented, and sluggish bureaucracy that has today become a synonym for the large, modern American corporation.

Since 1981, GE's top managers, with Jack Welch at the helm, have been energetically dismantling the firm's acclaimed culture and controls, shifting its priorities and rebuilding its capabilities. Driving the reorientation—what Welch calls the "Work-Out"—is simplicity: a simpler structure, closer relationships, less paperwork, entrepreneurship, more rapid sharing of information, and shared rewards. As Welch put it,

> the ultimate objective of Work-Out is so clear. We want 300,000 people with different career objectives, different family aspirations, different financial goals, to share directly in this company's vision, the information, the decision-making process, and the rewards. We want to build a more stimulating environment, a more creative environment, a freer work atmosphere, with incentives tied directly to what people do.[2]

The remaking of GE into an organizational model for the year 2000 is well under way. In the last decade, many layers of managers have been pruned. Businesses that proved unable to rise to the challenge of being number one or number two in their industries were sloughed off; others fused. Some key decisions (such as bonus allocations) have been decentralized while others have been brought into a streamlined corporate-level function. Indeed, GE's top managers are explicit about trying to write a new psychological contract with employees, one which, according to Welch, recognizes that "given today's environment, people's emotional energy must be focused outward on a competitive world where no business is a safe haven for employment unless it is winning in the marketplace."

And, most recently, there's IBM. Battered by intense competition in every segment of the industry, having systematically lost market share throughout the 1980s, the once mighty computer maker recently acknowledged that the time had come for a strategic change. On December 4, 1991, Chairman Akers flew in 500 of IBM's top managers from around the world for a presentation describing a radically decentralized corporate structure. The thrust of the transformation? Granting decision-making responsibility and autonomy to all major operating units to make them more responsive to market pressures. Even more heretically, Akers warned ominously that the old paternalistic culture that virtually guaranteed lifetime employment would be incompatible with the new structure—and so would be chucked. Already at IBM employment has dropped from a high of 410,000 in 1985 to 350,000 in 1991, with further cuts in the offing.[3]

Not every firm can be like AT&T, GE, or IBM. For one thing, few can lay claim to such rich histories. These three are exemplars precisely because they constitute extreme cases of firms whose prior successes, entrenched systems, inertia, and momentum virtually guaranteed *that they would not change.* Yet they are changing. First we must ask why. Then we can ask how. Whether these firms succeed in adapting to the new world order depends on how well their managers conceive the dimensions of their strategic changes, and how effectively they mobilize constituents to support these reorientations.

The Phases of Change

This book is one attempt to detail the processes that managers confront when they stand at such strategic turning points. Traditional views of change owe a significant debt to Charles Darwin's model of evolution: They contend that organisms—and, by implication, individuals, firms, and entire societies—change slowly and incrementally to adjust to changing environments. More recently, natural historians like Stephen Jay Gould have reminded us of the sudden change in life conditions that led to the extinction of the once dominant dinosaurs. They propose that evolution involves long periods of slow and gradual change, punctuated by intermittent epochs of radical change.[4] During these periods of turmoil, dramatic realignments take place.

We live in such a tumultuous era. Bankruptcies, technological innovations, social conflicts, and collapsing political regimes are shaking the foundation of economic and social relationships that managers rely on to conduct business. They place firms at a strategic turning point. To guide their firms through chaos toward renewed competitiveness, managers are increasingly compelled to conceive and execute metamorphic transformations of their firms' strategic postures and internal features.[5]—or else, like those legendary dinosaurs, to fail.

Table 1.1 proposes that we understand strategic change as a set of processes. As in mechanics, movement results from an imbalance between forces that stimulate change and forces that retard change.[6] In contrast to mechanical analogies, however, managers and employees experience these forces subjectively: They often succumb to individual biases that cloud their interpretations of events. The strategic directions that firms embark on therefore depend heavily on how managers think about environments, about their firms' capabilities, and about themselves. If particular managers select different strategic trajectories when faced with seemingly identical circumstances, evidently they must be interpreting those circumstances differently.

Analytically, the model proposes that strategic change involves three distinct phases. During Phase 1, managers struggle to make sense of the environmental turmoil surrounding their firms. They actively search for information with which to represent the changing face of rivalry in their industries. They interpret how threats are likely to congeal, and organize these interpretations around probable scenarios. Internally, however, firms' features create a degree of inertia and momentum that hamper change. Astute managers therefore carefully decipher how their firms' internal environments are likely to impede a strategic reorientation.

Phase 2 involves assessing how these internal and external conditions

Table 1.1. Modeling Strategic Change

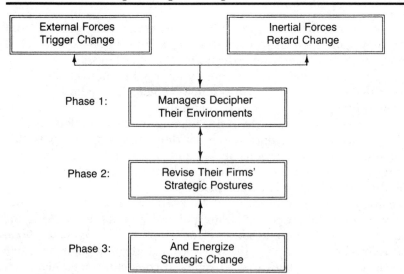

affect firms' strategic postures. Globalization and technological change tend to increase rivalry, and so magnify demands for efficiency and entrepreneurship. Simultaneously, demands for institutional responsiveness force attention to questions of fairness and ethics. To keep up, managers contemplate changes in business, corporate, and collective strategies.

To select a strategic posture, however, is not a unilateral act. Research recommends that those who carry out the plans should be closely involved from the start. Phase 3 therefore dissects the crucial role of leadership, company culture, and structure in energizing a strategic change. It suggests that strategic change requires a new mind set, a new way of organizing. It forces us to recognize that our tall pyramids no longer pass muster in an environment that demands more rapid informational exchange and more timely and effective decisions. A new kind of leader must therefore arise like a Phoenix from the ashes of our crumbling corporate hierarchies—one who recognizes that, at heart, if change involves managing emotions, then revolutionary change requires mobilizing collective passions.

Therein lies the challenge of carrying out strategic change.

Phase 1: Deciphering Environments

In 1986, BankAmerica, once the largest bank in the world, was in danger of decaying into oblivion, having accumulated $1.8 billion in losses in just one year. Much of the blame was laid at the California bank's encrusted systems and inertia in the face of mounting rivalry and declining margins. A paternalistic culture that coddled employees and guaranteed job security contributed to ballooning expenses across its 850-branch network. Where competing firms like Wells-Fargo and Security Pacific showed great aggressiveness in redeploying assets and going after new customers, BankAmerica had come to resemble a listless, bloated Third World administration.

Anxious about the bank's performance, BankAmerica's board asked former chairman and CEO A. W. Clausen to return from his five-year stint at the World Bank to spearhead a strategic change. After hiring a new top team of ex-Fargo executives, he urged a culture-busting effort, achieved by laying off employees, freezing salaries, introducing incentive pay schemes, and consolidating the structure. Selling became the centerpiece of a more competitive culture, the basic capability in dire need of reconstruction. Top managers instituted weekly sales meetings and bestowed awards on those responsible for the most sales of the week. The result: By 1991, BankAmerica appeared to be among the strongest of the leading U.S. commercial banks, with solid earnings, a steadily rising stock price, and good press.[7] It came as no surprise, therefore, when the bank announced in mid-1991 an aggressive merger with rival Security Pacific designed to consolidate its West Coast strengths and propel it to the number two position in the United States, behind giant Citicorp.

More than ever, firms like BankAmerica, IBM, AT&T, and General Electric face environments that command radical change but are difficult to interpret. For BankAmerica, uncertainty abounds about the shape of things to come in financial services. Will lingering regulatory restraints on commercial banks be removed or, following the savings and loan debacle, might they be strengthened? For AT&T, will technological changes facilitate or hamper the integration of communication and computers, and so its ability to capitalize on its merger with NCR? For IBM, will Akers' efforts to carry out decentralization prove sufficient to overcome the glorious history and mainframe orientation that will doubtless hold back change? And will GE's reputation recover from the trading scandals and media battles that have depreciated its acquisitions of Kidder Peabody and NBC?

Such questions are difficult to answer. Fundamentally, firms' environments are cloudy and difficult to read. They often operate in paradoxical, contradictory ways. For instance:

- *Efficiency vs. innovation:* Increasing rivalry places short-run stress on increasing efficiency. At the same time, however, rapid technological change compels managers to spend heavily on innovation-generating research to remain competitive in the long run.

- *Competitiveness vs. institutional effectiveness:* Attending to rivalry means streamlining functions, paying for performance, and eliminating dead-weight costs. Societal demands for fairness and conformity to ethical standards, however, place greater stress on equalizing rewards, monitoring work, and policing employees, thus adding to overhead.

- *Globalization vs. nationalism:* Economic forces shape increasing levels of interdependence between countries, compelling businesses to globalize. At the same time, in many countries, national and regional protectionism also looms larger, making economies of scale and globalization difficult to realize.

Take Whirlpool, the world's largest manufacturer of major appliances. In the search for global economies of scale, the U.S.-based company recently acquired Phillips' European appliance business. Yet uncertainties abound. It remains unclear whether the fragmented European market can be supplied from centralized manufacturing facilities like those in the United States. The company also has limited brand awareness abroad. Multiple national standards hamper the standardization of parts, and patriotic sentiments prevail.[8]

So seemingly simple changes in environments require considerable interpretation of how economic, social, and political forces will combine. They remind us that, fundamentally, to conceive a strategic change is a deeply subjective process.

In fact, although environments appear to have changed rapidly in recent years, few managers actually perceived them as doing so: Just as people generally do not notice small changes in ambient room temperatures, so many managers were desensitized to the piecemeal changes occuring in their firms' environments. By itself, globalization progressed incrementally since the mid-1970s, as did stakeholder activism, the end of the Cold War, and other contemporary pressures on firms for more efficient, entrepreneurial, ethical, and equitable management structures.[9] Although these forces were building up slowly and independently in historical time, they have come together suddenly in our own lifetimes, creating cataclysmic pressure for radical change.

The heady successes of the postwar era also fostered close ties between managers within firms and within the island-like business communities to which firms belong.[10] Managers' relationships with one another and with institutions such as governments, financial markets, universities, professional associations, and the media helped to insulate firms from their broader environments, blinding them and their firms to the gathering clouds of global competition.

Extraordinary as it now seems, the big three auto manufacturers, for instance, became fully aware of their dependency on oil only after the OPEC embargo of 1973. They then took a decade to acknowledge it. Similarly, large military contractors like General Dynamics, Northrop, Lockheed, and Grumman waited for the collapse of the Soviet empire before recognizing how extreme was their dependence on the Cold War for continued growth. Although the Pentagon's budget is expected to decrease by some 25 percent by 1996, weapons makers have done little to prune their operations.[11]

If, as managers, we initiate change only when our backs are to the proverbial wall, then the process by which particular issues reach a threshold of attention should prove central in generating strategic change. Many studies document how managers actively select information that confirms the merits of their pet projects, and downplay alternatives, thereby giving politically motivated decisions a rational interpretation. Concerned managers use formal planning as one way to overcome basic biases that dampen their ability to attend rationally to environmental trends. Still, in turbulent environments, planning itself proves insufficient, and biases threaten to overwhelm their ability to respond rationally.

Researchers point out how readily managers fall victim to processes of escalation in which they become wedded to preferred positions long after they have proven unproductive. Large public programs are notorious for this—the space program, for one. In 1984, the U.S. Congress committed itself to the planned space station as an $8 billion project. Seven years later, having already spent over $4 billion, estimates placed the cost of the station closer to $120 billion. Experts call it a case study in cost escalation, a demonstration of how psychological commitment combines with political interests to bias the decisions that our leaders make.

In the planning stages, advocates argued that the station would keep NASA in business after the windup of the Apollo program. As James M. Beggs, NASA's director in the early 1980s, conceded, "the feeling was that unless we could get a station, the manned activities would truncate and we'd run out of mission." In other words, rather than adopt a program of building modules, NASA opted for a single large unit that would function only when fully assembled. In bargaining for funds, negotiators were forced to make the station appealing to all constituents. So its purpose was continually enlarged to encompass first research, then employment, then commercial possibilities—thereby escalating the station's size and the investment required.[12]

Whether at NASA, among military contractors, or in everyday firms, these processes are pervasive. Since strategic issues tend to be ambiguous, background features of managers themselves and of their firms' cultures, controls, and capabilities, often lead managers to make very different interpretations of circumstances. If coping with revolutionary circumstances requires shared understandings among all of a firm's key employees, then in coming years managers are likely to grow increasingly concerned about how information and know-how are acquired, processed, and transmitted inside their firms.

Simultaneously, firms belong to larger business communities and so have relationships with rivals, suppliers, distributors, regulators, business schools, trade associations, and so on. Managers develop an understanding of what is hot and what's not partly through the networks of personal contacts that link them to one another. The strategic changes that they conceive and initiate therefore derive not only from personal characteristics, but also from features of firms and their inclusion in these larger business communities. So to encourage radical change is to explore avenues for emancipating managers from the closed mind sets that tend routinely to propagate within business communities.

Phase 2: Revising Strategic Postures

Radically changing environments command attention to the ways in which firms compete. In some firms, managers opt for conservative responses. They try to accommodate turbulence by making peripheral modifications that allow their firms to persist in orbiting along their historical trajectories. They deny that the system is broken, so they don't try to fix it.

In some vanguard firms, however, managers are recognizing that their internal systems are indeed beyond repair and require a complete overhaul. So they call for strategic change.

Change that is strategic alters a firm's trajectory, which means it is intended to overcome inertia and rebuild corporate momentum in a new direction. A strategic change modifies both the speed and the path of a firm's trajectory through time and space: It involves a redeployment of the firm's resources to a new configuration.[13]

During the 1980s, some visionary managers read environments well. They recognized the revolutionary circumstances their firms were facing and embarked on three types of key strategic changes: They made *business-level* changes in their firms' competitive positions, *corporate-level* changes in their companies' portfolios, and *collective-level* changes in their firms' external posture toward regulators and competitors. (See Table 1.2.)

Consider the Scott Paper Company. In the early 1970s, the maker of the famous tissue paper faced intense competitive pressure from Procter & Gamble, owner of Charmin. With costs some 15 percent higher than other tissue manufacturers, Scott Paper's managers chose to invest in rebuilding outdated plants, altering its resource deployments away from marketing. As competition fragmented the market, the company also struggled to innovate across market segments, introducing such premium brands as Cottonelle in the United States and Andrex in Britain. Supporting brands across segments, however, required reallocating resources between production, marketing, and distribution, altering the center of gravity of the company.[14]

Throughout the 1970s, Scott Paper's managers, following the national corporate fad, diversified out of the company's main business and into unrelated businesses such as leisure lighting and furniture. Increased competition in each of their businesses and low synergy across businesses, however, encouraged CEO Phillip Lippincott to reverse direction in the 1980s. He initiated a corporate-level strategic change to increase the

Table 1.2. Types of Strategic Change

Strategy	Change in configuration
Business-level	To alter competitive advantage
Corporate-level	To extend core capability
Collective-level	To broaden network of alliances

relatedness of the corporate portfolio by selling off businesses that were ancillary to the core paper business.

Recognition of the growing global market also encouraged Lippincott to form joint ventures and alliances abroad, a type of collective-level strategic change that could help Scott Paper quickly achieve a competitive position. The company's recent joint venture with Feldmuhle A.G., for instance, completed an alliance structure that arguably makes Scott the best positioned paper company in preparation for the pan-European market of 1992.[15]

Scott Paper might have moved fast, but it is no isolated case. Faced with intensifying competitive pressure, globalization, and other external challenges, leading firms today are challenged to make similar strategic changes at the business, corporate, and collective levels to improve their global positioning.

At the business level, many are looking to improve their competitive position by aggressively investing in developing a more differentiated market presence. Some firms are throwing money behind the idea that they can improve their ability to compete through new product introductions. Others are trying to differentiate better their products and services by cutting costs or improving product quality. Others still are more carefully targeting their products and services at narrower market segments.

The fashion industry is a case in point. In Paris' elite couture houses, designers are accustomed to command $10,000 for a suit. To cope with the recession, however, houses like Ungaro, Givenchy, and Yves St. Laurent have resorted to introducing secondary lines to target sales to the segment of consumers prepared to purchase the pricey but decidedly more affordable $100–$900 garments.[16] Among the most aggressive has been Italy's globalizing Giorgio Armani whose targeted brand strategy now spans couture-priced garments, designer-priced ready-to-wear, and, most recently, lower-priced clothing introduced in wholly owned retail outlets intended to compete with highly successful specialty chains like the GAP and the Limited.

In tandem, some firms are rapidly divesting assets to reduce their firms' exposure to environmental forces—a corporate-level strategic change. Because acquired businesses often were related only remotely to firms' original businesses, diversifications distorted the integrity of corporate portfolios, with nefarious consequences for operations within businesses.

Tax preparer H&R Block found it out the hard way. Through its 9000 outlets, H&R Block handles over 14 million tax returns a year. Its efforts to diversify into legal services and management seminars throughout the 1980s proved highly unsuccessful, despite apparent synergies. Disappointed with its merger with the Hyatt Legal Services chain, for instance, Block sold it back to private investors in 1987. In 1988, the company also sold off its seminar subsidiary, Path Management Industries, at a loss.[17]

Corporate consolidations of related businesses are enhancing profitability and producing large cutbacks. In the first months of 1991, no less stalwarts than Sears, Roebuck and IBM announced job cuts of 33,000 and 14,000, respectively. For Big Blue, this constituted a total trimming of 33,000 jobs since 1986. In the same period, AT&T cut 92,000 jobs.[18]

Most dramatically, perhaps, since 1986 Honeywell has systematically sold off its computer, semiconductor, and defense businesses and made acquisitions designed to consolidate its operations around its original business in automated controls. The restructuring has enabled increased global coordination of parts purchasing, marketing, and distribution, giving it a strategic edge.[19]

Finally, in a dramatic departure from tradition, many managers are now aggressively pursuing collective action. For one thing, shrewd managers have long recognized the benefits of having friends in the right places. So they try to shape institutional environments favorable to their activities by advertising aggressively, coopting regulators, or lobbying legislators for protective tarrifs, loan guarantees, favorable contracts, or tax benefits. In this way they hope to encapsulate competition within narrower, more profitable limits.[20] Sometimes, of course, they go to embarassing lengths to seduce potential allies, as John Sununu—then the White House Chief of Staff—demonstrated when his reliance on corporate jets for personal travel was brought to light, and contributed to bringing on his resignation.[21]

Many firms are also pursuing another type of strategic change at the collective level that involves developing network partners. Strategic alliances with rivals have proved increasingly vital to firms striving to maintain their competitiveness in industries such as telecommunications and financial services—sectors bombarded by bursts of technological innovation and deregulation. The recent agreement between Apple and IBM to share technology shocked the computer world.[22] It also highlighted the power of joint ventures and partnerships as a vehicle for improving firms' competitive postures without taxing scarce resources, and showed how increasingly competition is no longer simply between individual firms, but between *networks* of firms.

Phase 3: Energizing Strategic Change

Planning a strategic change is not enough: Much is required to get there. After all, old habits die hard. Current resource deployments constitute commitments around which employees and shareholders form work and career expectations. Previously announced goals, pay practices, recruitment systems, and administrative procedures place firms on strategic trajectories that create both inertia and momentum and inhibit change. To turn away from these trajectories requires, not only skill in selecting the most promising strategic changes, but also skill in overcoming inertia and remodeling institutions.

Resistance to change results because history constrains the conduct of firms and institutions. Much as geological crystals form when basic elements experience intense physical pressure, so, too, do firms' features crystallize from historical pressures on their internal capabilities and control systems.[23] As companies grow, their features tend to move into alignment: Managers design control systems to capitalize on their capabilities, and patterns of specialization induce employees to hold particular values. Over time, firms' capabilities, controls, and cultures fuse, creating inertia and building momentum that propels them along strategic trajectories.[24]

To carry out change also means to come to grips with the emotional implications of living through revolutionary circumstances. Transformations that disrupt the established order invariably create uncertainty and threaten vested interests, and so generate panic. Coping with the personal sentiments of employees is therefore one of the key challenges facing managers attempting to effect strategic change. To reinvent their firms, managers find themselves manipulating four key internal features: capabilities, controls, culture, and conduct. Change in any of these features generates emotional resistance. (See Table 1.3.)

Take Corning. In 1983, the company famous for its temperature-resistant glass products earned 70 percent of its declining profits from cyclical slow-growth businesses. In the following 8 years, under CEO and top shareholder James Houghton's tenure, the company redefined its strategic conduct by divesting marginal businesses, pursuing higher market share businesses, and forming a global network of over 19 marketing and technological alliances. It also transformed its basic capabilities by consolidating its operations into four groups: communications, laboratory services, consumer products, and specialty materials. To overcome

Table 1.3. Producing Change

Implement change in:	In order to:
┌─ Conduct	Redefine vision.
└→ Capabilities	Reallocate resources.
┌→ Controls	Modify systems.
└→ Culture	General commitment.

come the emotional resistance and parochial tendencies of a functional structure in a company town, internal controls were changed to emphasize product quality and innovation: All employees were sent through quality training programs; a 25-percent target was set for revenues derived from new products. And Houghton spearheaded the effort to revitalize the culture: The company's unions participated in key decisions involving plant design; barriers between research functions in different businesses were dismantled to enable technology sharing; managers strengthened relationships with minority groups and with the local community.[25]

Corning is just one example. In general, research suggests that firms successful in implementing strategic change do a good job of addressing:

1. Whether resources were reallocated in ways that enhanced firms' competitive *capabilities*.

2. Whether underlying structural *controls* supported the new strategic direction.

3. Whether careful attention was paid to the implications of the strategic change for firms' internal *cultures*.

4. Whether top managers showed visionary leadership and an ability to mobilize employees as they sought to redefine their firms' strategic *conduct*.

Altering firms' capabilities involves reallocating resources to projects more likely to assist in coping with changing environments. But it's tough to teach an old dog new tricks: New capabilities take time to build into the repertoires of established firms. So cultural resistance abounds. To produce strategic change, shrewd managers therefore instrumentally disseminate values throughout their firms. They discuss their rationales for change and try to persuade employees to buy into their interpretations.[26] Studies conducted by the *Business Roundtable* (1988), for instance, suggest that to cope with environmental concerns over firms' social responsiveness, corporate leaders have been increasingly conveying an ethical posture in their speeches. They try to galvanize employees into showing concern for customers and sensitivity to firms' other stakeholders.

So strategic change requires transformational skills: the ability to shape a vision of the future, mobilize employees behind the vision, and guide the company's different systems toward achievement of the vision.[27] A large body of evidence suggests that to fully involve employees is the surest way to produce a more mobilized work force, one willing to abandon established fiefdoms and hard-won perks in the pursuit of their firms' effectiveness. In contrast, isolation from decision making tends to breed emotional hostility and resistance, and sometimes active sabotage.

Both action and inaction by managers take on symbolic meaning and shape lower-level employees' interpretations about key events. Managers successful at carrying out strategic change point to the significance of active participation, coalition building, and up-front communication.

Change damages the political clout of some individuals and groups while increasing the visibility and prospects of others. Revised budgets disrupt ongoing relationships and the distribution of power among managers, producing internal machinations, negotiations, and coalition-building activity. So even when a strategic change can be justified by declining economic performance or forecasts that warn of gathering storms, proponents invariably get embroiled in complex political dynamics. The choice to invest more deeply in distinguishing a firm's products in the marketplace, for instance, not only means dedicating more resources to advertising, merchandising, and customer service, but also promises enhanced political clout for the firm's marketing managers, often at the expense of the firm's financial and operations managers. They will oppose the change.[28]

Similarly, programs for retiring outmoded factories, investing in capital projects, or deepening new product development all favor different groups of employees within a company. Reorientations empower some managers while they disenfranchise others. Just as elected officials find themselves routinely subjected to the political pressures of diverse interest groups, so, too, are senior managers lobbied by subordinates and pressured to conceive, select, and implement strategic programs that favor parochial interests.

Established firms often build up a reserve of slack resources from prior successes, which produces entrenched managers and sluggishness. In these firms, change easily gets mired in complex internal politics, so boards of directors frequently opt to hire outside executives for senior slots. Outsiders have fewer vested interests and so are more likely to redirect the firm toward objectives that the board favors. Symbolically, to hire an outsider is also to signal analysts, reporters, and rival firms about a no-nonsense commitment to change.

So successful efforts at accomplishing strategic change appear to require three skills: (1) *generating shared interpretations about firms' environments*, (2) *revising strategic postures*, and (3) *engineering the change program itself*. Failure can occur as managers misinterpret their firms' competitive circumstances, miscalculate rivals' actions, and misguide the process of change. Increasingly, savvy managers recognize that to overcome these barriers requires mobilizing all employees, shareholders, and key constituents to stand squarely behind managers' efforts. And that means extensive communication. Such a catalytic role may be the single most important function senior executives play when guiding their firms through strategic turning points.

Deciphering Environments

Strategic change does not happen automatically: It presupposes a group of managers that collectively recognize the need to initiate change. Chapter 2 points to a wide range of revolutionary forces that broadly affect all firms' economic and institutional performance and that are pressuring managers to contemplate radical reorientations.

But bureaucratic structures and entrenched cultures make change difficult, so Chap. 3 shows how inertia and momentum constrain managers' ability to carry out change. Indeed, although firms appear to be exposed to common environmental pressures, individual managers often disagree on what those pressures mean—on the magnitude and the effect they will have on their firms' operations. Chapter 4 follows up by clarifying the cognitive biases that managers inadvertently bring to bear in making strategic decisions, and how those biases create blind spots and induce inaction during revolutionary periods.

2
When Worlds Collide

Everything is collapsing.
MIKHAIL GORBACHEV (1991)

A revolution is under way. External pressures increasingly demand that managers conceive and execute strategic changes designed to alter radically how their firms function. Closer ties among nations and greater allegiance to market philosophies create unprecedented opportunities for growth. They also threaten many established firms with a sudden increase in rivalry on a global scale. As regional markets in Europe, North America, and Asia-Pacific consolidate, they establish economic battlefields for firms seeking growth. To capitalize on these developments, American, Japanese, and European firms all are searching actively for ways to improve their efficiency and innovativeness as they prepare for the coming global showdown.

Managers also recognize that they navigate in ever more pluralistic waters in which they can no longer attend simply to their firms' efficiency and profitability. Shifting environments require that firms curry favor with ever more diverse constituents; activist consumers, employees, suppliers, distributors, self-appointed public representatives daily remind managers of their responsibilities; and the threat of paralysis in decision making runs ever higher.[1]

Upheaval is driven by a combination of technological, economic, social, and political pressures. Globalization forces economic competition, which, in turn, goads firms to be more *efficient*—to search for ways of reducing costs and improving revenues.

It proves difficult, however, to squeeze profits from costs for very long. Rivalry therefore forces a long-run concern with established firms' ability to innovate. Constant technological breakthroughs accelerate change, compelling firms to be more *entrepreneurial* in identifying and exploiting new ideas.

While competition is on the rise due to a global convergence of technologies, economies, and political systems, our managers and firms are also experiencing significant institutional intrusions. In this changing world, we no longer seem content to ask firms that they simply be efficient, competitive, and innovative. We also expect them to be responsive to the activist concerns of an ever more fragmented audience, fair in the allocation of rewards and in sharing the burdens of change, and morally scrupulous in decision making. (See Table 2.1.)

So our willingness to discount externalities like environmental pollution, the risks associated with advanced technologies, or the hazardous by-products of firms' production processes appears to be falling by the wayside. Catastrophes like Union Carbide's Bhopal, Exxon's oil spill in Prince William Sound, and the Soviet Union's Chernobyl fallout, serve to heighten our concern with how firms contribute to the destruction of the ecological environment. Together with change in the demographic makeup of employees and recurring evidence of dubious conduct by managers, environments draw increasing attention to the *ethical* underpinnings of corporate acts.

Finally, laissez-faire philosophies that have demonstrably disenfranchised many groups lead to questions about the basic *equity* of corporate schemes that unfairly distribute income, perks, and privileges. Awareness of the skewed distribution of benefits heightens infighting and forces greater attention to questions of fairness in the allocation of corporate perquisites, particularly following a strategic change. People ask that the burden of changing be borne fairly by all. At a revitalized *New York Post*, for instance, renewed profitability in 1991 meant returning concessions

Table 2.1. External Triggers of Change

Environmental sector	External trigger	Pressure on firms for:
Economic	• High rate of innovation • Linked global markets	Efficiency
Technological	• Computerization • Telecommunications	Entrepreneurship
Social	• Global demographics • Moral/ecological damage	Ethics
Political	• Deregulation • Distribution of wealth	Equity

to the tune of some $8 million of the $21 million granted by the company's unions 8 months before.[2]

To meet the challenge of radical change requires of firms, not only new strategies for competing, but also a new approach to managing, one that can overcome the limitations of practices that produced bloated bureaucracies, alienated employees, social injustice, and moral turpitude. As savvy leaders and managers contemplate the tremendous opportunities open to their firms, they recognize a need to balance more carefully the simultaneous and often contradictory pressures on their firms to demonstrate efficiency, entrepreneurship, equity, and ethics in dealing with stakeholders.

Global Convergence

Combative adversaries threatened the stability of established industries in the U.S. throughout the 1970s and 1980s. Various estimates suggest that United States firms' global market share fell by more than 50 percent in many industries between 1970 and 1980, whether in cameras, stereo components, medical equipment, color television sets, radial tires, electric motors, food processors, microwave ovens, athletic equipment, computer chips, industrial robots, electron microscopes, machine tools, and optical equipment. By 1985, U.S. firms had also lost competitive advantage in sophisticated manufacturing industries such as automobiles, trucks, machine tools, semiconductors, and consumer electronics, among others.[3]

The ground swell of rivalry derives mainly from the sudden and dramatic interpenetration of nation-states caused by globalization, itself precipitated by either technological change or deregulation. Heightened rivalry directs us to explore ways for improving the competitiveness of our firms and for exploiting latent sources of synergy.

In the postwar era, nations have increasingly recognized their interdependence, formed social ties, and promoted global norms to stabilize international relations. Stability enabled domestic specialization and international trade, and eased corporate expansions into multiple national markets.

Developments in transportation, information technologies, and telecommunications have shaped growing levels of interdependence in the world, and caused a proliferation of social exchanges linking countries through trade and transportation. Because communication reduces social distance between disparate countries, the world has grown progressively more homogeneous and more prone to sharing goods and services, lifestyles, attitudes, and even ideologies. Convergence on global norms and a global culture is facilitated by the proliferation of regional and international associations devoted to coordinating economic and political activities, by the decline of traditional east-west distinctions, and by the de facto adoption of English as the language of international business.

A good example of global convergence was the common ideological front presented to Iraq's occupation of Kuwait in the fall of 1990. In a remarkable show of unity, East and West joined in multiple United Nations resolutions. They began by condemning the invasion and demanding Iraq's withdrawal. They then placed an embargo on trade with Iraq and passed increasingly severe restrictions on enforcement of the embargo, which brought about a coordinated war launched in January 1991 and Iraq's defeat a few weeks later. Such unprecedented acts speak to a new role for the United Nations as the world's principal agent for sanctioning international norms and propagating shared values.

In fact, many strategic changes we ask our firms to initiate are designed either to capitalize on the opportunities that a more structured global environment provides, or to respond to threats posed by competing firms actively seeking global advantage. Increasingly, then, managers confront problems rooted in an evolving economic interdependence that promotes intersecting relationships between national markets and global firms.[4]

Economies That Interpenetrate

Arguably the most profound developments of the postwar era have been: (1) dramatic improvements in transportation systems, facilitating the movement of people and goods, and (2) the incremental convergence of computer and communications technologies. Just as the steam engine and the factory system begot the industrial revolution, so, too, have transportation and communications technologies placed firms on the cusp of a second industrial divide, at the threshold of the information age.[5]

Rapid change in transmission and switching technologies after World War II increased competition in a sector until then treated as a natural monopoly. In the United States, the Federal Communications Commission gave permission to use microwave transmission for private networks as early as 1959. In 1969, it authorized an independent company to offer microwave services—AT&T's now famous rival MCI. Providers like MCI could broker discount services because they did not bear the overhead costs of an AT&T. By 1975, a series of landmark judicial decisions led to the complete deregulation of foreign firms and their entry into the telephone equipment market.

The declining cost of microprocessors that underlay the microcomputer revolution also furthered a convergence of analog and digital technologies that merged computer and telephone networks. Falling costs of converting voice signals into digital data made it attractive in the late

1970s for networks to incorporate both phones and computers. As switching costs declined relative to transmission costs, the efficient network increasingly resembled, not a pyramid, but a geodesic dome in which switches (such as telephone exchanges) and intelligent nodes (such as personal computers) proliferated, and in which transmissions were minimized.[6] Parallel developments in fiber optics eased the combined transmission of voice and data, further undermining established competitive positions.

These technological developments induced in national infrastructures shifts that are still working their way through the economies of leading nations. In the United States, they heightened competitive pressure to such an extent that managers themselves petitioned for the deregulation of long-distance telephone services and the breakup of the AT&T–Bell system.* In Japan, foreign computer companies made inroads on Nippon Telephone and Telegraph throughout the 1980s, while privatization of telephone services continued in the United Kingdom and West Germany.

Improvements in telecommunications and transportation fostered closer financial, social, and political ties among firms and nations. These ties constitute the heart of a dramatic mutation in the global infrastructure that is nowhere more apparent than in the mobility of goods and, especially, capital.† Today, stocks and bonds change hands around the clock as traders leapfrog from New York to London to Tokyo. Their unencumbered trades virtually tie local exchanges into a single global auction market that fosters converging rates of return on similar financial assets from different countries. Most observers conclude, in fact, that few obstacles to long-term capital mobility exist in the United States, Canada, and the United Kingdom, while Germany, Japan, the Netherlands, and Switzerland have extensively liberalized their markets.††

In the last 30 years, outward investment by U.S. firms has grown at an average rate of 9.5 percent, a near ninefold increase since 1960.[8] The lion's share (97 percent) flows out from the seven leading industrialized

---

*The Bell saga is far from over. Since the divestiture of the Bell operating companies, start-ups relying on new technologies like fiber optics and wireless phones have begun encroaching on the markets of the regulated phone companies. The pressure to deregulate local phone monopolies is now under way.[7]

†World trade as a proportion of gross domestic product for the major industrial countries grew dramatically between 1953 and 1985. The rapid upturn in trade's importance to the economies of these countries since 1965 is striking. Also remarkable is the degree to which world trade has outpaced production within countries.

††Various studies point to the increasing substitutability of assets held in those industrialized nations that face minimal political risk. They demonstrate financial integration by either: (1) correlating changes in return on assets traded in different national markets, or (2) testing for evidence of interest rate parity between countries. Both long-term and short-term capital flows appear to behave in ways consistent with a globalization of financial markets, making assets substitutable across countries.

nations (the United States, United Kingdom, West Germany, Japan, the Netherlands, France, and Canada) and into each other's economies. Indeed, the industrialized nations host over 60 percent of all inward direct investment, with North America receiving the largest share. A serious concern, therefore, has been the flight of investment from the developing nations, and their incremental isolation from the principal economic trading blocks.

Finally, an estimate of the global character of banking is provided by the international holdings of banks, that is, assets representing cross-border claims. U.S. and Japanese banks hold the largest shares of international business, with some 25 percent each. Most of these international assets involve claims by banks on other banks, showing how the infrastructure of the financial community itself has grown more tightly linked.[9]

Crumbling National Barriers

Economic bonds call for greater global coordination. More than ever, countries collaborate within regions, and the axis of global dialogue has shifted away from the East-West and North-South descriptions of the post–World War II era. Today, most firms with a global presence contemplate strategic changes designed to capitalize on the policies of individual nations and of the triad of trading blocks in North America, Western Europe, and Asia. As firms attain global status, however, they also become more flexible and able to avoid responding to nationalistic demands.

North America. Canada and the United States generate the world's largest volume of bilateral trade, over $150 billion in 1988. In 1986, 78 percent of Canada's exports and 69 percent of its imports were with the United States. Canada absorbs only 22 percent of U.S. exports. In addition, direct investment in Canada by the United States in 1986 amounted to over $50 billion, making the United States Canada's principal foreign investor.

In 1989, the United States and Canada signed a free trade agreement that essentially created a North American community, paving the way for the unencumbered flow of goods and capital between the two countries. Canadian investment in the United States topped $40 billion in 1990, and trade could double by 1995. Spurred by lower wages in the United States, cheaper real estate, and lower tax rates, hundreds of Canadian companies, such as industrial giant Varity Corporation (better known by many as the former Massey-Ferguson) are moving south of the border.[10]

On the United States' southern border, efforts by Mexican leaders to open the economy to foreign trade offer the possibility that a low-wage partner could enhance the global competitiveness of the North American community.[11] The Maquila Program, begun in 1965 and renamed the

Mexican Industrialization Program in 1986, created export-processing zones for U.S. firms throughout Mexico. In 1987, some 1100 manufacturing firms participated in the program, 67 percent of which were U.S. majority-owned and 93 percent of which lined the U.S. border with Mexico, employing some 280,000 workers. Major U.S. firms include General Motors with 23 plants, General Electric with 14 plants, and Zenith with 7 plants.[12] Government-level talks in the early 1990s aim to add Mexico to the existing U.S.–Canada free trade zone, creating a market of 364 million consumers with a total GNP of $6 trillion, some 25 percent larger than the European community.[13]

Europe 1992. Leaders of the 12 member nations of the European Economic Community (EEC) agreed to eliminate the regulatory patchwork inhibiting free trade in Europe by 1992, creating a single market of 320 million consumers. By 1997, individual countries are expected to stop issuing their own money and forfeit control over interest rates: Consumers should be relying on a common currency—the European Currency Unit or ECU—managed by a single central bank (the European Monetary Institute) scheduled to open in 1994.

A united Europe is expected to deregulate sectors previously run as government monopolies, including financial services, telecommunications, and advertising. Experts predict that sales of communications equipment, for instance, will increase at double the U.S. rate, expanding from $70 billion in 1988 to $105 billion in 1992. Where individual governments once tightly rationed ad time and licensing to private broadcasters, European advertising billings are already increasing at 12 percent a year, twice the U.S. rate. Grey Advertising doubled its European billings to $1.4 billion between 1988 and 1990. Whereas in 1990 a patchwork of national barriers meant a Volkswagen Golf cost 55 percent more (before taxes) in Britain than in Denmark, such variations will quickly disappear in a united Europe.*

Nonetheless, fears remain that Europe 1992 may mean a "fortress Europe," confronting non-European firms with an unsurmountable wall of legal, technical, and cultural barriers. Giant U.S. toy retailer Toys 'R' Us experienced it firsthand when it struggled to enter the German market in 1986. The German Toy Manufacturers Association boycotted the company's efforts to open stores, local manufacturers refused to supply them, and regulators denied construction permits for the sprawling

---

*As one observer put it, "in the decade of the 1990s Europe will become more and more a U.S.-style consumer society. Countries will retain their own tastes, cultures, langauges, and almost certainly their own currencies. But for the first time, Europe won't be severely handicapped by its divisions. Economically, 320 million consumers will be speaking with one voice. Catering to Europe's finicky new consumers will take companies that are big, agile, and pan-European" (*Fortune:* 10 April 1989, 114).

stores on the outskirts of town. It took the financial muscle of the U.S. parent, as well as extensive local hiring, to overcome local resistance.[14] The experience stood the firm in good stead when, after facing similar resistance, it successfully entered the Japanese market in December 1991.

Asia-Pacific. Nations of Southeast Asia constituted the world's fastest growing economic region in the late 1980s. Their growth rates exceeded 8 percent between 1988 and 1990, reaching double digits in the four clusters of nations led by China, Thailand, South Korea, and Singapore. Spurred by Japan's rapid growth, these trading nations form an increasingly dynamic community: Between 1987 and 1991, trade among East Asian nations nearly doubled. Japan buys 21 percent of all Asian nations' exports, provides 64 percent of all nonmilitary aid, and accounts for between 20 percent and 50 percent of foreign investment in all Asia-Pacific nations, except for oil-rich Brunei and the Phillipines.[15] Japan has superseded the United States as the largest aid provider to the world (Japan doles out some $7 billion a year within Asia alone, while more of its production gets delegated to lower-wage countries in the region). Indeed, some worry that a Japanese "coprosperity sphere" is evolving which could seal off the dynamic region from rivals, much as fears abound that a "fortress Europe" might develop.[16]

The Triumph of Market Capitalism?

Interdependence has also prompted dramatic changes in the world's ideological and cultural coherence. Three indicators suggest that macroscopic changes are stimulating increasing homogeneity of ideas and thought structures worldwide: The capitulation of socialist ideals and dismantling of the Soviet empire; the rise of English as the language of politics and business; and the export of U.S. cultural products overseas. In the global competition for ideas, even as the United States has declined economically, it is settling into a position of near ideological hegemony over world affairs.

A new world order is rising from the ashes of the Cold War. The mass defection of Poland, Hungary, Romania, Czechoslovakia, Bulgaria, and East Germany from the Warsaw Pact; the introduction of multiparty structures in Eastern block countries and popular elections that swept communist parties out of power and elected democratic candidates; the destruction of the Warsaw Pact's most visible symbol, the Berlin Wall, and the reunification of the two Germanies; the splintering of the Soviet Union into independent republics—all these events have spelled economic and military chaos for Eastern Europe in the early 1990s. At the same time, they have opened new markets to global firms as liberated countries look for assistance in building their antiquated infrastructures, as local businesses struggle to achieve efficiency, and as consumers long starved for Western goods demand satisfaction.

Global liberalization is also evident in the number of key industries worldwide that were deregulated. In the United States, deregulatory acts instigated under the Carter administration were pursued aggressively by the Reagan administration, and implemented in two ways: (1) by opening to competition firms traditionally shackled such as trucking, airlines, telecommunications, and financial services; and (2) by attacking the social regulations introduced since 1964 that were designed to protect the health and safety of consumers and workers and to safeguard the environment.* Between 1980 and 1986, for instance, the *Federal Register* documented a halving of proposed and adopted regulations, from 87,012 to 47,418 pages.[17]

Consider financial services in the United States. The International Banking Act of 1978 and various regulatory changes culminated in the Depository Institutions Deregulation and Monetrary Control Act of 1980 and the Garn–St. Germain Act of 1982. By removing restrictions on firms' activities, these laws melded the historically segmented sectors represented by savings and loans associations, commercial banks, investment banks, insurance firms, and brokerage houses into a financial services community. Competition also increased due to a burst of financial innovations, the development of offshore capital markets, and the growing role played by assets bundled into securities in international capital flows.[18]

To capitalize on industrial convergences in the late 1970s and early 1980s, firms that previously specialized in offering a narrow range of products began diversifying across industry lines. Following Merrill Lynch's entry into retail banking through its innovative Cash Management Account, other nonbank intermediaries also joined the fray. Most aggressively, Sears Roebuck purchased brokerage firm Dean Witter and converted its store card into the Discover credit card in a search for synergy between its retail operations and the delivery of financial services to its customers. Banks and savings and loan associations retaliated by petitioning legislators to rescind the Glass-Steagall and McFadden Acts. They also raised interest rates and worked hard to keep up by introducing such new products as money market funds, interest-bearing checking accounts, annuities, and insurance policies.

As competition intensified, the search for higher returns to cover increased costs encouraged old-time financial managers to make riskier

---

*Cf. Harrison, B. and Bluestone, H. in *The Great U-Turn* (New York: Basic Books, 1990). H. Reagan also encouraged privatization of government controlled businesses like Conrail, following in the footsteps of the more aggressive Thatcher in the U.K. who sold off British Airways, British Telecom, and Jaguar, among others.

investments in commercial real estate, junk bonds, and foreign currency—one result of which was the S&L crisis whose cost, borne by taxpayers, could exceed $500 billion.[19] Anticipating the dissolution of the McFadden Act that restricted interstate banking, many prominent banks like Citicorp and Chemical Bank diversified across state lines by purchasing regional banks. Money center banks also broadened their business and product portfolios in anticipation of becoming one-stop financial supermarkets.

Jointly, then, the globalization of industries, spurred by technological developments, political transformations, and deregulation, has provoked in banking, as in other sectors, a convergence of industries that traditionally were protected. It has heightened competition and forced managers to reassess their firms' strategic trajectories.

Toward a Global Culture?

Agreement about the merits of markets constitutes only one aspect of our progressive global homogenization. In a world fragmented into multiple religions, tribes, and cultures, language also provides an important vehicle for developing greater levels of integration. Early excitement over man-made Esperanto as a universal language points to our collective wish for a medium of communication through which to manage our global interdependence. Far more than Esperanto, English now appears to have taken on the role of medium in the conduct of world affairs.

In a pioneering study, linguist Otto Jespersen documented the increasing use of the English language between 1500 and 1930. He attributed the spread of English to the "political ascendancy" of the English-speaking world, one aspect of its growing hegemony over world affairs.

Today, his words ring true. An estimated 300 million people are native speakers of English in the world; another 450 million command English as a second language. Although Chinese boasts more indigenous speakers, none of its many dialects have diffused significantly outside China. With one of every seven people in the world conversant, English is manifestly the leading medium of international communication for both advanced study and the conduct of business. It serves as the native language of 12 nations, and an official or semiofficial language of 33 others.*

---

*In 56 other countries, English is a required subject or widely studied in school. A recent study confirms the global pervasiveness of English by highlighting the growth of English in non-English-mother-tongue countries. They report that English mother-tongue countries host more than 40 percent of the non-English-speaking world's foreign students; that English book production is more than double that of French in all nonnative countries, making English the most viable medium through which ideas are presented worldwide; and that some 16 percent of all primary school students, 77 percent of secondary students, and over 98 percent of tertiary students receive significant exposure to English as a second language (*U.S. News & World Report:* 18 February 1985, 49–52).

Additionally, newspapers such as the *International Herald Tribune* and magazines such as *Newsweek* and *Time* help to diffuse English further. Over 47 countries of Asia and Africa publish English-language dailies, suggesting extensive local familiarity with English as a second language. These data suggest that as firms seek global opportunities, English increasingly will be the medium for sharing business information.

Western culture and lifestyles are also transmitted through exports of films, books, television programs, theater, and music. Statistics documenting the export of U.S. films indicate how ascendant U.S. cultural products have become in global consumption. In 1988, U.S. films generated some 60 percent of worldwide theatrical showings, accounting for 45 to 65 percent of local box office receipts. Between 1984 and 1988, the fastest growing markets for theatrical films were outside the United States, in the United Kingdom, Sweden, West Germany, and Spain—each with an increase greater than 100 percent. In Japan and Italy, U.S. film imports grew by more than 80 percent. Because the pattern of film exports also mirrors that of other cultural goods such as popular music and television programming, it suggests that Western values and ideas disseminate ever more widely abroad. So perceptions of mutuality are becoming singularly Western and probusiness, supporting the globalizing efforts of corporate managers.

The Moral Dimension

While globalization, technological change, and deregulation have forced interpenetration of nation-states and industries, institutional environments place greater urgency on the task of controlling the managerial and corporate excesses brought to light during the freewheeling decade of the 1980s.

Two principal trends combined to shape the greed decade: (1) sociodemographic effects associated with the postwar baby boom moving through the workplace, and (2) economic consequences of a liberal canon of beliefs that swept throughout the United States and Western Europe, promoting laissez-faire within industries and firms. This marriage of opportunity and skill gave birth to a decade of economic growth, on the one hand, and to widespread ecological and ethical transgressions, on the other. The 1990s result is greater concern with the deficiencies of competitive markets, the distortions of corporate actions, and firms' inadequacies as institutions.

Enhanced international cooperation increased firms' flexibility in allocating resources across countries and regions. As governments negotiated more bilateral and multilateral agreements, they created the institutional framework that now drives managers' global strategic actions. Historical mistrust of multinationals has fallen by the wayside as nations vie to attract firms that can transfer valuable skills to their local populations and contribute to building the human capital that constitutes the basis of domestic development.

Reigning in Laissez-Faire

As firms have developed into global institutions with more autonomy and less oversight, we have become increasingly concerned that they should somehow factor into their decision making the viewpoints of environmentalists, consumers, and other stakeholders—that they should own up to fundamental social responsibilities. U.S. industrial history is punctuated with similar calls for scrutinizing the conduct of managers, firms, and industries. The so-called robber barons of the turn of the century were reviled for their single-minded pursuit of personal wealth despite the cost in human lives that fulfilling their ambitions entailed.

Throughout the 1980s, the aggressive attacks by corporate raiders on many established firms highlighted the opposition between images of raiders as entrepreneurial swashbucklers championing industrial efficiency, and their depiction as modern day robber barons, selfishly motivated to gain at all cost. By breaking up large firms into smaller units, closing plants, and restructuring whole industries, they gathered enormous profits, while causing layoffs, community anguish, and human distress.[20]

Social displeasure with firms' actions was accentuated with revelations of pervasive insider trading on Wall Street. Dennis Levine, Ivan Boesky, and Michael Milken headlined in government's charge that the industry violated securities laws regarding use of private information in issuing, transferring, and manipulating stocks and bonds. Their widely publicized condemnations to multi-million-dollar restitutions and jail terms made salient the degree to which markets sit squarely on an edifice of norms—norms that they had overstepped—the moral dimension of the marketplace. Having ignored the cultural rules that enable markets to function, having behaved like Tom Wolfe's omnipotent "masters of the universe" in *The Bonfire of the Vanities*, managers were held responsible for disrupting the smooth functioning of society.

In sentencing Michael Milken to 10 years in prison, for instance, Judge Kimba Wood argued that he set an example:

> When a man of your power in the financial world, at the head of the most important department of one of the most important investment banking houses in this country, repeatedly conspires to violate, and violates, securities and tax laws in order to achieve more power and wealth for himself and his wealthy clients, and commits financial crimes that are particularly hard to detect, a significant prison term is required in order to deter others.[21]

Scarcely had Milken's prosecution left the front pages before allegations of wrongdoing—this time by no less stalwart than the world's number one brokerage house, Japan's Nomura Securities—provoked further soul searching in the financial community. Nomura's chief executive officer resigned after admitting the firm's illegal reimbursement of top clients for stock market losses, and ties to organized crime.[22] Other leading brokerage houses like Daiwa, Nikko, and Yamaichi soon confessed to making similar improper payments, embarassing Japan's regulators.[23]

Within weeks, however, embarassment would give way to consternation as the global money-laundering activities of the Arab-owned Bank of Credit and Commerce International, secret parent of Washington's largest bank holding company, First American Bankshares, came to light. Through a complex web of cross-ownership in Britain, the United States, the Middle East, and throughout South America, BCCI apparently engaged in fraudulent transfers, bribes, and bad loans, with links to drug barons, dictators, and terrorists.[24]

This scandal was only to be pushed off the front pages by yet another tawdry revelation: that mighty Salomon Brothers, one of the United States' premier investment banks and a leading purchaser of government securities, had sought to corner the market in some Treasury issues and subsequently altered records in an attempted cover-up. Resignations quickly followed, culminating in the departure of one of the investment community's most powerful figures, John Guttfreund.[25]

Clearly these indictments of some of the world's most prominent firms and their managers raise deep questions about the ethical postures lodged within companies' cultures; about the moral basis of the strategic decisions managers make as they seek to maintain their firms' competitiveness.

The Gilded Age

Not Michael Milken's condemnation, however, but the ringing of the bell at the New York Stock Exchange on October 19, 1987 actually signaled the end of a decade of continuous economic expansion that produced dozens of new billionnaires, hundreds of new decamillionaires, and thousands more centimillionaires and elevated the yuppie, the raider, and the MBA to the status of cultural icons.[26]

The money culture these gilded financiers helped to fashion represented a nexus of supply and demand: In the United States, the liberal policies of Ronald Reagan's administration created a tremendous supply of growth opportunities. It found a receptive audience in the United States' most educated and ambitious generation in history, the postwar baby boomers, about to make their first foray into the workforce. Liberal policies provided a heady environment indeed for recently minted, achievement-oriented MBAs, eager to parlay their training at some of the best business schools into wealth.

Tax reforms introduced in the United States between 1981 and 1983 lowered personal income tax rates by 25 percent. Instead of initiating a personal savings boom, however, the discretionary income returned to consumers brought on an unparalleled spree of spending, a burst of conspicuous consumption unseen since Thornstein Veblen described the rise of the "leisure class" at the turn of the century. Tax cuts also lowered corporate rates by 50 percent to encourage managers to reinvest in plant and equipment. Unfortunately, absolute capital investment in the United States grew only 12 percent from 1981 to 1984, and not until 1985 did it match the capital investment levels of 1978.[27]

By providing firms and consumers with excess cash, many argued that Reagan's liberal tax policies actually transformed the United States into a "casino society," one more interested in financial speculation than production.[28] Lower taxes, especially when combined with the tight monetary policy of the U.S. Federal Reserve and with massive government borrowing to pay for mounting deficits, pushed up interest rates and unearned income. The rise of over-the-counter market trading in the stocks of smaller, riskier firms; the increased trading of risky financial instruments such as futures and commodities; and the startling popularity of high-yielding junk bonds, all pointed to the increasing involvement in speculation by individuals and institutions.

On the corporate side, speculation was nowhere more visible than in the proliferation of leveraged buyouts and hostile takeovers of large firms like Nabisco, General Foods, and Revlon. Burdened by debt, managers restructured their firms by selling assets, retrenching, and consolidating lines of business, with all the social dislocations to employees, families, and communities that these cutbacks entail.

The generation of baby boomers entering the work force stood poised to capitalize on the opportunities afforded by the liberal expansion. Well credentialed, ambitious to a fault, they struck out into the working world to achieve rapid success and wealth. Between 1982 and 1988, Wall Street itself absorbed tens of thousands of newly minted MBAs, willingly paying them $100,000 starting salaries and bonuses, with the promise of far more to come.*

---

*As John Taylor put it in *The Circus of Ambition* (1990: 218): "That generation of young professionals—who made staggering and unprecedented sums of money while still in their twenties—represented a sort of cultural and economic avant-garde in the eighties. Together with the hordes of new lawyers and accountants who service Wall Street firms, they were a primary force in the creation of the money culture. They were behind everything from the surge in value of American antiques and the proliferation of expensive restaurants to the rising price of housing in cities like New York, Boston, and San Francisco."

As the decade ended, however, many self-appointed "masters of the universe"* suddenly found themselves unemployed, forced to recognize that they had created only an illusion of wealth; many of their financial innovations had damaged important sectors of U.S. industry; some deregulated markets would require reregulation. Under Reagan's successor George Bush, as one observer put it, "the garden of government is once again teeming with an abundant growth of new regulations."[29]

New Rules

Other demographic trends also feed the social pressure we now place on managers to address firms' institutional effectiveness. With more than 70 percent of women between the ages of 20 and 44 working, for instance, companies today find themselves forced to confront employee concerns about child rearing, day care, and mobility. Estimates show that by 1995 some 66 percent of preschool children and 75 percent of school-age children will have mothers who work outside the home.[30]

As single parents and dual-career families proliferate, we expect ever greater assistance from firms in managing the work-family interface. And firms are complying: According to the Conference Board, more than 3500 U.S. companies now provide some form of child care assistance, and the number is rapidly increasing. Even previously unheard of paternity leaves have become an option at companies like Aetna, 3M, Lotus, AT&T, and Eastman Kodak.[31] In 1989, IBM created a $22 million fund to be distributed over five years, to increase the availability of child care services for its employees. Three million dollars were spent in 1991 to build five child care centers in the United States, and an additional $500,000 were spent to improve facilities in communities with large numbers of IBM employees.[32]

The mixing of races, long a challenge to governments the world over, now also affects firms more deeply. The Bureau of Labor Statistics projects increased participation of minorities in the 1990s, with 74 percent growth in hiring of Hispanics and a 29 percent increase in hiring of African-Americans—in contrast to only 15 percent growth in the white labor force. With social attitudes and educational backgrounds different from the prevailing mix, these groups will need training to work in the knowledge-intensive fields that are the most rapidly growing sector of corporate America. To this end, many firms already participate in educational programs, forming public-private partnerships with local schools

---

*Author Tom Wolfe's (1989) colorful and ironic description of successful urban professionals in his best-selling *Bonfire of the Vanities*.

to reduce high school dropout rates and promote skill building. As the costs of replacing older employees increase as firms compete in a tighter labor market, former bastions of cultural conformity increasingly realize the merits of accommodating cultural diversity.

Changing demographics also influence firms' marketing strategies. Targeting products to the 76 million baby boomers proved lucrative to marketers in the postwar era as they harmonized their offerings with the life cycle of schooling, dating, marrying, and family building. As the postwar babies age, their tastes and interests shift, and marketplace concerns are likely to be dominated more by middle-age concerns such as care for the elderly, health and well-being, convenience, comfort, and product quality. Once begun, these overhead items on corporate income statements will not quickly dissipate.

Spaceship Earth

Our awareness has grown in recent years of firms' role in damaging the natural environment, with global implications for humanity. Consumers and other interest groups voice our concern about firms' actions by lobbying governments, boycotting products, sponsoring ad campaigns, and generating media hype through attention-getting events. Not coincidentally, public activism is forcing firms to develop significant savvy in public and government relations.

TRI published a report in 1989 listing the top 500 polluters in the United States. Topping the list were firms involved in oil and mineral extraction and chemicals production. Of the so-called Toxic 500, Table 2.2 lists the 10 firms responsible for releasing the most toxic pollutants into the environment.

Table 2.2. The Top Ten Polluters

Rank	Firm	Pollutants released in 1989 ($\times 10^6$ lbs)
1	Aluminum Company of America	1984
2	National Steel Company	440
3	E.I. Du Pont	396
4	British Petroleum	341
5	Monsanto	275
6	American Cyanamid	224
7	Shell Oil	216
8	Kaiser Tech	199
9	Freeport-McMoran	144
10	Reynolds Metals	125

Partly because of consumers' concerns over degradation of the environment, fast-food giant MacDonald's Corporation announced in November 1990 a planned phaseout of styrofoam packaging for its hamburgers. A few weeks later, leading soft drink bottlers Coke and Pepsi took their rivalry one symbolic step further by announcing that they would each be first to sell soft drinks in plastic bottles made with recycled materials.[33]

Spurred by medical findings and industrial accidents, many communities in recent years have initiated lawsuits and received multimillion-dollar awards against companies involved in producing oil and chemicals. To avoid pollution and damage claims, some of these companies go so far as to buy up homes around their plants to create "safety zones." Exxon, for example, spent some $4 million to buy and remove 110 homes and businesses near its refinery in Baton Rouge. Some of these homes had been damaged in December 1989 by an explosion that killed two workers, injured seven, and generated 8000 damage claims. Across the Mississippi River, Dow Chemical began a similar home buyout program that could cost it $10 million. Conoco is preparing to spend some $18 million to buy 377 homes near its refinery in Ponca City, Oklahoma, after settling a lawsuit over pollution.[34]

As public attention turns to the decaying natural environment, concern builds for how managers' carelessness with risky technologies produces industrial accidents; how manager's decisions create industrial waste and air, water, and land pollution and make inefficient use of energy; and how manager's local choices about plants and production processes have global consequences.

Industrial Accidents.   Over half the most serious industrial accidents in this century occurred since 1977. Indeed, the 1980s provided many instances that showed how managers are prone to underestimate the catastrophic potential of new technologies.[35]

The danger of nuclear power, for instance, was never more clearly proved than in April 1986 when one of four reactors at Chernobyl in the Soviet Union's Ukraine republic exploded, releasing between 50 and 100 million curies of radioactive material into the environment. Health effects were significant and immediate, in contrast to the 1977 Three Mile Island accident in Pennsylvania where a thousand times less energy was released. At Chernobyl, 29 people died of radiation poisoning in the first few months, and 200 others have poor long-term prospects, with high probability of developing cancer later in life. One hundred million people throughout Europe fell under mandatory or voluntary food restrictions as the radioactive cloud spread over the continent and contaminated fruits, vegetables, and grass for grazing livestock. Experts estimate an additional 135,000 cancer cases and 35,000 deaths will result from the fallout.[36]

Our reliance on fuel combustion places oil extraction and transport as a leading source of both pollutants and industrial accidents. Still, oil spills actually account for less than a third of the oil released. The bulk of pollutants comes from washing tankers out with seawater and releasing into the ocean oily ballast water that kills and harms marine life.

Nonetheless, tankers contracted by oil companies spill between 3 and 6 million metric tons of oil into the ocean each year—about a ton of pollution for every thousand tons transported by sea. After a Swedish tanker spilled 300 tons of oil into the Baltic Sea in 1987, some 60 tons of mollusks and crustaceans perished. In 1989, the Exxon Valdez disaster off the Alaska coastline spilled more than 10 million gallons of oil, killing some 23,000 migratory birds and 730 sea otters.

In 1984, what was probably the worst industrial accident of this century occurred when a storage tank at Union Carbide's pesticide plant in Bhopal, India, leaked methyl isocyanate gas into the neighboring community, killing some 3000 people, 2000 animals, and injuring over 300,000 others. In a settlement reached with the Indian government in 1989, Union Carbide agreed to a $470 million payment to compensate victims of the disaster.

Especially because the Bhopal accident involved the transfer of a risky technology to a developing nation, managers felt prompted to sponsor many studies of their firms' practices regarding toxic hazards. In 1985, for instance, Monsanto Co. audited each of its locations worldwide. Surveys of chemical industry associations revealed that most of these firms' managers modified their structures and systems to coordinate better global safety programs.[37]

Industrial Waste.   Solid waste consists principally of paper and plastics, each of which is the lifeblood of a highly profitable industry. Although these materials are at least partially recoverable by recycling, in the United States only about 11 percent was recycled in 1986. Of the remainder, 9 percent was incinerated, and 80 percent was dumped in landfills. But because landfills present serious threats to ground water and surface water pollution, the number of U.S. landfills dropped from 20,000 in 1978 to 6000 in 1988.

Wastes include dredged material, sewage sludge, incinerated hazardous waste, and industrial waste. The Dutch government recently reported that the North Sea is among the most polluted seas in the world. In 1984, about 5.6 million tons of industrial waste, as well as 5100 tons of sewage sludge and 97 million tons of dredged material were dumped into its waters. PCB pollution is believed responsible for massive fish poisonings and high rates of infertility and miscarriages among local seal populations.

In 1983, the London Dumping Convention adopted a resolution banning the dumping of low-level radioactive waste generated in medical research and industrial activities. However, many plants that reprocess nuclear fuels release radioactive wastes into coastal areas not covered by the Act. Discharges from reprocessing plants in the United Kingdom and France have been linked to local illness and death.

Some 250 city sewage facilities and 627 industrial operations routinely dump toxic waste into U.S. waterways. A recent study by the Environmental Protection Agency documents nearly 7000 accidents involving hazardous substances between 1980 and 1985. U.S. firms generate over 250 million metric tons of hazardous waste each year, two-thirds of which is disposed through injection wells and pits that threaten to pollute water supplies.

As a principal contributor to solid waste, plastics present a disconcerting challenge. Each year, firms produce and we toss out more than 6 million metric tons of shipboard litter into the ocean. We also discard some 5 million plastic containers each day. In a three-hour cleanup sweep covering 157 miles of Texas coast in 1987, volunteers collected 307 tons of litter; two-thirds of it was plastic and included 31,733 bags, 30,295 bottles, and 155,631 six-pack rings. Up to 2 million seabirds and 100,000 marine mammals, including some 30,000 fur seals, perish each year after eating or becoming tangled in plastics. Sea turtles choke to death on plastic bags they mistake for jellyfish. Birds eat plastic pellets floating on the surface, mistaking them for fish eggs or larvae. A study on Midway Island in the Pacific found that 90 percent of the albatross chicks examined had plastic debris in their digestive systems. With plastic production doubling every 12 years, the amount of waste can only increase.

Pollution. Pollution forms when firms and countries disregard the effects of their products and production processes on the global ecology. Firms pollute because the social costs of production are not incorporated into managers' decision-making frameworks. Nations pollute either because they lack the infrastructure necessary to monitor and control firms, or because of bellicose acts like the polluting inferno created by Iraq's Saddam Hussein after he set fire to Kuwaiti oil fields in early 1991.

Industrial and mining operations are a major source of toxic pollutants: petroleum, petrochemicals, pesticides, herbicides, fertilizers, steel, and paper products. Major industrial pollutants include chlorinated organic compounds, phenols, nitrogen, phosphorous, mercury, lead, and cadmium. In 1987, for instance, world fertilizer and pesticide sales exceeded $16.8 billion. Fertilizers and pesticides, however, contain phosphates and nitrogen that damage drinking water. Pesticides and herbicides are also toxic, not only to target pests, but to people and wildlife: Some 45,000 annual cases of accidental pesticide poisonings are reported in the United States alone.[38] Indirect public health costs of pesticide use have been estimated at between $1 and $2 billion a year.

Industrial activities routinely produce gases that pollute water and air and contribute to global warming. Reliance on motor vehicles for transportation and oil combustion for fuel causes annually the release of about 110 million tons of sulfur oxides, 69 million tons of nitrogen oxides, 193 million tons of carbon monoxide, 57 million tons of hydrocarbons, and 59 million tons of particulates. As these gases accumulate in the stratosphere, they create a shield around the planet, trapping radiant heat—the greenhouse effect.

Acid rain results when water condenses around molecules of sulfur and nitrogen oxides released from electrical power plants, industrial boilers, mineral smelting plants, and motor vehicles. Acid rain harms U.S. forests, agriculture, and aquatic ecosystems to the tune of some $5 billion annually. Reactions between nitrogen and organic compounds influence the levels of ozone in the atmosphere.

At ground level, excessive ozone damages human health, trees, crops, and buildings. In 1988, 96 U.S. cities and counties failed to meet EPA standards for ozone. Indeed, average ozone concentrations in industrialized cities were three times higher than the level at which damage to crops and vegetation begins. The U.S. National Crop Loss Assessment Program estimates that damage to corn, wheat, soybeans, and peanuts due to lower atmosphere ozone results in annual losses of $1.9 to $4.5 billion.

For lack of ozone, however, earth's upper atmosphere no longer screens out as much harmful ultraviolet radiation from the sun. Over the last 20 years, ozone levels have dropped by as much as 40 percent over Antarctica during the spring. The thinning ozone layer increases incidence of skin cancers and eye disorders and aggravates nutritional deficiencies and infectious diseases. Chlorofluorocarbons (CFCs), nitrogen oxides, carbon dioxide, halons (used in fire extinguishers) and methane destroy upper atmosphere ozone. CFCs are used in such consumer products as aerosol propellants, refrigerants, coolants, sterilizers, solvents, and blowing agents used in foam production. Although the United States has already banned the use of CFCs as aerosol propellants, they continue to be used in other products and countries.

Turning Points

Globalization, technological change, deregulation, and social recklessness are creating a revolution in corporate environments. They place sometimes contradictory and sometimes convergent pressures on managers to make their firms increasingly attentive to efficiency, entrepreneurship, equity, and ethics in strategic pursuits. Efficiency has become the salient driving force of strategic change for firms based, not only in North America, but also in Asia-Pacific, Western Europe, and, increasingly, in Eastern Europe as firms defend their domestic turf and compete for regional positioning within blocks of trading nations. Rivalry seems all the more ominous as globalization pits American firms against Japanese and European rivals bent on consolidating the successful forays they made throughout the 1980s into highly visible industries in the United States. Rivalry means pressure to improve competitiveness by making operations both more efficient and more entrepreneurial.

Convergences due to technological innovations and widespread deregulation are providing additional spurs to strategic change. Technology has made many previously noncompeting products or services into close substitutes and rendered more permeable the boundaries of established industries. Similarly, deregulation has altered the features of firms that enabled competitiveness and forced managers to form ties to firms in neighboring industries.

Managers are also experiencing increasing social pressure as labor force and consumer demographics change. As women and minorities grow more visible in the workplace, work-family, life-career, and public-private dichotomies become less meaningful. Simultaneously, consumers and other corporate stakeholders demand that greater attention be paid to environment-friendly waste reduction, energy efficiency, recycling, composting, and incineration in forming firms' competitive strategies. To share the burden of change means ensuring that managers make choices that are perceived as fair by all key constituents.

In companies whose activities span the globe, more than ever ethical quandaries abound. Faced with different local standards, managers easily adopt a form of cultural relativism which asserts that behavior should conform solely to local norms. Relativism, however, justifies using different standards in every community—an unsatisfying basis for global operations. In a world growing more homogeneous day by day, pressure is increasingly brought to bear on managers to resist relativism by promulgating unified codes of conduct and stronger integration across all of firms' subsidiaries.[39] Even within national cultures, disagreement about ethical standards prevails: witness the debates spawned by Milken's condemnation and the differing interpretations placed on the common practice of brokerage firms in Japan of giving gifts and reimbursing losses to prominent clients.

These institutional forces impel managers to adopt a more cautious and conciliatory stance toward their many stakeholders. They challenge them to scan environments continually, to improve their ability to interpret strategic issues, to develop consensus views about the implications of ongoing changes, to assess carefully employees' ability to mobilize around core values, to formulate objectives in light of stakeholders' concerns, to balance conflicting demands, and to design internal practices to meet those objectives.

So we face simultaneous demands for efficiency, entrepreneurship, equity, and ethics. These are the forceful triggers and often contradictory pressures that today are provoking strategic change in our leading companies and institutions.

3
Why Companies Resist Change

We make our fortunes and we call them fate.
BENJAMIN DISRAELI

In 1973, more than three years before Steve Wozniak and Steve Jobs put together the first of their now legendary Apple computers, and some eight years before IBM brought out its own PC, researchers at Xerox's famous Palo Alto Research Center had the Alto running—the first personal computer ever designed and built. In July 1975, however, Xerox's board, dismayed at the operating losses of the computer division, unanimously voted to end the business by writing off a $1.3-billion loss. By 1981, when IBM entered the fray, the personal computing market, commercialized by Apple in 1975, would total revenues in the multibillion-dollar range. How could Xerox fail to foresee the Alto's market potential? Why did Xerox not capitalize on its early technological lead?[1]

From 1860 to 1930, U.S. steel makers grew slowly and steadily into a powerful oligopoly that dominated world production. Between 1930 and 1960, the industry was characterized by high margins, manageable competition, stable prices, and extensive reinvestment in increasing plant capacity. The next 20 years, however, would prove disastrous for U.S. steel makers as steel imports from Japan and Europe rose from 4 percent in 1960 to over 16 percent of total domestic supply in 1980, while U.S. global market share dropped from 50 percent in 1945 to less than 20 percent by 1980. How could an industry widely recognized as a dominant force in global markets decline so quickly?[2]

These are not isolated occurrences. Similar stories of missed opportunities, rapid decline, and even outright failure can be told about such household-name firms as Chrysler, ITT, the *Saturday Evening Post*, Penn Central, Rolls Royce, and others. They constitute much of the historical, biographical folklore that inspires fashionable books and that populates business magazines like *Forbes*, *Fortune*, and *Business Week*. Throughout the 1980s, in fact, many of our largest firms either failed entirely or disappeared from view either through takeover or leveraged buyout. Their laid off workers and liquidated assets litter the corporate landscape. If the recent spate of pessimistic assessments of bureaucracy at IBM, AT&T, and GM is to be believed, others appear poised for decline as they face the incursions of more fleet-footed and aggressive rivals.

Why do so many of our large established firms decline and fail? Why do our managers, trained in the most advanced management techniques, seem so easily caught off guard by technological change, by the incursions of competitors, by changes in regulatory policy, or by consumer activists championing, say, product safety or ecological protectionism? Do these firms and their managers lack any fundamental skills, systems, or resources necessary for adaptability? Are they guilty of duplicity, complacency, or outright ignorance?*

Probably not. In fact, many firms and entire business communities appear to be done in by a combination of inertia and momentum that produces entrenched managers, systems, and administrative controls, and circumscribes firms' capabilities. Although these internal features enabled competitiveness in earlier periods, they prove disabling during revolutionary eras.[3] And managers soon find their firms saddled, like leopards, with their spots: Witness the liquidation of the once proud Eastern Airlines, the dismantling of Pan Am, the takeover of the mighty brokerage E.F. Hutton, and the scandal-ridden demise of Drexel Burnham Lambert. In one way or another, they fell victim to a combination of inertia and momentum.

What Produces Inertia?

What we loosely term *inertia* in fact consists of powerful forces that obscure managers' ability to discern looming threats and so to implement needed changes. These inertial forces derive from crystallized features of firms and the business communities in which they operate.

---

*Although we generally recognize that small firms experience a "liability of newness" and that most start-ups fail in their first year for lack of funding and lack of experience, far less obvious is the frequency with which large firms also decline and fail, despite their accumulated assets, know-how, and goodwill. Indeed, although older firms certainly are more likely to survive than smaller firms, a surprising 13 percent of well-established 100-year-old firms never make it to 105. See Starbuck and Nystrom *Handbook of Organization Design* (NY: Oxford University Press, 1981, xiv).

The Entrenched Features of Firms

Managers invest capital in purchasing equipment and hiring employees. The skills workers bring to bear in creating products and services create firm-wide *capabilities* that managers then rely on to compete. The basic capabilities of even large companies like Exxon or Ford are built up from their core technological and human skills: The particular factories, offices, and laboratories they own; their capital stock; the skills of their labor force; and their strengths in research, communications, transportation, and distribution. Insofar as firms' capabilities provide them with an advantage in the marketplace, potential for performance exists. (See Fig. 3.1.)

To realize this potential, to capitalize on their firms' capabilities, managers design *controls*—systems for administering and coordinating the many transactions involved in putting out products and services. Most of our companies today, for instance, continue to rely heavily—and I will argue, excessively—on bureaucratic hierarchies to control activities. They also devise complex systems for systematically recruiting, evaluating, and compensating employees; and administrative systems for monitoring expenses, making decisions, and assigning tasks. When well crafted, these systems serve to channel interactions between employees and so produce good job performance.[4]

Employees also abide by many beliefs and norms that are part of their companies' *cultures*. For example, over time they acquire a shared understanding of firms' competitors, their products, and strategies. A company-wide culture, often made evident in "corporate credos" and codes of conduct, delimits the actions deemed legitimate for everyone to pursue, including the social and ethical postures taken in dealing with clients and other stakeholders. Like controls, cultures require people to act in ways consistent with shared beliefs and company norms about, say, punctuality, product quality, customer service, or social responsibility.

Ultimately, a firm's *conduct* consists of the strategies through which it competes. A firm's conduct is constrained by its underlying capabilities, controls, and cultures. Firms lacking capability in R&D, for instance, find

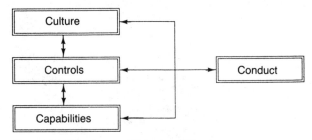

Figure 3.1. The internal features of firms.

it difficult to pursue a strategy designed to achieve first-mover advantages. Firms relying on low-wage labor tend to routinize production facilities and develop authoritarian hierarchies, making it difficult for managers to motivate the commitment and involvement of employees. The passage of time tends to align capabilities, controls, and cultures, and so constrains firms' conduct.* The munificent environment of the postwar era, for instance, encouraged many of our larger firms to develop stable configurations of internal features, only to find that they hampered their ability to adapt when the environment subsequently changed.

Xerox is a case in point. Born as the Haloid Company, an "also ran" to Eastman Kodak throughout its early years in Rochester, the company's success can be traced, not to internal innovation, but to the savvy acquisition in 1947–1948 of patent rights to xerography, a technology pioneered by entrepreneur Chester Carlson. Careful engineering and shrewd marketing created a market larger than Xerox had imagined, and justified the company's evolving identity: first Haloid-Xerox in 1958, then simply Xerox by 1961. The name changes would mirror the company's growing commitment to the technology.[5]

That commitment and capability in copier technology soon translated into protective bureaucratic controls and an inertial culture that would frustrate Xerox managers' efforts to enter the personal computer market in the early 1970s despite an early technology lead. The company's prior successes at creating a steady 15 percent rate of growth had led managers to design controls anchored around copier technologies, a single-product hierarchy, and a shared identity. This configuration of internal features prevented managers from imagining the company as a diversified office products company competing directly with IBM. Later, the internal configuration would continue to frustrate managers' attempts to break away from the mature copier business into mainframe machines, word processors, computer peripherals, workstations, and even document processing systems.[6] Recognizing how much the company has been paralyzed by a continued inability to capitalize on its own innovations, Xerox named in 1990 a new CEO whose stated aim is to break down the bureaucratic walls between R&D, marketing, and manufacturing, and "... to change the company substantially to be more market driven."[7]

Some managers recognize the need for their firms to change only after

---

*For an ecological view of how inertia develops because core features of firms are difficult to change, see Michael Hannan and John Freeman "Structural Inertia and Organizational Change," *American Sociological Review*, 49: 1984, 149–164. For ecologists, change occurs only when external forces such as the discovery of the steam engine, the postwar spurt in births between 1945 and 1955, or developments in miniaturization come to disrupt the stability of the configuration. For a life-cycle interpretation of corporate growth, see Kimberly, J., Miles, R., & Associates, in *The Organizational Life Cycle* (San Francisco: Jossey-Bass, 1980).

it is too late. The demise of retail giant W.T. Grant in 1976 is a case in point. By the time its managers took stock of its overly decentralized structure and its failed internal controls on inventories and receivables, the company was unable to satisfy suppliers, and time had run out.

Other, perhaps more vigilant, managers, however, arrest decline in the nick of time. At Sears Roebuck, for instance, rising competition from specialty catalogues and discounters prompted a slow but systematic response that fostered cost containment and prompted a bold diversification into financial services. Although the jury is still out on Sears (the company has lost over 15 percent of its market share since 1971 and earnings dropped 8 percent between 1984 and 1989), recent internal consolidations suggest a concerted effort to arrest further bottom line decay.[8]

Often dramatic external events are the only force capable of triggering change in long-lived firms. Take defense firms. Over the years of the Cold War, traditional dependence on government contracts lulled them into complacency. With the disintegration of the Soviet empire and sudden liberalization of Eastern economies, they find themselves struggling to reinvent themselves.

A case in point is General Dynamics. By 1995, the defense contractor expects to lose over a third of its sales. To prepare, top managers have already initiated dramatic cutbacks in personnel, capital spending, and R&D. Over 27,000 jobs are scheduled for elimination by 1994. To spur productivity, the company has launched an incentive compensation plan that is tied to its stock performance.[9] Efforts to overcome inertia typically involve managers in such a reshaping of their firms' internal systems and cultures.

In *Rude Awakening*, auto analyst Maryann Keller showed how a close correspondence among corporate elements nurtured insularity at General Motors. Over the years, GM became a paternalistic organization in which managers spent their entire careers—in which elitist privileges such as company dining rooms, heated parking spots, and lavish offsite meetings accrued to executives who conformed to the GM way—in which finance reigned supreme and lorded it over production engineers—in which profits overshadowed product quality—and in which a parochial sense of God-given infallibility and inherent superiority over competitors, especially foreigners, prevailed. Not suprisingly, self-satisfaction and complacency most typified GM, catching the firms' managers completely unprepared for the oil crisis of 1973 and the changed consumer preferences for smaller, more efficient cars; and unable to match Japanese know-how in addressing these consumer needs.

Until the early 1980s, the giant telephone monopolist AT&T was also an inertial system, lumbering into the future with an antiquated mission, a meaningless competitive strategy, and a complacent, bureaucratic culture. The judicial decree that split up the Bell System on January 1, 1984 created a new AT&T along with seven regional companies (the "baby Bells"). Numerous observers have depicted the difficulties AT&T and the baby Bells have experienced in penetrating the competitive computer and telecommunications markets since 1984. Observers ascribe much of the blame to carryover from the centralized structure of the original company whose implementation-oriented culture had always discouraged risk taking, innovation, and change.[10]

Close Ties Within Business Communities

A similar convergence of capabilities, controls, and cultures guided the development of entire business communities since the early 1960s. In autos, for instance, individual firms like General Motors were not the only ones experiencing inertia; the entire community of firms associated with auto production itself was inertial. Stable relationships among GM, Ford, and Chrysler, their parts suppliers, advertising agencies, and investment bankers, all impeded managers' ability to recognize market share erosion by Japanese rivals such as Honda, Toyota, and Nissan, and the changing basis on which they competed: quality and innovation rather than volume, technology rather than marketing.

Partly to blame, of course, were outdated conceptions of strategy formulated within single industries. By the 1980s, the convergence of many industries in one another's markets became so common that strategy was better thought of in the context of what some of us called business communities—the natural groupings of firms whose members routinely interact.* As prominent sectors such as telecommunications and financial services have continued to merge in recent years, the dynamics of change in the context of business communities have only grown more salient.

Because business communities join firms that share a common commitment to a particular technology (e.g., the internal combustion engine), they tend to develop an island-like mentality, a shared world view. Various researchers have suggested that business communities form around a "technological paradigm," a set of thought patterns that are widely shared

---

*Of course, if we focus solely on competitors, it is true that industries try to regulate the activities of their member firms through trade associations. In some industries, collusion among competitors results in price setting and control over distribution. [See Scherer, F., *Industrial Market Structure and Economic Performance* (2nd ed.) (Boston: Houghton Mifflin, 1980). In other industries (such as agricultural products), firms develop lobbying expertise and successfully co-opt powerful figures and agencies of government to achieve price supports or get tax benefits. Just as firms' conduct is constrained by the correspondence of their internal capabilities, controls, and cultures, so is the conduct of industries limited by the correspondence of their particular capabilities, controls, and cultures. Much of the time, however, what we refer to colloquially as industries are in fact business communities.

and provide managers and firms with easily agreed-on solutions to problems. Paradigms act as guideposts to innovation, channeling managers' allocations of funds toward improvements on existing technologies rather than a search for innovations that could detract from their accumulated expertise.[11]

Recall the saga of the VCR. Today, the American film community earns a large part of its revenues from releasing video versions of its feature films. Yet when Sony first introduced the VCR in 1975, the community actively sought to ban the new device. It took over 8 years of litigation and a legal contest that ran all the way to the Supreme Court before the new technology was legalized in the United States. Imagine if they had won!

Or consider the set of firms involved in "keeping people clothed," a business community that joins chemical companies, whose capabilities lie in producing man-made fibers, to textile and apparel manufacturers with capabilities in weaving cloth, to garment designers, jobbers, wholesalers, specialty retailers, and department stores. The community's existence is predicated on a chain of technologies that relates multiple industries competent in fiber development, textile production, apparel manufacturing, equipment manufacturing, parts supply, wholesaling, and retailing.[12] Various controls bind firms across these sectors: Chemical firms not only make the fibers, but also weave fabrics with those synthetic fibers. Yet no single company actually bridges all sectors. Instead, a network of alliances among firms from the different industries ties them into a community.

Since the late 1960s, for instance, the study and exploitation of developments in recombinant DNA has fused into an emerging biotechnology community consisting of a wide variety of firms from traditional industries such as pharmaceuticals, chemicals, agriculture, and energy. Well known start-ups like Genentech, for instance, rely on multiple relationships with other firms that supply equipment, fund research, disseminate information, and regulate genetic manipulation. Development and commercialization of therapeutic products from biotechnology requires active cooperation by many firms, and they rely on extensive networks of contracts, joint ventures, and other alliances to cope with the financial, legal, technical, and social impediments to innovation that they face.[13]

As firms such as these interlace across specialized communities, they form national networks that crisscross the industrial landscape and bind some sectors more closely together. In the United States, the flows of raw material inputs and commodity outputs linking all 370 industries loosely cluster into seven principal communities diagrammed in Fig. 3.2.* As

*The mapping was produced by clustering the supplier and consumer transactions across industries in the U.S. economy. For additional information, see Burt, R.S. and D. Carlton "Another Look at the Network Boundaries of American Markets," *American Journal of Sociology*, 1989, 95: 645–672.

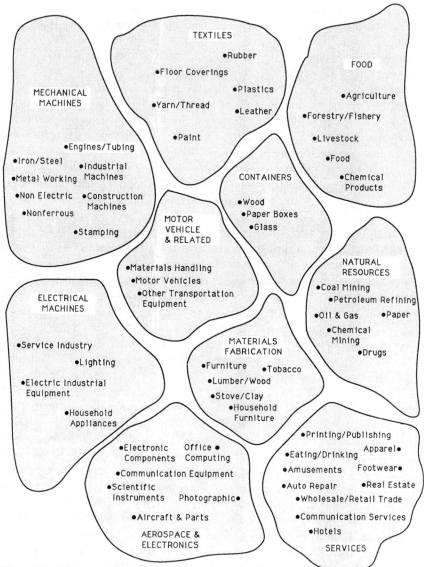

Figure 3.2. Business communities in U.S. industry.

might be anticipated, textile-related activities, for instance, demonstrate an underlying coherence, as do firms involved in electronics, oil, food, and the production and marketing of machinery.[14]

Individual companies are more likely to participate in joint bids, license each other's technologies, pursue joint ventures, and cooperate through trade associations and strategic alliances within business communities. These relationships constitute a community's controls. In turn, a community-wide culture develops as managers agree on product standards, exchange personnel, and participate in joint conferences. As with individual companies, the resulting configuration of capabilities, controls, and culture constrains the conduct of the whole constellation. Just as a family cares for its own, the community favors stability and defends itself against innovations that disrupt member firms' established capabilities.

The garment community itself, for instance, has a pronounced culture. New York symbolizes it well, with its hundreds of specialized garment manufacturers huddled in a small but densely populated part of midtown Manhattan, vying to retain market share in a rapidly changing environment. Perhaps most significant in binding the community together has been the high public profile firms enjoy, their links to the worlds of celebrity and glamour, and their extensive inbreeding through community-wide personnel exchanges. Despite developments in the technologies of design, cutting, and sewing of woven cloth, however, the community demonstrates high levels of inertia, with dozens of firms founded and disbanded each season—few of which show a willingness to adopt novel technologies.[15]

So, Momentum Builds...

Although inertia principally retards change, it also contributes to building momentum that propels firms and communities forward along strategic trajectories. Just as planets are constrained by gravitational forces to move along well-defined orbits around the sun, so too are managers held in check by forces that impede change. In recent years, many firms have succumbed, not only to inertia, but to accumulated momentum that has catapulted them past critical turning points. (See Fig. 3.3)

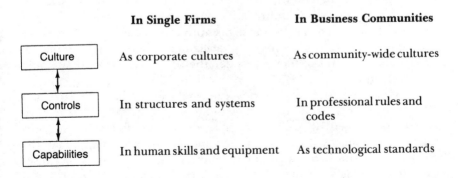

Figure 3.3. How inertia and momentum crystallize.

Trapped on Strategic Trajectories

The close correspondance that develops over time among firms' distinctive capabilities, structural controls, and corporate cultures not only fosters tunnel vision, but blinds managers to events inconsistent with their shared assumptions. Historical success affirms managers' prior commitments, encouraging them to underestimate the need for change.[16]

Success also entrenches incumbents. Initiating change requires a reallocation of resources that threatens the balance of power among managers. Politically savvy subordinates therefore filter information to protect their mentors' vested interests and inhibit change.[17] In his famous study of the Kennedy White House during the Bay of Pigs crisis, for instance, author Irving Janis showed how Kennedy's advisors sheltered the president from relevant information that might have damaged the group's sense of moral righteousness and invulnerability.

Corporate examples abound: Established firms like GE, RCA, and Raytheon proved unable to convert their expertise in older vacuum tube technology into a commercial presence in new transistor-based products; American Viscose failed to recognize the potential of polyester to displace rayon Ampex introduced the first videotape recorder in 1956 but then proved unable to transform its expertise base in recording tape and lost the VCR market to Sony, Matsushita, and JVC; Transitron ignored silicon as a substitute for germanium in semiconductor fabrication; AT&T relied on its government monopoly to delay the diffusion of innovations in communications, only to find itself struggling today to convert its expertise in voice-based systems into a commercial presence in computers—a solo effort that appears to have failed given its acquisition in 1991 of computer maker NCR.

Most large firms and institutions decline and fail from a combination of environmental conditions, strategic actions, and internal characteristics. As environments lose their munificence, competition for a diminishing market generally heightens, and firms whose managers are slow to act, whose structures lack administrative coherence, go out of business.[18] Because their managers do not speak with one voice, these companies tend to initiate erratic responses. By vacillating in their strategic replies to environmental threats, they squander the scarce resources that would return them to health.

A comparative study of 57 large-scale bankruptcies between 1972 and 1982, for instance, showed that few failures were sudden: Most experienced a prolonged 10-year decline in accounting performance, suggesting that, as managers, we are typically much slower to change than the environments our firms inhabit. Ultimately, these companies' trajectories came to resemble a downward spiral. A period of marginal existence and strategic dithering was followed by one in which managers used up their firms' accumulated slack. The decaying trajectory built up to a fatal death struggle as stress precipitated more wavering in their final two years of existence.[19]

Long-lived firms do not suffer only from debilitating inertia. They are also carried forward by the accumulated momentum generated from past and ongoing activities. Much as individuals develop habits, so do firms cajole employees into behaving predictably, encouraging them to respond to even novel circumstances according to past practice. Firms gather momentum as managers repeatedly initiate these well-learned routines. Centralization begets further centralization; specialization begets more specialization.[20] Failure results when managers initiate favored activities that propel them onward but are no longer appropriate to the conditions for which they were designed.

The rapid decline of Chase Manhattan Bank throughout the 1980s demonstrates how inertia and momentum can weigh a firm down. Insiders readily depict Chase in the early 1980s as burdened by a corporate culture that resisted change. While rival financial services firms broadened their portfolios and diversified into advisory work, financing, and other fee-generating services, Chase's tradition-minded managers rejected risk-taking efforts. They actively sabotaged efforts to grow the kinds of investment banking services that were propelling J.P. Morgan and Citibank upwards. Having grown up in a culture that revered personal relationships, Chase's managers resented the impersonal deal-making mentality of the new breed that eschewed promotion from within for job hopping, and skewed pay scales by demanding sky-high bonuses. Bureaucracy, tradition, and risk aversion proved a deadly mix during the heady decade of the 1980s. It cost Chase its leading position in American banking.[21]

An empirical study of the airline industry between 1926 and 1985 found that carriers exhibited, not only inertia due to age, but built-up momentum over time: Managers were more likely to repeat changes in routes, labor contracts, and marketing agreements that their airline had experienced in the past. Follow-up analyses found that companies with a particular competency often were trapped into routinely calling on that competency, thereby generating momentum for change even when change was unnecessary.[22]

In the *Icarus Paradox*, Danny Miller proposed that many familiar firms like IBM, Polaroid, Procter & Gamble, Chrysler, Sears, and Walt Disney Productions bore the distinct capabilities of prototypes he described as Craftsmen, Builders, Pioneers, and Salesmen. When pursued vigorously by managers, however, their core capabilities placed them on strategic trajectories that ultimately led to their decline.*

---

*Bob Hinings and his colleagues at the University of Alberta describe a concept of "tracks," which are archetypes of change, see Hinings et al., *The Dynamics of Strategic Change* (Oxford, England: Basil Blackwell, 1989). I use trajectories in a more limited way as a description of only one type of track, the inertial.

So, commitment to engineering quality in Craftsmen-like firms frequently turns them into Tinkerers, carrying perfectionism to the point of rigidity. Early entrepreneurial Builders tend to become Imperialists, overextending their managerial abilities. Inventive Pioneers become Escapists, converting their commitment to innovation into pie-in-the-sky chaos. And aggressive Salesmen firms indiscriminately proliferate products, becoming aimless Drifters. Even though some firms recover, it appears that frequently managers persist in pursuing strategies beyond the point where they are effective in providing their firms with a competitive advantage.

Consider Steinway, the famous maker of top-of-the-line concert pianos. A total of 12,000 parts and 26 types of glue go into the making of a Steinway grand. The company relies on 400 workers to turn out about 2500 of these pianos a year. Internally, an inbred culture glorifies traditional handwork in the making of the instrument and defies modern principles of parts standardization in manufacturing.

Yet competitive pressures from highly automated Yamaha and other piano manufacturers that turn out some 200,000 pianos a year threaten Steinway's niche, calling for strategic change. Since no one can dispute Steinway's demonstrated success in producing unique, first-rate, and long-lasting pianos, however, change is difficult: It threatens what workers do and how they relate to one another; it challenges their expectations for the future. Who from within the firm would dare to break with tradition and spearhead change? As often happens, to overcome inertia and rebuild momentum the board recently chose to go outside: It hired a former General Electric executive to shake up the firm.[23]

Community Pathways

Just as many companies like Steinway resisted change, so did inertia and momentum force entire business communities to move along obsolete trajectories throughout the 1980s. The history of U.S. industry demonstrates how quick managers from rival firms have been to join forces in an effort to stabilize competition and erect barriers to new entrants. The resulting convergence of an industry's basic capabilities, controls, and culture erected mobility barriers by bonding firms into units, and shielded members from direct influence by the environment and enhanced their profitability. Sheltered from all-out competition, managers then favored incremental changes that built on established capabilities.[24]

Comparative studies of technological innovations suggest that once an industry is founded, its core technology tends to act as a guidepost to its future development. A study that compared airlines, cement manufacturers, and microcomputer manufacturers confirmed that competence-destroying innovations rarely came from firms within an industry—

designers could not invent them, and managers would not encourage them.[25]

Industries themselves are separated into more or less homogeneous groups of firms pursuing similar strategies and achieving different but consistent levels of performance. Firms within these groups compete aggressively. Competition between groups, however, is limited, as managers experience mobility barriers that prevent shifts from one group to another. Studies of beer, pharmaceuticals, and insurance providers suggest that membership in particular subgroups within these industries significantly constrains managers' ability to alter their firms' strategies.[26]

Noted economist F.M. Scherer provides a long list of settings in which start-ups introduced innovations that altered mobility barriers. They illustrate how business communities are anchored around basic technologies from which managers find it difficult to depart. Much as they do for individual firms, community-wide controls and cultural guidelines create momentum that constrains firms' conduct and sets communities moving along stable trajectories.[27]

Most observers now recognize that U.S. auto manufacturers were part of a business community that developed an insular mentality between 1945 and 1970 and led us to minimize the threat of Japanese imports, despite abundant warnings to the contrary.[28] Similar closed-mindedness appears to have characterized integrated steel makers in their initial dismissal of the minimills, and mainframe computer manufacturers in their early disregard for the personal computer.

The community of firms involved in watch production in Switzerland was slow to react to Timex's early distribution of disposable watches through drugstores and other mass outlets. Harvard's Michael Porter argues that they were paralyzed by fear of alienating the jewelry stores that were their prime distributors. However, they also appear not to have recognized the threat posed by the concept of disposability, much as Timex itself later failed to capitalize on the highly lucrative niche of fashion watches subsequently targeted by the retaliatory coalition of Swiss manufacturers known as Swatch.[29]

Familiar high-tech business communites like Silicon Valley in California and Route 128 in Massachussetts also exemplify remarkable coherence, and a perhaps surprising tendency to suffer from inertia. Most firms in these communities are highly specialized, both horizontally in the products they make and vertically in the functions they perform (design, manufacturing, marketing). Despite intense competition, a proliferation of start-ups, and a high failure rate, established firms like Advanced Micro Devices, National Semiconductor, and Intel came to dominate general purpose semiconductor production. Various accounts suggest that by the early 1980s, pursuit of low-cost strategies had bureaucratized these firms' structures and reduced their agility. Employees complained that they were growing increasingly isolated from customers and that their companies were reluctant to pursue promising technical opportunities.

The largest wave of start-ups in the industry's history took place between 1980 and 1987 as entrepreneurs like Cypress Semiconductors' T.J. Rogers and Chips & Technologies' Gordon Campbell quit their jobs and pursued niche markets in the industry, much as the original founders of the Valley had in the 1950s and the 1960s. Whereas the larger established firms had come to discourage interfirm relationships, start-up firms relied heavily on collaborative relationships with customers and competitors: They would meet at trade shows, industry conferences, and trade associations. The resurgence of network ties helped to facilitate community-wide change and Silicon Valley's rebirth in the 1980s.[30]

Dynamic Communities

The mind sets that induce tunnel vision in many of our industries and communities derive, not only from inertia and momentum, but from relationships between firms and key institutions in their environments. AT&T's ability to retard the diffusion of transmission technologies in telecommunications, for instance, resulted from its protected status as a regulated monopoly. In the United States, a legal system of patents and copyrights protects innovations from theft by competitors. More subtly, firms fund associations that routinely lobby legislators and regulators on behalf of industries and communities. The movement of personnel between firms and regulators tends to produce shared mind sets that perpetuate established industrial trajectories.

Japan demonstrates more clearly, perhaps, than the United States how the social environment can influence the strategic directions that firms, industries, and entire business communities take. Most Japanese firms are affiliated with one of nine major business communities (the six older *financial keiretsu* Mitsui, Mitsubishi, Sanwa, Fuyo, Sumitomo, Dai Ichi Kangyo and, of more recent origin, the three *production keiretsu* Toyota, Hitachi, and Matsushita). Firms within these communities closely coordinate their activities through regular meetings to protect the interests of all member firms. Each community often constitutes the principal market for its firms: They invest in each other's stock and buy each other's products, acting much like paternalistic governments in supporting member firms' attempts to be competititive.

Take the Mitsubishi Group. Its three flagship companies are Mitsubishi Corp., the trading company; Mitsubishi Bank, the group's banker; and Mitsubishi Heavy Industries, the group's leading manufacturer. A second tier of 28 core members are bound by cross-ownership ties, interlocking directorates, long-term contracts, and diverse social and historical links. Beyond the core are hundreds of other Mitsubishi-related companies. Clearly these firms constitute a business community with considerable internal coherence. Some 25 Mitsubishi companies have set up shop in the United States. Their mutual support practices defy traditional U.S. notions of antitrust laws.[31]

As a production-oriented community, the Toyota group is a network of closely linked manufacturers and suppliers. Their long-term outlook and mutual commitment create an incentive structure that drives efficiency and cost control. In a very real sense, the community functions much like a structure that decentralizes accountability and motivation to each unit, while encouraging them to minimize total costs.[32]

In Japan, moreover, close ties between government and business are facilitated by culturally sanctioned practices such as *amakudari* (descent from heaven), in which senior officials from the powerful government ministries retire into industry positions. Common understandings develop between firms and their regulators, which sustain the existing capabilities of industries and communities. Japan therefore illustrates how key institutions constrain managers' actions and their ability to conceive, initiate, and implement strategic changes.[33]

If Japanese firms were so constrained by their institutional context, how then were they able to lead the way in globalizing industries like electronics, semiconductors, and autos? The answer appears to reside in the collective apparatus that both maintains competition and mobilizes Japanese firms' cooperation against a common enemy: the non-Japanese firm. In contrast, in the United States, economic tradition and its canonization in antitrust legislation misled managers for years into believing that cooperation was the source of all evil. Recently, managers have begun to pursue partnerships with rivals and to lobby government in favor of cooperative ties. In so doing, they indicate growing recognition that, in fact, the enemy is us.

Sidetracked by Institutions

In a widely publicized article written in the late 1970s, two Harvard professors blamed the global decline of American business squarely on managers' shortsightedness. In truth, their thesis targeted far more than corporate managers. After all, if firms take a short-run view to managing, they are encouraged to do so by: (1) business schools, who instill in managers a worship for short-run financial manipulation instead of a long-run investment orientation; (2) investors, eager to uncover and capitalize on short-run fluctuations in firms' securities; (3) government, for requiring quarterly financial reports; (4) unions, for insisting on wage increases regardless of corporate profitability; and (5) boards of directors, for not clearly linking executive compensation to firms' long-term performance.

Institutional pressures contributed significantly to building momentum and defining trajectories that made firms less responsive to their environments in recent years.[34] Five key institutions stabilized how companies related to their environments throughout the 1970s and 1980s: the media, the financial markets, business schools, the labor markets, and regulatory agencies. In the United States, these sectors heavily reinforced the inertial tendencies of firms and communities, and encouraged them to attend less to change and more to perpetuating the status quo. As many firms have found, the collective network structure of many countries, not only insulated domestic competitors, but created an institutional barrier to entry that dampened innovation. The experiences of U.S. firms in both Japan and Germany confirm the continued existence of these institutional barriers to competition and change.[35]

Scrutinized by the Financial Markets

Most firms fund operations by raising capital, principally through financial markets. They list their stocks and bonds on major exchanges such as the New York Stock Exchange, the American Stock Exchange, and the over-the-counter market (NASDAQ), with the NYSE accounting for 85 percent of all shares traded in the United States. Listing facilitates funding capital projects.

Investors, creditors, and analysts assess a company's prospects through information drawn from public financial statements. Firms engage auditors to verify their claims about capital allocations and to influence the judgments prospective investors and employees make. Rating agencies like Moody's, Dun & Bradstreet, and Standard & Poor's also regularly assess firms' creditworthiness and communicate their appraisals to outside publics. Since a company's ability to raise funds in the capital markets depends on its ratings, managers are highly attuned to maintaining policies and strategies likely to curry favor with ratings agencies.[36]

By constantly reacting to announcements about firms' economic value, riskiness, managerial skill, technological soundness, competitiveness, and future prospects, the financial markets have encouraged managers to make decisions likely to produce favorable short-run assessments by investors. They therefore discourage making investments in strategies with longer-term pay-offs, be they for more basic research or for replacement of still productive but inefficient plant and equipment.[37]

Moreover, accounting practices sanctioned by the FASB enable firms to shape financial statements in ways that continue to mislead investors. Indeed, existing accounting rules allow firms sufficient leeway in accruing uncollected revenues and valuing inventories that many failing firms are actually able to report strong earnings immediately prior to declaring bankruptcy.[38] These practices are unlikely to help firms plan and execute timely strategic changes.

Through the Media's Looking Glass

Reporters do not simply report facts when they assess managers and their companies: They actively interpret firms' activities and their prospects. Research suggests that the omnipresence of the media may dampen firms' proclivity to take risks: Risky strategies get negative publicity from the press, and since they are frowned on by investors, tend to lower market value.

Firms also advertise through the media to maintain demand for their products. Tobacco is a case in point. Early recognition of advertising's success at building demand for tobacco products led to a ban on television advertising of tobacco. Many expected tobacco manufacturers to abandon quickly what was described as a declining industry. Although most firms diversified somewhat, only Liggett and Myers actually left the industry altogether. In contrast, Philip Morris invested heavily in improving operations, becoming the industry leader as early as 1975.[39]

Tobacco companies have had to side-step television in order to maintain a youthful consumer base. Constrained by regulation, companies advertise largely through sponsorship of sports events (e.g. Virginia Slims) and through print ads. Managers of tobacco firms also heavily fund their industry association, the Tobacco Institute, using it to support counterresearch and to shield firms from direct public scrutiny. Despite aggressive antismoking lobbies, boycotts, and pressure on boards to sell off their institutions' investments in the stocks of tobacco firms, the tobacco industry has shown a remarkable ability to sustain itself: Demand continues to grow for products uncontestably associated with cancer, and the industry's success highlights the role that media advertising, sponsorships, and trade associations have played in enabling firms and industries to postpone a strategic change.

Under Government Control

Government acts directly on firms' environments as legislator, regulator, and arbiter of conflicts of interest. Regulators define the boundaries around sectors of activity and their jurisdiction, and influence the unity of firms subject to their scrutiny. The legislative system offers protection to innovating firms in the form of exclusive patents and copyrights. An agency like the Securities and Exchange Commission (SEC), for instance, unwittingly promotes the short-run orientation of firms by requiring filing of quarterly earnings statements that fuel speculation and stifle managers' attempts to fund strategic endeavors such as long-term R&D. Governments also raise money by taxing firms and consumers. Through arbitrary rules that define taxable income, taxing agencies like the United States' Internal Revenue Service (IRS) induce companies to channel their resources in advantageous ways. For instance, rules that provide tax deductibility for charitable contributions and political donations enable firms to target otherwise taxed income to these ends, thereby conjuring public debate about how managers manipulate the political environment when they back elections.

Managers often succeed in neutralizing a regulatory agency by placing former executives inside the agency. A study of U.S. foreign relations between 1886 and 1905 concluded that foreign policy came to reflect a set of business interests that were vested in the internal structure of the State Department.[40] Another study showed how aggregate economic concentration has influenced U.S. business tax rates, suggesting that in times of greater political unity, managers successfully lobby and obtain lower levels of taxation for their firms.[41] Jointly, these analysts propose that regulators promote a placid environment for firms, protecting them from disruptions either by regulating entry into the corporate community or through price controls.

In the airline industry, between 1938 and 1978 the Civil Aeronautics Board not only controlled the extent of competition, but allocated air routes, granted ritualistic fare increases, limited agreements, provided subsidies, and otherwise sheltered established firms from the vagaries of competition and the need to minimize costs. Following deregulation fares declined, many new firms failed, mergers proliferated, service quality and airline profits fell, while the variety of services increased. Clearly in all these industries government played a key role in maintaining an industry structure that departed from competition, and therefore retarded strategic change.[42]

Facing Compulsory Miseducation

Less visibly, perhaps, schools and universities also contribute to propagating mind sets that encourage managers to perpetuate established trajectories. Social scientists point out that the educational system operates largely to promote the reproduction of the industrial structure unchanged over time. Schools, educators, and texts filter information, present consensus values, and suppress controversy. The limited kinds of information provided to students naturally circumscribe their world views by playing on their cognitive biases. Company schools, training institutes, modern business schools, the MBA, as well as corporate training and development programs are vehicles for distributing propaganda about how companies function, what techniques to use in managing employees, and how to finance operations. As students graduate from these programs, they enter work organizations where they call on these common frames of reference to solve problems.[43]

Much as adherence to shared views of the world binds scientists into invisible colleges, so too does socialization by common exposure to an MBA, for instance, produce shared values among firms' managers. Critics suggest that the failure by industry to invest in operations technology resulted in part from the overemphasis placed on financial wizardry in the business schools to which our managers were exposed. "Managing by numbers" obviously distances managers from core activities and erodes their control over underlying factors that influence firms' relative competitiveness in many industries.[44] By contributing to an orthodox view of management designed to preserve the status quo, our schools discouraged strategic change.[45] Increasingly, business schools throughout the United States appear to be performing a collective *mea culpa*, with deans of leading schools spearheading efforts to overcome some historical impediments to change: The tenure system that emphasizes research at the expense of teaching, the low contact hours with students, the extreme division of labor that specializes faculty and isolates them into departments. Top-notch business schools like Penn's Wharton School and NYU's Stern School have recently publicized major efforts designed to increase their institution's responsiveness to student concerns by improving teaching quality, strengthening the integrative character of their programs, and downplaying purely technical skill building.

Gagged by Unions and Professionals

As firms move up the value-added chain into high-tech sectors or by automating production, they come to rely more and more heavily on human skills. So characteristics of the nonmanagerial work force increasingly affect firms' ability to respond to changing technologies and global competitive conditions. Where craft skills were once acquired by apprenticeship and protected by guilds, labor unions and professional associations now guard the skill content of many jobs, provide workers with career progressions, and discourage change.[46]

Moreover, in 1990, a rapidly declining but still significant 12 percent of the U.S. labor force was unionized, working principally in the manufacturing sector. Unions constrain firms' ability to respond to their environments: They negotiate work rules that reduce flexibility in combining tasks and redeploying people to more efficient uses. They also lock into labor contracts cost of living increases that escalate firms' fixed expenses, regardless of profitability. These dynamics create inertia by reducing managers' ability to implement strategies designed to cope with changing circumstances.

For instance, in 1985 the Chicago Tribune faced a conflict with its unions over the introduction of productivity-enhancing technology. After a lengthy strike from which management emerged victorious, the Tribune spent $200 million in automating its plant, slashing costs, and eliminating over 400 jobs—more than 25 percent of its production work force. Since 1985, revenues have increased from $460 to $680 million, while profits have more than doubled from $65 million to approximately $160 million in 1990.[47] Because technology displaces labor, unions clearly resist its introduction, reducing the competitiveness of firms and inhibiting strategic change. A similar conflict between the Chicago Tribune and the New York unions representing the drivers, printers, and newsroom employees of its unprofitable Daily News division was repeated in the fall of 1990, culminating in sale of the tabloid to British entrepreneur Robert Maxwell.

If the trend continues, however, by the year 2000 unions' share of private sector workers should shrink to less than 5 percent,[48] and other forms of representation will take their place. Take Weirton Steel, the subsidiary of Bethlehem Steel that was bought by its workers in 1984 through an employee stock ownership plan. After years of success, Weirton's managers were forced to eliminate over 1000 of its 8200 jobs in 1991. The pressures of competing in the global steel market compel modernization, greater capital intensity, and reorganization, to the dismay of its laid off employee-owners whose union continues to contest the actions of the firm's managers.[49]

In nonunion settings, professional groups act to create and diffuse typical thought patterns among professionals. Because of their cosmopolitan outlook, professionals do not necessarily respond to managerial pressure. In hospitals, for instance, the conflict between health care professionals and administrators is well documented. Despite increasing cost pressures, respected medical professionals resist attempts to economize, thereby inflating the indirect burden placed on society through taxation.

The personnel policies designed to benefit managerial staff also places constraints on the most efficient deployment of resources. Routinized recruitment, appraisal, and compensation systems prevent firms' managers from quickly altering the skill mix of the labor force or implementing changes in strategy. In fact, research suggests that in firms with more elaborate, functional, and centralized administrative systems, employees are more likely to resist changes initiated by upper-level executives.[50]

Finally, in recent years the finger has been heavily pointed at accountants, lawyers, and other professionals for helping firms to disguise their problems from shareholders and the public. In the collapse of the savings and loan industry, a seeming conspiracy of self-interest among professionals appears to have made it possible for these thrift institutions to travel on a trajectory that took them into ever riskier territory. Unchecked appraisers artificially inflated real estate values; insolvent customers received ever larger loans; preoccupied auditors carelessly overlooked fraudulent billings. Rather than check the industry's momentum, these professionals appear to have facilitated the excesses that finally led to the industry's collapse.[51]

Why Then Do Firms Fail?

Firms fail because their internal features generate inertia and momentum that seduce managers to opt for the status quo, favoring established directions that proved successful in the past; because their activities embed them in business communities that shield them from the wider environment; because their relationships with institutions such as the media, government, the financial markets, unions, and professions exacerbate inertia and accelerate momentum. (See Fig. 3.4.)

But of the many ironies that plague corporate life probably the most vexing is the observation that the same relationships that managers forge to implement strategic change also lock them into networks that contribute to furthering momentum and inertia. Just as acquired capabilities limit a firm's attempts to go beyond those capabilities, so do the social structures, interlocks, and institutional relationships that managers create prevent them from recognizing external pressures and implementing strategic change. Within firms, shrewd managers recognize the importance of building into their corporate structures autonomous elements and programs that can challenge the core assumptions undergirding existing strategic directions.[52]

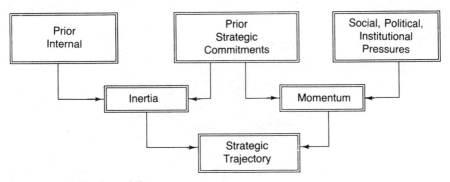

Figure 3.4. Why firms fail.

At the national level, we should welcome such an autonomous function for extracorporate institutions such as government and the media in undermining the status quo. When competition prevails, institutions should stimulate managers to collaborate toward collective ends; when collaboration produces tunnel vision, those same institutions should incite competition. MITI has played this role successfully in Japan, to the benefit of firms like Matsushita, Sony, Honda, Nissan, and Mitsubishi. The European community also favors this model—witness the multination collaboration that created and nurtured Airbus, the successful airplane manufacturer which, in a few short years, has become Boeing's chief rival.

Figure 3.3 shows how firms, like planets, come to move along relatively narrow strategic trajectories. The next chapter shows how inertia and momentum jointly work to blind managers to the pressing need for strategic change in an environment that has become both more competitive and more institutional.

4

Why Managers Misinterpret Reality

There are no facts, only interpretations.
FRIEDRICH NIETZSCHE

Information that we form into images comes to us after being filtered by other peoples' interpretations and analyses. For instance, the popular image of Mozart as an impish and precocious genius with a scatological sense of humor and intense self-absorption has attained near-legendary status in the hands of biographers. A recent study by William Stafford, *The Mozart Myths*, scrutinizes these images and shows us how biographers and scholars have continually selected and amplified material that supports these popular myths. In the process, they inadvertently reinterpreted certain facts and ignored others that might have challenged the received view.

And so it is with all people. Over time, we form images for which we routinely seek confirmation, seldom recognizing how our interpretations actively shape what we see and what we think. This is why even during times of revolutionary upheaval, there are those who disagree that a change is under way. Vested interests in the status quo often blind people to the reality of even the most terrifying events. The 3-day coup d'état that threatened to halt the progress of Mikhael Gorbachev's *perestroika* in the Soviet Union in August 1991 showed how misperceptions induced by an inertial structure within the Politburo could lead to poor decision making. A group of Stalinist-era bureaucrats, raised under the precepts of absolute power, accustomed to mass obedience, and incapable of conceiving of

life outside received communist doctrine failed to anticipate active resistance by a newly liberated population.

In similar ways, although corporate environments changed dramatically in the last two decades, managers often disagreed on the magnitude
and the effect these changes were having on their firms. Following the
1973 oil embargo by OPEC nations, for instance, some U.S. energy
companies invested billions of dollars in developing synthetic fuels;
others pursued coal gasification, shale oil exploration, or solar energy—at
great expense. Their efforts were predicated on varying assumptions
about the future prices of oil. When, contrary to all expectations, prices
subsequently fell, most programs were abandoned.

It happened again following the Iranian revolution of 1979; and yet
again in 1990 when we rode the roller coaster of prices back up after Iraq
invaded Kuwait. Encouraged by the Bush administration, many firms
dusted off their old alternative fuel programs and resuscitated them, only
to let them flounder as oil prices again tumbled. Collectively we act like
substance abusers: We demonstrate a collective unwillingness to denounce the dependency on petroleum products that hampers our ability
to develop a sustained solution to domestic scarcity.

Or consider the banking industry. It turns out that bankruptcy is in the
eye of the beholder. That is because the level of a bank's capital depends,
not only on its losses from bad loans, but quite critically on who does the
measuring. Banks set aside reserve funds in order to cover their estimated
losses. If, as critics contend, banks' loss estimates are too low, then so are
their reserves. Based on estimates of losses for various types of loans, a
recent analysis by the *New York Times* concluded that, as of September
30, 1990, four of the top 10 U.S. bank holding companies could not meet
minimum recommended capital-to-asset ratios of 3 percent, and so were
insolvent, namely Citicorp, Chase Manhattan, Security Pacific, and
NCNB.[1] Clearly, regulators, bankers, and analysts differ in their interpretations of the solvency of the U.S. banking industry, and so in the
actions they deem necessary to redress the situation.

Bad Maps

Psychologists like to point out how cognitive limitations impede our
efforts to understand complex relationships. As managers we have a
limited capacity to deal with all the information in our environments and
to assimilate what we do perceive. Mental maps help us formulate alternative plans for allocating corporate resources to achieve stronger positions
against rival firms. Plans provide cognitive guidance in envisioning and
implementing strategic change—what psychologists call schemas. They

help organize the way information gets collected and represented, and so influence the strategic directions firms take. Much as generals use cartographers' maps to deploy armies, so do managers rely on cognitive mappings of the competitive landscape to deploy their products, resources, and personnel.[2]

But maps are only representations of the world. They, too, are incomplete: A road map does not advise a driver about road conditions, nor does it indicate traffic congestion. In the boom years of the mainframe computer, for instance, many computer gurus vaunted the merits of centralizing data processing. Enormous effort was expended and resources committed to developing technical capability in isolated centers, with remote access by distant terminals. Leading firms like IBM and their mainframe customers, blinded by a commitment to centralized processing, ignored mounting protests from users, and dismissed the alternate technology of the PC network. Dominated by a cadre of specialized engineers and technicians trained to appreciate the wonders of mainframe machines, top computer makers and their clients failed to think of the computer as a network until the PC was virtually thrust on them. Now most users prefer to distance themselves from mainframes.[3]

To cull data about environments and highlight trends, managers rely on information-gathering systems and on rules of thumb, experience, and expert systems to interpret events. Royal Dutch/Shell Group, for instance, was among the few oil companies to anticipate successfully the oil price increases of the 1970s and their subsequent collapse in the 1980s: By collecting vast stores of information and articulating simple scenarios, the company chose to build new refineries before oil prices rose and to postpone purchasing new oil fields until prices fell.[4]

But planning and decision support systems themselves filter some types of information and call attention to others. By monitoring and presenting only the data that the systems' designers programmed them to observe, planning systems ensure that all corporate managers are exposed to the same kinds of information. In so doing, they artificially restrict managers' range of vision, and thereby distort the environmental conditions to which firms respond.

Many observers have reported how managers attend disproportionally to information that confirms the merits of their pet projects and downplays alternatives, thereby making their decisions appear rational. Subordinates often act as mind guards, screening out weak signals that contradict or challenge assumptions built into existing plans. Managers' perceptions of changing environments are, therefore, edited by the established relationships they have with peers and subordinates within firms, and by the external ties that senior executives establish with media reporters, regulators, and other actors.[5]

Despite having common information, even shrewd managers tend to disagree about how to address changing environments because they look at the world through the refractive lenses of their differing backgrounds. To develop a common viewpoint in the simultaneous pursuit today of efficiency, entrepreneurship, equity, and ethics poses enormous challenges to decision making. The polarized interpretations of environments that these diverse objectives induce are the stuff of much partisan politics within top management teams. To grapple with strategic change, therefore, requires an appreciation of how even our best companies distort information and how managers bias decisions.

A recent analysis of the banking industry in metropolitan Chicago showed how perceptions of the competitive environment differed among banks' top managers. Despite the high geographic similarity of firms, the lengthy 18.5-year average tenure of employees, and the stability of their local environment, planners showed a surprisingly low level of agreement about the important dimensions of competition in the industry, with only 2 of 331 possible dimensions (geographic scope and lending target market) agreed on by more than 80 percent of those surveyed.[6]

If managers lack consensus in their perceptions of environments, then they should favor different strategies. And they do. Many analysts have shown how managerial perceptions of strategic issues systematically influenced the range of solutions considered, the amount of resources committed to particular projects, and the steps taken to carry out strategic changes.[7] Indeed, in a detailed investigation of the top 300 U.S. financial services companies, I found that firms competed more aggressively with companies whose managers perceived their environments in similar ways. The combinations of strategies that managers chose appeared to split up the industry into groups in which managers with similar perceptions of their environments showed stronger rivalry towards one another than to managers with dissimilar views in other firms.[8] During periods of environmental upheaval, developing a consensus viewpoint becomes particularly critical if managers are to mobilize their firms' attention to a shared vision of the future.

We Often Distort Reality

It often surprises people to learn that the human brain systematically distorts information and routinely biases our decisions. In a world that idealizes science and technology, in which humanity has come to dominate nature through the dazzling application of rational thought, it seems paradoxical that we should suffer such a distressing failing. For managers raised in firms that glorify executives' ability to rule and control, such biases are anathema, a curse on success.

Yet the record seems clear: Like the rest of us, managers have often fallen victim to prosaic prejudices in observing environments and in deducing their likely effects on firms. Understanding the origins of these blind spots could prove key to overcoming the distortions they induce when managers respond to environmental upheavals.

No matter how smart, people have often assumed that events are correlated just because they are similar, negative, or unexpected when, in fact, they were entirely unrelated. For instance, many scientists and practitioners have observed a correlation between the occurence of sunspots and agricultural harvests, stock market peaks, levels of manufacturing production, and influenza epidemics. Illusory correlations like these quickly entice us to search for a plausible theory to explain why sunspots, for instance, should cause these observed events—even when none makes sense.[9]

As managers, we readily assign blame to the most visible of all possible causes, even if unrealistic. People and events who become salient capture more of our attention, and so appear causal. Much as owners of sports teams routinely laud or castigate coaches for teams' seasonal results, so we blame our top managers for firms' failures and strategic successes, even though their actions have little short-run impact. The coincidence of a new appointment and heightened performance is probably illusory, but it often affects how much a board will pay the company's top executives. Ironically, it seems quite likely that new CEOs mostly benefit from (or pay for) the strategic initiatives taken by predecessors whose actions only now are taking root.

Prior experience sensitizes our brains to receive and process information in particular ways. These mental scripts help us to decode external occurrences. Salient events are stored more prominently in our memories, and so are more readily available in making decisions.[10] When information does not fit into our mental scripts, we therefore disregard it: We insist that events did not occur when they did, or dismiss surprising events as inconsequential aberrations.

Finally, when we are heavily invested in a situation, psychologists tell us that we distort information that is presented to us. Quite naturally, most managers noticeably favor news that confirms their beliefs and enhances their self-concepts—and ignore self-deprecating and contradictory data. Not surprisingly, then, we find that chief executives tend to consistently claim positive corporate performance as a result of their own efforts, while they blame negative results on uncontrollable factors like the weather.[11]

A detailed analysis of the letters to shareholders contained in annual reports for a group of 18 firms over an 18-year period showed that managers were 3 times more likely to credit themselves for positive outcomes and to blame negative results on the environment. Moreover, executives of the most unstable firms, lacking any real control over their companies' performance, tried harder to convey an illusion of being in control by claiming responsibility for both positive and negative results.[12] Clearly managers not only distort information about environments but also broadcast self-serving presentations *into* those environments.

We Tend to Escalate Commitments

Just as people often feel paralyzed by personal threats, so do environmental threats invite rigidity in managers' strategic responses. Changing circumstances test our ability to cope effectively and induce psychological stress and anxiety. Stress naturally increases the likelihood that managers will distort information and muddle important decisions.[13]

Threats also bring top teams closer together, encouraging corporate managers to close ranks and restrict information likely to challenge the good feelings they share. The noted social psychologist Irving Janis studied policy-making groups in the U.S. government and showed how critical decisions that led to the Korean War, the Vietnam War, and the Bay of Pigs fiasco in Cuba were heavily influenced by social pressures forcing conformity of team members to consensus beliefs.

More recently, an examination of 100 firms involved in the computer, chemical, and natural gas industries showed how characteristics of top management teams contributed significantly to strategic inertia. Firms whose top managers had longer tenure proved less likely to experiment with innovative strategies, more likely to imitate competitors' strategies, and more likely to mimic the most typical strategic profile of competitors.[14] So effectiveness at carrying out strategic change may depend heavily on having the right mix of managers in a top team.

Unfortunately, even well-balanced top teams can fail. The record suggests that top managers tend to react perversely to inimical environments by taking company-wide actions that usually restrict information flows and impair their ability to cope. When faced with adversity, managers habitually centralize control, cut costs, and formalize responsibilities—all of which make firms more rigid at a time when flexibility would be more helpful.

Finally, program directors often throw good money after bad, persisting in unprofitable pursuits. Like those of us who, irrationally, continue to invest in a declining stock or whose fondness for an old car leads them to spend in repairs far more than the car is worth, managers have shown a propensity to escalate their commitments to pet projects and strategies far beyond the seemingly rational point. Indeed, it seems that the more important a decision, and the greater managers' disappointment with initial losses, the more likely they are to persist in a losing course of action. Commitment results because managers want to justify their initial positions, both to themselves and to their peers. Perseverance demonstrates heroic leadership and—who knows?—could also prove them right in the long run.

An analysis of British Columbia's strategic decision to host a world's fair in 1986 (Expo '86) in Vancouver, showed how just such a process of escalation led the prime minister of the Canadian province to increase his commitment to the fair, despite mounting estimates of financial losses. In 1978, Expo '86 was a $78-million project with a worst-case deficit of $6 million. By 1985, the fair had become a $1.5-billion project with a deficit of $311 million. In the 7 years of planning, decision makers increasingly discounted economic costs, allowing them to recede while making social and political costs loom larger in the overall picture.[15]

Similar processes within our best firms limited managers' abilities to assess and respond to the environmental upheaval of the 1980s. The systematic nature of these biases reduces the magnitude and speed with which they conceived and carried out strategic changes.

Wrong Interpretations

Whereas the 1980s epitomized the logic of profit at any cost, the competitive and globalized environment of the 1990s presents us with the greater constraint of having to reconcile the frequently contradictory demands placed on firms by their multiple stakeholders. Everyone demands heightened attentiveness and responsiveness. Shareholders and bondholders require greater competitiveness, that is, efficiency and innovativeness. Consumers expect quality and value. Employees demand satisfying work environments. Suppliers and distributors want predictability. Public interest groups petition for social responsibility. Yet low-growth environments, coupled with rapidly changing technologies, compel a restructuring of industries that is making it more difficult for firms to accommodate these diverse demands.

Strategic concerns deriving from the demands of stakeholders gain greater or lesser visibility in different companies and industries. In turn, visibility confers varying degrees of urgency on particular issues. When companies' activities and competitiveness appear jeopardized by an emerging issue, we are more likely to discern and attend to signals from environments early on. For better or worse, public exposure commands our attention, as Fig. 4.1 indicates.

A "strategic issue" describes trends, developments, or events that may have a major and discontinuous impact on firms.[16] Globalization, new technologies, and ecological awareness all constitute trends. Not all of us regard these trends as equally important. To assess changing market conditions, we actively construct interpretations: We pick the trends to

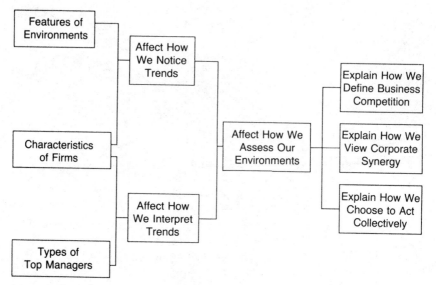

Figure 4.1. Discerning and interpreting trends.

which our firms attend and determine how they will affect us. In turn, the meanings we attach to apparent trends create momentum for strategic change at the business, corporate, and collective levels.

Even when broad tendencies like globalization and competitiveness became widely visible, managers often interpreted them differently. Some see threats where others saw opportunities: They disagreed on the dimensions that constituted an environmental issue and naturally debated its implications for their firms. In an era of environmental turmoil in which firms confront radical change, managers can benefit from carefully assessing the factors that: (1) generate attention and (2) influence interpretation.[17]

We Don't Always Pay Attention

Many industries were caught sleeping in recent decades, whether in auto, steel, or tires. As numerous reporters have pointed out, their managers lent a deaf ear to loud warning bells and mountains of data that indicated trouble was brewing. How could it happen?

Managers are driven to act only when environmental triggers cross a minimal threshold of visibility. When triggers lack visibility and a sense of urgency, managers often delay, postponing costly resource redeployments and corporate reorientations. Since visibility creates urgency, to trigger strategic change requires that managers invest heavily in systems and processes designed to build attention.

Systematic information gathering can increase confidence in a diagnosis of external events. When scanning environments, managers rely heavily on information supplied by peer and professional networks, by reporters in the media, and by firms' leading stakeholders. Professional and trade associations routinely identify issues of interest to their membership, and scrutinize their implications. The media regularly spotlight trends affecting the general public; and employees and other stakeholders predictably call attention to their special interests.

Triggers become more noticeable when managers believe they will affect their firms' performance. Issues that affect what media reporters and financial analysts think of firms, for instance, normally become very visible to corporate decision makers and encourage rapid remedial action. Reporters magnify events they expect their readers to find interesting, and so attend more to incendiary statements and negative information about firms.

Ratings agencies like Moody's or Standard & Poor's draw inferences about firms' creditworthiness and future prospects from their managers' responses to environmental events. Events likely either to heighten firms' financial riskiness or to lower their future profitability lead to negative appraisals that quickly propagate throughout the financial community and translate into declining stock prices. When firms have few evaluators with which they have strong relationships, their managers more readily discern and agree on key environmental issues.[18]

If strategic issues become more noticeable as they attain widespread visibility, it is also true that visibility encourages managers to dwell more heavily on short-term triggers than on more long-term changes in environments. Rapid-fire environmental changes command quick responses, whereas slowly building triggers cajole top managers into complacency, reducing the likelihood that they will initiate strategic change. As key brokers of environmental events, stakeholders therefore play a potentially central role in making external triggers more visible to a firm.

Internal features of firms also influence whether or not managers notice an external trigger. The more internally participatory, interactive, and informal a company, the more faithfully and quickly information flows among employees, encouraging differences of opinion and discussion. By circumscribing interactions, hierarchical, centralized structures increase the likelihood that negative information gets filtered before reaching top decision makers, thus impeding strategic change.

The more attention managers pay to a set of events, the more information they collect about them, and the greater the confidence they have in their diagnosis of impending shifts and discontinuities. One study of top management teams in the hospital industry defined their ability to process information in terms of three key dimensions: How extensively they participated in strategic decisions, how much they interacted, and how formalized their activities were. The results showed that top managers functioning in participatory structures, and those who were accustomed to accessing and analyzing lots of information, experienced a greater sense of mastery and control over strategic decisions. High participation and interaction, combined with low formalization, facilitated collecting information, and so encouraged its application.[19]

Of course, individual managers also differ in their relative influence over top management teams. Where a single person (sometimes, but not always, the CEO) overpowers a management team, extensive conformity can result. Should that manager happen to be an engineer, the team as a whole could end up paying greater attention to technology-related issues, and acquire greater sensitivity to technological innovation.

Similarly, were the dominant person in a top team to be from some functional area other than engineering. Early research by Nobel laureate Herbert Simon suggested that areas of specialization would color managers' interpretations of problems. The bias of marketers is to meet sales projections, regardless of cost. Manufacturing managers favor expediency at the expense of marketability. Financial managers focus strictly on the bottom line, all too often ignoring human costs.[20] Top teams dominated by one or the other invariably bias the group's interpretations.

Managers' educational backgrounds also have implications for the initiatives firms take. Studies of hospitals and banks indicate that more innovative firms have more educated managers, while firms pursuing successful growth strategies are more likely to have managers experienced in marketing and sales.[21] In young semiconductor firms, the characteristics of the founding team appear to influence heavily companies' future growth: More successful firms had founding teams with more prior experience working together and the firm's managers were more dissimilar.[22]

Finally, firms' strategies themselves affect how managers scan environments and how they notice trends. Existing strategies embody firms' past experiences, and facilitate filtering out the critical from the unimportant. In firms pursuing aggressive service-oriented strategies or widely diverse product lines, managers demonstrate greater cognitive complexity, and so pay greater attention to information about their firms' environments. In firms pursuing defensive strategies, in which firms compete more narrowly within niches, managers generally pay attention to fewer pieces of information.[23]

We Sometimes Misread Trends

Not only did companies' environments differ in triggering awareness throughout the 1980s, they also led managers to construct distinct interpretations about what salient events meant and how they should respond.

Consider recycling. Only a few years ago, many firms considered anti-litter campaigns a nuisance and most managers dismissed environmental concerns as leftist-inspired propaganda. Some still do. Others, however, attend to statistics that depict a growing population of 8 million U.S. homes who already sort their refuse into recycling bins. For firms like Procter & Gamble or McDonald's, which use enormous quantities of plastics, recycling offers an opportunity to clean up their image and protect their markets. A joint venture of eight chemical companies, which includes Dow and Amoco Chemical, now operates the first two polystyrene recycling plants in the United States. Similarly, Du Pont formed an alliance with Waste Management of North America to operate five recycling plants by 1994: Du Pont will buy the recycled plastic to mold into park benches and traffic barricades.[24]

Managers impose order on information that has already garnered their attention by discussing how a particular issue impacts their companies. Discussion clarifies differences, generates consensus, and builds confidence in the available response options. For some firms, globalization might be viewed internally as an opportunity for growth, while to others foreign competitors constitute an ominous threat. For some, the growing concern with ecological damage is a threat; for others, it represents an opportunity to demonstrate responsiveness to consumers and to secure a competitive niche. Some of us would meet the rising threat of competition with drastic cost reduction; others would favor improving quality or looking for opportunities to diversify.

How do managers arrive at these interpretations? What explains the different strategic responses firms make to similar external triggers?

Interpretations are heavily influenced by characteristics both of firms and of their institutional environments. For instance, in firms with few formal controls, where employees are treated like members of an extended family, managers tend to favor strategic changes that promote lateral cooperation and shared ownership by employees. In hierarchical firms, however, managers are more likely to interpret external triggers in terms of their effects on the bottom line, and disregard the significant long-run but intangible costs of employee alienation. Similarly, firms with limited information-gathering systems often interpret strategic issues as threats rather than opportunities.[25]

Corporate cultures condition the interpretations that managers make. Widely shared values throughout a firm place blinders on our ability to conceive solutions to visible issues. In hierarchical firms, for instance, deference to authority is the norm. The corporate culture forbids employees to question the assumptions of decision makers. Covert, behind-the-scenes coalitions form to control the corporate agenda. By contrast, in decentralized firms we are often more forthright in sharing information, reducing political behavior, and broadening the interpretations of environmental trends that are made.

In May 1975, San Francisco's physicians called an unprecedented strike against Bay area hospitals. A detailed study of how 19 hospitals dealt with the strike showed how the responses companies make to an environmental change are heavily influenced by their managers' interpretations, over and beyond the objective reality of the strike as an event. Hospitals differed greatly in their internal structural features, particularly in employees' shared values. As it turned out, these characteristics of hospitals' internal cultures were instrumental in predicting whether managers perceived the strike as a dilemma, an opportunity, or an aberration.[26]

In hospitals whose cultures emphasized efficiency, predictability, and self-reliance, managers regarded the strike as a temporary decline in revenues, and opted to deplete financial reserves rather than take drastic action to cut costs. In hospitals whose cultures accentuated innovation and professional autonomy, managers perceived the strike as a dramatic upheaval requiring extensive cost cutting, layoffs, and centralization. In a third group of more diversified hospitals, managers interpreted the strike as a short-run aberration requiring a temporary reallocation of resources, and largely ignored it.

In general, then, corporate cultures legitimize certain actions, render other actions heretical, and create meanings for events that have yet to occur. Firms with more conservative internal cultures seem often to get caught unprepared by radical environmental changes. They monitor their environments only perfunctorily and often overlook or disregard early tremors that foreshadow discontinuities. In contrast, firms with more aggressive entrepreneurial cultures appear most likely to detect early tremors and so better prepare for jolts and discontinuities.

Much as they influence the visibility of environmental events, so too do characteristics of executive teams influence how those events are interpreted. Managers evaluate the impact of strategic issues as either opportunities or threats. Opportunities are associated with positive impacts, gains, and controllability, while threats are associated with negative impacts, losses, and uncontrollability. The more formalized and less interactive a company's top managers are, the more restricted is their capacity to process information, and the less likely they are to perceive positive stimuli. Under such circumstances, managers attend more to threats than to opportunities. Lacking appropriate structures to assist them in gathering and processing information, managers routinely experience overload, high levels of stress, and anxiety. In turn, these conditions sometimes lead to a sense of helplessness—a belief that environments are uncontrollable—and overwhelm managers' ability to control the fate of their firms.

The capabilities that companies develop over time also affect managers' perceptions. Where firms compete principally on the basis of costs (e.g., producers of generic drugs), managers are more likely to focus on enhancing short-term efficiency and productivity rather than innovation or growth. Where corporate successes derive more from new product introductions (e.g., ethical drugs), managers more often interpret environments as requiring intensive research and enhanced skill building. Similarly, in firms pursuing defensive, imitative strategies, managers typically act to preserve traditional product-market positions, and so tend to see events in their environment as corporate threats. By contrast, managers of firms pursuing more aggressive strategies view issues as opportunities, ones their firms can act on, and through which they can realize their business, corporate, and collective strategies.

In a comparative study of 148 universities, administrators were asked to assess the impact of a major change in U.S. demographics: the dramatic decline in the number of 18–22-year-olds. Universities differed significantly in how they interpreted the imminent decline in clientele. Administrators of universities with stronger internal cultures and a sense of identity tended to perceive the change as more of an opportunity than a threat, and felt more secure about their institutions' ability to cope with the plunging applicant pool.[27]

Externally, firms' linkages to a network of institutional actors also constrain how they respond to events. Companies closely tied to technological centers and professional groups are more likely to interpret external events as calling for research, innovation, and entrepreneurship. Companies whose relationships are strongest with concentrated cultural centers such as the media and universities may emphasize training, education, and other learning-oriented responses for coping with external triggers. If Japanese firms opt for competing through product quality and service, for instance, it partly reflects their extreme proximity to a densely connected web of institutions that includes schools, government, and the media, whose managers share a view of firms' central function as an instrument of collective welfare rather than as an economic vehicle for generating individual wealth, as we do in the United States.

We Believe in Crystal Balls

Most firms and institutions use planning systems and forecasts to help managers screen and respond to environmental changes. Unfortunately, these systems are themselves imperfect and seldom overcome the fundamental biases we all experience as individuals, as members of executive teams, and as employees of complex organizations.

For instance, a study of 50 manufacturing companies revealed that top managers relied more heavily on both systematic scanning (provided by the media, by special studies, in reports, or from information services) and use of personal information sources such as business associates, officials, and customers, as environmental uncertainty increased. Uncertainty impels managers to search for more information and to use multiple sources to supplement interpretations of environmental events. Personal contacts facilitate detecting subtle signals and thereby help to elaborate the understanding managers derive from formal scanning systems. Centralized and hierarchical firms also tend to rely more heavily on comprehensive planning.[28]

A detailed study of 129 planning executives of *Fortune* 500 companies explored how planning systems had helped them in making over 1000 explicit decisions between 1982 and 1986. Managers were asked to describe the bottom line importance and riskiness of these decisions, and the contributions that their firms' formal strategic planning systems made. The results suggest that large firms' managers tend to assign considerable value to these systems, particularly for key decisions involving large and risky global deployments.[29]

Even nonprofit organizations make use of planning processes: In an analysis of planning processes in 179 Southern Baptist churches, researchers found a strong relationship between church leaders' perceptions of the environment and their sophistication in planning. The more they interpreted their environments as complex and changing, the more likely they were to engage in scanning and formal planning. Larger, growing churches also tended to have larger staffs and facilities, and so to adopt more formal planning processes.[30]

Reliance on formal planning processes also results from firms' institutional relationships. Managers who routinely seek strategic advice from trade asociations and who hire business school graduates are more likely to develop sophisticated planning systems in their firms. Even if the systems do not produce especially valuable data, managers may implement them to signal a degree of savoir-faire to their observers, and so to appear legitimate. One account of how a simple financial reporting rule was progressively adopted by *Fortune* 200 firms between 1962 and 1984 suggests that managers experience conformity-inducing pressures placed on them by a network of professional associations such as the Securities and Exchange Commission, the Financial Accounting Standards Board, and the Interstate Commerce Commission—all of which have jurisdiction over aspects of firms' financial statements. Similar forces may induce managers to adopt planning systems to conform to stakeholders' expectations.[31]

Among planning tools, managers often invest much time and money in sophisticated forecasting models to assess environmental trends, but to little avail. Forecasts rely on past observations to predict future events. One review of forecasting methods pointed out some basic, and perhaps surprising, limitations of complex forecasts and simulations. In particular, the analysts concluded that most forecasts are no better than rather naive linear extrapolations; that expertise adds very little to the accuracy of forecasts; and, most importantly, that forecasts can never identify turning points.[32]

As with forecasts, most planning systems probably overquantify environmental conditions. Numerical accuracy misrepresents the value of planning and misleads managers by inducing an illusion of control over the future. This is partly why so many corporate watchdogs suggest that the benefits of planning lie, not in the quantitative estimates they generate about environmental changes, but in probing and questioning assumptions, and in exploring the underlying biases that hamper what we notice and how we interpret environments.

Building Strategic Schemes

If anything, planning and forecasting can only help to distill information about rather general environmental issues. In fact, managers formulate their strategies around:

1. Specific actions taken by competitors at the business level.

2. Targeted opportunities for diversification at the corporate level.

3. Unique relationships at the collective level.

To understand how companies actually are responding to the revolutionary circumstances they face therefore requires an appreciation for the cognitive processes through which managers interpret competition at the business level, conceive synergy at the corporate level, and discern the costs and benefits of cooperating with competitors at the collective level.

To Assess Business Competition

As everyone recognizes, an ever more central feature of environments is competition. Globalization, technological convergences, and increasing ecological sensitivities magnify rivalry within industries. The psychological processes that lead managers to notice and interpret these environmental forces also narrow their view of who are their firms' competitors and on what dimensions they will compete: Rivals are those firms whose managers regard environments in similar ways.

Through experience, managers develop mental classifications of firms. They collapse firms' structural features into typical profiles. By pigeonholing, managers highlight the key similarities and differences among their firms and competitors, and simplify the process of collecting information for strategic planning. When asked to describe their key competitors, for instance, bank managers appear to rely on a limited number of dimensions such as geographic scope, target market, and size, as well as location and their perceptions of competitors' managerial competency.[33]

Managers also think in terms of hierarchies. Each type of firm that managers identify as rivals is nested within a broader category. For instance, when asked to describe their competitors, managers of a group of Scottish knitwear firms produced the five-level hierarchy shown in Fig. 4.2.[34] Such a hierarchy does not easily recognize or encourage innovative fabrications that combine knits with lace, natural fiber with synthetics to create new products.

The greater are managers' product familiarity and industry experience, the finer are the categories into which they classify competitors, and so the more attuned they are to information describing changes in their environments and estimating the likely responses of rivals. Those who come into daily contact with other managers in rival firms, for instance, tend to develop a much finer understanding of the similarities and differences between firms.[35] Conferences, trade and professional associations, and hiring from competitors, therefore, constitute one way through which managers are able to incorporate within firms a more complex understanding of competitors.

Placing competitors into categories also solidifies managers' self-concepts. To assign a firm to a category is, implicitly, to identify rivals and the dimensions on which firms compete. Categories implicitly define competitive rankings in which some firms appear stronger and others weaker; some firms leaders, others followers. Naturally, managers attend more closely to information about better ranked firms and create strategies around close rivals' likely actions.

If our thinking about firms' competitors is guided by this kind of enduring classification, it may lead managers either: (1) to misrepresent rivals and so misperceive their actions, or (2) to ignore the intentions of other firms that are not currently direct rivals but whose managers are themselves planning diagonal attacks from neighboring niches. In rapidly changing environments, categories are no longer stable, and they distort managers' thinking about competition.

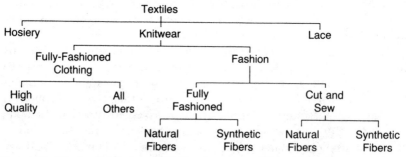

Figure 4.2. The Scottish knitwear community.

Strategy making is also a game in which managers of one firm try to outdo managers of rival firms. As chess players know, calculating the likely actions of your competitors and incorporating them into your game plan—difficult as that is—proves key to winning the game. Unfortunately, we often ignore or underestimate the responses of rivals and commonly fall victim to blind spots.[36]

For instance, the decision to invest in capacity expansion within an industry is a key aspect of many firms' competitive strategies. Managers try to preempt rivals by being the first to acquire capacity and thereby deter other firms from also building capacity. Still, most industries overbuild: Too many firms try to preempt their rivals. Once the process has begun, managers escalate commitments to capacity expansion despite competitors' responses.[37]

A similar process may describe the seemingly irrational price wars that airline managers initiate on a cyclical basis and that lead to unprofitable operations for all firms. Managers undercut rivals in an attempt to draw travelers to their airline. However, they neglect to anticipate sufficiently competitors' retaliatory responses. When competitors strike back by lowering their prices, they launch a downward spiral of revenues and profits.

In an analysis of prices paid at wine auctions, economist Orley Ashenfelter found that the first lot of a wine auctioned off at Sotheby's ended up costing 31 percent more than the third lot of the very same wine.[38] Since the true value of a lot is unknown, the most optimistic bidders tend to put in winning bids. A similar blind spot explains why managers systematically overvalue acquisition targets and produce positive returns only for the seller. The acquiring firm pays a market premium for a takeover because it essentially competes in an auction with incomplete information about the value of the target firm. Like buyers of wine and art at auction, managers must therefore guard against taking actions that do not incorporate assessments of their rivals' likely reactions.

To Conceive Corporate Synergy

Historian Alfred Chandler eloquently described how managers of Dupont, General Motors, and Standard Oil turned to diversification once the profit opportunities available within their original industries ran out. A corporate-level strategy of diversification enabled them to capitalize on latent synergies in related businesses.[39]

In diversifying, however, managers face common pitfalls. For one, they easily overestimate their own ability to apply expertise to managing the resulting portfolio. For another, managers readily rationalize acquisitions and escalate their commitment to acquisitions despite failure to create synergies with existing businesses.[40]

The number of failed acquisitions that firms concede were mistakes (often after cumulating enormous financial losses) testifies to the illusion of control to which managers so easily fall victim. Overconfidence in their ability to create either operational or managerial synergies not only encourages managers to make acquisitions, but also persuades them to hold on to these acquisitions even after they prove unable to produce synergies. Having committed large sums, managers are loath to intimate failure to their shareholders and peers, and so become trapped in funding acquisitions at levels that exceed their economic value.

Much as managers are limited by their understanding of competition at the business level, so too they are constrained by their interpretations of synergy at the corporate level. In selecting the businesses into which they diversify, executives implicitly adhere to a dominant logic that expresses their particular understanding of industry-level dynamics, and the potential for creating value from combining operations.[41]

In particular, the top team in a corporate structure is made up of individuals with distinct backgrounds and experiences, who wear different lenses in assessing businesses. Similarities and differences between businesses themselves also influence the team's ability to identify and exploit synergies. So managers pursue corporate-level strategies to exploit what they perceive to be similarities in the success factors, time horizons, and variables influencing performance across businesses.[42]

Managers of firms with strong capabilities in technical areas naturally incline their firms to diversify into industries that require these skills. Differences in backgrounds influence the degree of consensus among top managers: Having similar training, schooling, age, and specialty reduces conflicts in direction setting. In turn, greater consensus facilitates implementing strategies.[43]

When Robert Daniell was named CEO of United Technologies in 1987, for instance, he began holding regular weekend meetings at the conglomerate's Hartford headquarters to swap ideas and share experiences. These efforts to "put the united back in United Technologies" began a process of building synergy among previously isolated businesses. In contrast, when the tire companies Uniroyal and B.F. Goodrich merged in 1986, there was considerable animosity between Goodrich and Uniroyal people. Top management exacerbated the problems by operating the company as a joint venture, maintaining two distinct sets of engineers, accountants, and management systems.[44]

Corporate controls also affect the types of synergies that managers identify and choose to implement. Stable hierarchical firms are not likely to identify entrepreneurial firms as acquisition candidates. Where firms attempt to move quickly into emerging fields by acquiring new ventures, they frequently fail to demonstrate the dexterity needed to build synergy. Exxon's failed entry into high-technology businesses in the late 1970s is easily traced to the differences in the controls required for its traditional petroleum business and the controls suitable for the entrepreneurs working in Exxon Enterprises, the new venture group. By trying to impose the Exxon way on the new venture group, Exxon's top managers botched their diversification attempt.

Various analysts suggest that acquisitions produce high turnover because acquired managers face culture shock and balk at complying with the "foreign" management practices that acquiring firms' managers want to implement. Close to 59 percent of all acquired companies' top-tier managers depart within 5 years of a merger; of these, half leave in the first year. Differences in the beliefs shared by members of both companies cloud an acquiring firm's ability to build synergy (encouraging acquired managers to leave) and hinder a homogenization of accounting, budgeting, and human resource practices between the firms.[45]

Corporate cultures influence whether companies diversify through internal growth or through acquisitions. Many firms are heavily identified by their external images and internal cultures, and managers resist implementing change that goes against the historical trajectories set in motion by firms' founders. The more intensely these cultural beliefs are shared among a company's top managers, the less likely they are to consider a range of alternatives. Managers quickly converge on the most visible and least controversial acquisition candidate, the one whose strategic profile is most similar to the focal firm, and whose purchase is unlikely to be contested by shareholders.

To Pick Network Partners

Just as managers' interpretations affect business and corporate strategies, so do they play a central role in influencing managers' predispositions to initiate collective-level strategies. On the one hand, large firms have access to more resources and so have less need to participate in alliances. Lacking capital and capability, small firms seek out partners to achieve a critical mass. On the other hand, because alliances constitute a small part of their total portfolio, managers of large firms are more favorably disposed to pursuing alliances than are managers of small firms because large firms do not fear losing control. Despite their needs, smaller firms may shy away from alliances because they dread being overshadowed by their alliance partners. Such contrary motives are at work and affect a company's predisposition to pursue an alliance strategy.

A study of the chemical industry, for instance, demonstrated how firms whose managers interpreted environmental conditions as opportunities were more likely to enter into joint ventures. Managers who saw environments as threatening preferred to retain control within their firms by emphasizing internal development.[46] Another study of the financial services industry found that managers who viewed their firms' competitive environments as creating growth opportunities tended to form more alliances with commercial banks.[47]

Firms whose managers underscore the importance of internal control over operations and outputs in their principal business are less likely to embark on alliances in which they have less than majority ownership, or over which they lack managerial oversight. Alliances bring together multiple cultural viewpoints, and each managerial team tries to design into its collective agreements the idiosyncrasies to which it has grown accustomed on the home turf.

Institutional pressures also encourage managers to conceive and pursue similar collective actions. In firms that belong to more coherent business communities, managers tend to interpret environments in similar ways. One study demonstrated how managers' external relationships can have important consequences for their firms' actions: Among commercial banks in St. Louis, business lending patterns closely mirrored the relative centrality of these banks in a network of directorships that tied them to large local corporations.[48]

Corporate charitable and political contributions also appear to reflect the social relationships among firms. One study found that patterns of political contributions were heavily influenced by firms' indirect ties through major banks and by banks' shared ownership in firms within an industry. The same network also predicted the similarity of political contributions made by 57 large U.S. manufacturing firms in 1980. In another study, social relationships between decision makers were found to determine the level and type of charitable contributions firms made in Minneapolis–St. Paul, and also indicated that networks induced shared beliefs among a group of professionals.[49]

Just as managers' assessments of the extent of competition and the potential for synergy involve cognitive interpretations, so their understandings are colored by their relationships with neighboring firms and institutions. Clearly, the features of environments that managers notice and interpret lead them to conceive and implement idiosyncratic business-, corporate-, and collective-level strategies.

What About Rationality?

We like to think of ourselves as rational. Hard as we try to be, in fact, we probably are not. As managers of large institutions, to recognize our innate biases is important if we are to improve our ability to make decisions wisely—decisions that have pervasive impact on the lives of others. During periods of revolutionary change, the only way to develop a map of the world is to explore our own individual intepretations and look for areas of broad consensus.

To successfully conceive and implement strategic change, managers must first notice and recognize key trends in their environments. Not all trends are equally significant, however, nor do we interpret information describing trends in the same ways. After all, we are biased: We fall victim to familiar human processes through which we distort information and escalate commitments in unproductive directions. To overcome these biases, managers often rely on planning systems to develop complex forecasts of the future. However, forecasts and plans are themselves imperfect tools for representing changing environments. At best they enrich the mental maps which managers rely on to screen environments.

In responding to environmental conditions, managers also routinely classify competitors into groupings, from which they derive the dimensions along which to compete and the likely responses rivals will make to their strategic initiatives. The resulting business, corporate, and collective-level strategies that get implemented crystallize managers' interpretations of how environmental changes are likely to affect the strategic positions firms assume and to which their competitors react. Sound management of strategic change requires that managers carefully scrutinize the groupings they choose because such groupings constitute the foundation of competitive planning and, so, of strategic responses.

Because these innate biases are built into managers' social interactions, overcoming them proves difficult. Simple and seemingly simplistic guidelines for safeguarding against them involve: (1) making expectations explicit, (2) recognizing the merits of counterplanning, (3) actively searching for discrepant information, (4) creating forums for testing and debating key assumptions, (5) and avoiding universal rules. In the final analysis, understanding environments means producing consensually validated assumptions about the world. A useful prescription may be that managers should regularly solicit the interpretations of all key constituents of their firms and so define domains of consensus against which to juxtapose areas of difference. Only from active discussion can they derive a useful understanding of the environment.

In our increasingly complex and competitive environment, achieving a degree of social rationality is important. That means recognizing the organizational limitations on our own decision-making abilities and working to overcome undesirable features of working under corporate umbrellas. Failure to consensually perceive and interpret changing environments will prove costly to employees and shareholders alike as managers prepare to compete in the complex global context of the twenty-first century.

PHASE 2

Revising
Strategic Postures

Having deciphered the contours of the revolution—the broad
scenario of environmental forces currently compelling a
fundamental reorientation of industries—managers face the
daunting task of conceiving anew the strategic profiles of their
firms: at the business level, at the corporate level, and at the
collective level. Chapter 5 shows how environments have
heightened rivalry and placed pressure on firms to become more
aggressive through timing, differentiation, and segmentation.
Specifically, managers are trying hard to increase the speed with
which they bring products to market, to magnify the features that
differentiate them from rivals in consumers' minds, and to focus on
serving narrower niches.

Chapter 6 shows how managers are becoming more preoccupied
with capitalizing, at the corporate level, on synergy—the marriage
of resources, skills, and technologies across business units. Where
portfolio management once dominated discussions of growth, more
than ever corporate conversations revolve around the more
difficult issue of how to benefit from extensions of existing
businesses and from related diversifications.

Chapter 7 turns to the collective level and discusses how
cooperation among competitors has taken center stage as managers
struggle to cope with rivalry on a global scale. As revolutionary
forces sweep through the corporate landscape, managers and
regulators are recognizing the benefits of forming joint ventures,
strategic partnerships, alliances, consortia, and other forms of
collective action. Competition is no longer between firms but
between cooperative networks of firms and institutions.

5

Competing More Aggressively

My right has been rolled up.
My left has been driven back.
My center has been smashed.
I have ordered an advance from all
directions.

GENERAL FOCH, World War I

Differences in interpretation affected how many U.S. companies perceived environmental problems and why so many lost ground in the crucial post-OPEC embargo years during which Japanese companies prepared their offensive. Many managers of U.S.-based firms refused to recognize changing environmental circumstances and allowed their firms to forge blindly ahead on their historical trajectories. Ultimately, declining market shares forced them to heap loads of debt on their balance sheets in an attempt to recapture a competitive position.

Surely this was not a good time to doze off. In the 1980s, the United States entered yet another entrepreneurial period. The first was the Industrial Revolution of the 1880s and 1890s. Another occurred in the 1920s, when visionaries like Alfred Sloan and Henry Ford put together their giant enterprises.[1] Each of those entrepreneurial booms produced a dramatic restructuring of industries as firms struggled to adapt to innovations. The boom that climaxed in the 1980s confirmed the rule: It called for firms to rethink dramatically their competitiveness.

Entrepreneurial eras tend to follow bursts of technological innovation. They represent attempts by ingenious individuals and resourceful firms to produce commercially viable applications. Basic innovations encourage efforts to commercialize these innovations, fostering a cycle of incremental change as entrepreneurs and firms launch new ventures and vie to attract a market.[2]

In the last century, radical technological innovations clustered at four discrete intervals: around 1825, with electricity, steel, and cement; around 1885, with the railroad, telegraph, telephone, electric motor, and steam turbine; around 1935, with the jet engine, plastics, and electronics; and around 1975, with biotechnology and the microprocessor.[3] In each case, the cluster of basic innovations was followed by a swarming of incremental innovations and entrepreneurial start-ups that spurred established firms to initiate strategic changes.

Basic innovations often challenge the competencies of established firms, making it difficult for their managers to create commercial applications. A comparative study of how the cement, glass container, and minicomputer industries evolved showed how technological innovations first promoted an era of ferment during which old and new technologies rivaled for superiority. After a dominant design emerged, change became primarily incremental.[4]

Still, before a dominant design appears, entrepreneurial firms are key players. In the declining steel industry, the specialty steel producers (the so-called minimills) spurred large integrated steel manufacturers to rethink their operations and contemplate disintegration. Similarly, after the deregulation of the airline industry, entrepreneurial upstarts like PeopleExpress forced established carriers to compete more aggressively.

The explosive number of start-ups and bankruptcies filed in the United States since 1970 is symbolic of the quantum change in competitive rivalry over the last decade. Although many were high-technology related, a significant proportion were also ventures designed to capitalize on opportunities created by deregulation and by the boom in food, financial, and personal services. Another subset of these ventures also resulted from the breakup of larger firms faced with increased competition and from new forms of organizing such as franchising that grew in popularity throughout the 1980s. In older technologies, these trends heightened competitiveness and encouraged established companies to spin off product lines and businesses and to decentralize operations. In new technologies, newcomers like Apple and Compaq boldly challenged the dominant positions of firms such as IBM.

Savvy managers implement change at the business level in order to develop more advantaged postures within their industries—monopolistic positions that can shield their firms from all out competition, increase their autonomy, and enhance their profitability. Typically, business units successfully monopolize markets and achieve higher margins by following strategies that distinguish their products from competitors' through a combination of: (1) timing, (2) differentiation, and (3) scope.

In response to the quantum change in environmental conditions, many managers are contemplating strategic changes within business units that involve either intensifying commitments to their firms' existing patterns of advantage or shifting to a new source of advantage. Competition erodes barriers between firms and demands that managers become ever more aggressive—that they increase the speed with which their firms act, deepen their differentiation, and narrow their scope.[5]

Improving Strategic Timing

Companies can compete either by being first to develop and market new products or designs, or by allowing industry innovators to bring out new products, then quickly copying successful characteristics. Since the early 1980s, the pace of change has accelerated, forcing managers to confront more carefully questions of timing in new product development and introduction. In many cases, first movers have benefited from capturing markets early on. In other cases, imitators have fared better. In a competitive environment, managers must choose between deepening their commitment to innovation or relinquishing their leadership position in favor of a strategy of imitation.

Speeding Up

First movers routinely pioneer in bringing new products to market. Many historical first movers are today household names: IBM in mainframes, Xerox in copiers, Ford in autos, GE in appliances, Federal Express in overnight delivery. More recent examples of first movers have included Sinclair, Osborne, and Apple in personal computers; Advanced Memory Systems in microprocessors; Genentech in biotechnology. Early entry generally translates into higher profitability, thereby providing pioneering firms with a competitive advantage over later entrants. All too many early pioneers, however, go bankrupt or move on: RCA pioneered black and white television but no longer produces any; Osborne built the first portable computer but subsequently closed shop. First-mover advantages may be durable, but clearly they are not impregnable.

During periods of radical change, when established practices are disrupted profoundly, opportunities for innovation abound. Many firms today are aggressively pursuing opportunities to position themselves as first movers.

Managers try to create first-mover advantages either by achieving technological leadership or by making it too costly for consumers to switch to competitors.[6] Whereas building technological advantage has significant structural implications, increasing switching costs involves only designing sticky product features. Examples of sticky features that have produced first-mover advantages include airlines that raised consumers' switching costs by instituting frequent flyer programs, and TV and VCR manufacturers who made it costly for consumers to change equipment suppliers by making their systems incompatible. So Apple's unique graphical style provided them instant recognition and a distinct advantage in the early years of the personal computer. But software developments (e.g., Microsoft's Windows program) have made it possible for IBM clones to look and act just like Apple Macintosh machines, eroding Apple's advantage and forcing prices down.[7]

In contrast, structural first movers tend to invest heavily to secure patents and quickly move down the learning curve. To develop a head start and deter rivals, their managers spend aggressively on research and development. By being first with a technology, first movers can obtain patents that shelter them from rivals. Often these patents enable innovators to define standards to which the industry as a whole then gravitates. Take Du Pont's famous Lycra, the original fiber whose generic name is spandex. Although the 31-year-old product's patent has long since expired, savvy marketing has enabled Du Pont to retain its hold over two thirds of the world market for spandex.[8]

In the last decade, for another instance, Japan's Sharp Corp. has developed a significant lead in optoelectronics, with first-mover advantages in flat-screen TVs that hang on walls, dual cassette recorders, solid-state calculators, color desktop fax machines, and HDTV projection systems using LCD screens. In all of these areas, competition is likely to be brutal in the years ahead, forcing ever greater commitment of financial, human, and organizational capital to innovation.[9]

In PC hardware, Compaq has routinely outdone giant IBM by being first to sell machines that incorporate the latest technology—a strategy that has secured the company a stable 4-percent share of the market. In the days when Big Blue had yet to offer a portable PC, Compaq's was a hit. Later, Compaq was invariably first to feature the newest and most powerful microchips. Maintaining first-mover status, however, has become increasingly difficult as IBM and other PC makers such as Dell Computer, Packard Bell, and AST Research bring out competing clones more and more quickly. Recently, both IBM and Hewlett-Packard beat Compaq to market with products featuring the latest 486 chip.[10] To meet the challenge will require of Compaq either accelerated innovation or a strategic change designed to capitalize on global expansion while adopting an imitator strategy in the U.S. market.

In global environments, however, domestically granted patents, have proven less than effective as a source of advantage. For one, there is no adequate global system for enforcing patents and registrations. So competitors in foreign markets can more easily knock off products with impunity. Moreover, the time between filing and approval can be as long as 7 years, limiting the period for recovery of development costs, and so reducing the firm's advantage.

Moreover, if a patent is for a unique design rather than a new technology, it can prove entirely ineffectual. Take Zelco, maker of the Itty Bitty book light so popular with bedtime readers. Introduced in 1982 in a clever book-like packaging, within a year exact copies, down to the packaging, were introduced in Korea, Taiwan, Germany, Italy, and Australia. According to the U.S. Trade Representative's office, design knock-offs cost U.S. companies up to $40 billion in lost sales, royalties, and licensing fees annually.[11]

Besides relying on patents, many firms create advantage by emphasizing learning by doing. In a comparison of the largest U.S., British, and German firms, historian Alfred Chandler found that advantages accrued historically to firms who were first to exploit scale economies by investing in product-specific facilities and management-led administrative structures.[12] By leading in the decision to adopt improved production processes, to invest in efficient systems of distribution, to install research laboratories, and to train technicians, these managers ensured that their firms would move quickly down the learning curve. Rapid learning guaranteed that latecomers would have to make larger and riskier outlays of capital. A detailed study of the chemical industry confirms that cumulative experience increases the annual number of patents filed and leads to rapid reductions in product prices, which discourages new entrants.[13]

Only a few years ago, for instance, high-tech giant Motorola seemed destined for a takeover, with its key markets in chips, pagers, and cellular phones taken over by Japanese competitors such as NEC, Toshiba, Hitachi, and its U.S. nemesis, Texas Instruments. In a dramatic gamble, since 1986 the company has poured billions into research and development to recapture a leadership position in semiconductors. The result: In 1988, Motorola was the first to introduce a new breed of digital signal-processing chip (DSP) that is expected to feature prominently in the combined handling of image and voice signals. Aggressive R&D is also paying off in cellular phones, from which Motorola derived $1.3 billion in revenues in 1989.[14]

First movers are defending themselves against encroaching rivalry by obscuring their competencies. The more complex the combination of technologies involved in making a product, for instance, the less rivals are able to identify the critical skills they need to compete. Insofar as pioneering firms have developed unique internal cultures, they also erect barriers to imitation: Rivals cannot reproduce the deep-seated cultural features that led pioneers to innovate. Additionally, by establishing unique relationships with complementary suppliers and distributors, pioneers are heightening the ambiguity of their competencies and impeding imitation.[15]

Global competition is compelling first movers to allocate more funds to R&D than ever before. In order to spread risk, companies introducing products with short life cycles and relying on rapidly changing technologies have lobbied U.S. officials successfully under Ronald Reagan's presidency, getting them to set aside antitrust laws that prevented cooperative R&D both with domestic competitors and across borders. In the early 1980s, a group of U.S. Silicon Valley companies formed an R&D consortium, Sematech, funded half by industry and half by government, to reduce growing dependence on Japanese chip manufacturing. Similar cooperative R&D programs have been established in Europe.

At the same time, U.S. and European companies have been spending more aggressively than ever to develop products tailored to the European market. While research results suggest that centralized R&D costs less and is easier to coordinate, we also know that gains from commercialization are more difficult to capture when R&D is too far removed from ultimate markets.[16] The familiar tension between the functional areas of marketing, R&D, and manufacturing gets exacerbated as firms struggle to compete in global markets by trying, on the one hand, to reduce scale economies within functional areas, while responding, on the other hand, to the requirements of differentiated markets.

The pressure on first movers has therefore grown more acute. It comes from two sources: globalization that has heightened rivalry, and aggressive encroachment by imitators eager to reap the advantages of leadership.

When Followers Play Leapfrog

Humbled by the complexities of maintaining a first-mover position, some firms are electing a back seat, "second-mover" strategy when they expect that patent or other barriers will not prevent them from imitating an innovation at a cost substantially below the pioneer's development costs. In many industries, patents and R&D offer only weak protection to innovating firms, and new products are easily imitated. A comparative study of 48 product innovations, for instance, showed that 60 percent of successfully patented innovations were actually imitated within 4 years. Patents appear most significant in prescription drugs where imitation costs traceable to patents are some 30 percent higher, compared with about 10 percent in chemicals and only 7 percent in electronics.[17]

If following sometimes proves cost effective, which firms are doing better as imitators?

In the PC market, firms like AST, Dell Computer, and Packard Bell have grown rapidly in the last few years to catch up to leaders like Compaq, Tandy, and IBM. Between 1987 and 1989, while Tandy's share fell from 7.1 to 4.8 percent, Packard Bell's share in selling PC clones rose to 3.7 percent. Key to their success has been a combination of lower prices, distribution through mass merchandisers like Sears Roebuck rather than dealers, and customer service.[18]

Large sample studies of the semiconductor industry suggest that early followers have tended to be subsidiaries and divisions of large, established firms with existing businesses in related areas, firms such as Fairchild and Texas Instruments.[19] In a study of 129 start-up ventures, for instance, one researcher found that imitators had widely diversified parent firms, spent less on marketing their products than rivals, and had lower product quality and customer service than first movers.[20] What appears to drive early followers, then, is principally rapid learning from pioneers and swift capture of experience gains.

To quickly imitate pioneers and capture market share, astute followers develop efficient external information gathering. By cultivating competitor intelligence, constantly scanning environments, and rapidly responding to opportunity, imitators can often capitalize on the large investments made by pioneers in R&D, buyer education, and personnel training. In semiconductors, for instance, Fairchild benefited from the early efforts of Shockley Transistors, the firm started by transistor pioneer William Shockley which was dissolved and whose employees then joined Fairchild.[21] The training programs of money center banks also serve to diffuse accounting standards and product innovations. Empirical studies of the diffusion of innovations suggest that imitators gain access to detailed information on products and manufacturing processes within only 1 year of development through the interpersonal and exchange networks that exist within technological communities.[22]

Because imitators rely on other firms to pioneer, they invest little in basic research and dwell more heavily on product development in related technologies. By focusing on price as a means of competing with first movers, they strive quickly to acquire experience gains. Competitive intelligence enables them to avoid the technological mistakes made by pioneers, and to incorporate into their product designs the timely feedback of the product's initial consumers.

Revolutionary environments present managers with a unique opportunity to swerve from their original business strategies. Early innovators find it more difficult to maintain their position of leadership as specialized start-ups aggressively attack their narrow niches. Similarly, as early imitators grow in confidence and expertise, they often aspire to take over the leadership role from established firms. As attractive as it may appear, however, shifting from an imitator to a first-mover strategy is a risky endeavor: Imitators have relatively primitive skills in product development and lack the internal fiber needed to move quickly to commercialize them. When managers contemplate a fundamental reorientation within business units that involves altering the speed and timing with which their firms innovate, they must carefully assess whether their internal systems are strong enough to withstand the transformation.

Cultivating Distinctiveness

Companies can regain advantage from pursuing business strategies that rely more heavily on image and reputation as a source of differentiation. To build reputation is to signal publics about the merits of one's firm's products, jobs, strategies, and prospects relative to those of competing firms. Being held in high regard enables a company to obtain premium prices because it raises the value of the company's products to consumers. Firms with strong reputations are also able to recruit better skilled applicants for comparable pay, have greater access to the capital markets when they try to raise funds, and are more likely to attract investors in new ventures.[23]

Throughout the 1980s, many firms tried to distinguish themselves to consumers by developing a distinctive reputation either for selling at a low price, for making better-quality products and excellent service, and even for demonstrating social responsiveness. As competition escalates, managers today are trying to solidify aggressively the basis on which their firms are perceived to differ from competitors. Insofar as these dimensions prove valuable to buyers, they lower competition and increase profits.[24]

Cutting Costs

In firms competing as price leaders, the principal stress is on tightening control of operating costs. Because efficiency and productivity now loom ever higher as a source of competitive advantage, many managers are rediscovering manufacturing and investing heavily in smart factories and automated production. Indeed, many leading business schools, once more closely attuned to the rarefied subtleties of finance and strategy, have taken steps to reintroduce operations management into the core curriculum of their MBA programs. Indeed, an estimated 40 percent of the University of Chicago's MBA class of 1991 accepted jobs in manufacturing industries. Meanwhile, at MIT, an innovative program called Leaders for Manufacturing was started to prepare technically oriented students and revive shop floor management skills.[25]

In recent years, technological developments in manufacturing have steadily made scale economies less salient as a source of advantage by reducing the number of units needed to produce efficiently.[26] Controlling costs has therefore meant: (1) pruning administrative ratios and centralizing decisions; (2) investing in computer-aided design and manufacturing (CAD-CAM), robotics, and flexible production; and (3) developing Japanese-inspired just-in-time relationships with suppliers to reduce inventories and stock-outs and thereby lower operating costs.

Take the F117-A Stealth bomber, the lean, mean fighting machine that played a pivotal role in the allied air war against Iraq in 1991. Its builder, Northrop Corp., contends that it is the most complex mechanical system yet conceived, engineered, and produced totally by computers. So intricate and precise was the computer model of the aircraft that Northrop never even bothered to build a mock-up version. The result: All but 3 percent of some 30,000 parts fit perfectly the first time—a dramatic improvement over the typical 50 percent fit.

To further improve manufacturing efficiency, the Air Force is now funding 80 percent of a $19 million, 40-month project to develop with Northrop Corp. the Automated Aircraft Assembly Plant (AAAP), an expert system that will integrate all of the disparate databases scattered in different parts of the company, whether in design, purchasing, warehousing, manufacturing, or distribution. Getting different programs and databases to coordinate has been the principal stumbling block to developing computer integrated manufacturing.[27]

To achieve lower cost and price positions, many managers are making early preemptive investments either to monopolize scarce raw material inputs (e.g., buying up mineral-rich land at low prices) or to build excess production capacity designed to deter rivals. By building scale economies in production, distribution, or advertising in order to lower marginal costs, managers hope to lower product prices.

In turbulent environments, however, a low cost position is a source of advantage difficult to achieve, as U.S. auto makers have known all along: Despite spending $50 billion to retool and modernize its plants in the last 10 years and cutting costs by some $13 billion, GM has proved unable to lower its cost structure sufficiently to match the price advantage Japanese manufacturers enjoy.[28]

The most successful price leaders constantly look for ways to standardize products and activities, preferring to capture a large component of the market with a basic configuration of their product, than to customize its characteristics to particular segments.[29] Take the fast food industry. Taco Bell has been a shining star for its parent Pepsico. Because most fast food outlets are located side by side in high-traffic areas, competition among them is principally on the basis of price. With its "value menu," Taco Bell has emerged as the industry's discount leader, growing at some 10 to 15 percent annually compared with the 2 to 4 percent average growth of its rivals.[30]

In manufacturing, labor cost savings are usually obtained by jointly emphasizing managerial efficiency and adapting new technologies to operations. CAD-CAM and robotics technologies have enabled U.S. auto manufacturers, for instance, to dramatically reduce the average cost of producing cars domestically. To lower costs and maintain price leadership (or at least achieve parity), many U.S. managers are trying to emulate Japanese practices by developing closer relations, not only with employees but with suppliers; sharing information with vendors; helping them improve quality; and jointly solving production problems.[31] Similar process interventions have been documented at plants owned by Kodak, Timken, and Corning, among others. Through selective plant closures, layoffs, cost cutting, and quality control, entire industries have recast their operations in an attempt to compete with lower-cost foreign producers in globalizing markets.[32] Eastman Kodak, for instance, cut 11,000 workers in 1983, 13,000 in 1986, 5,000 in 1989, and 3,000 in 1991 as it focused more closely on its core photography business.[33] At 3M, running a leaner shop has not meant layoffs. Rather, in one program dubbed Challenge 95, the company has targeted cutting unit costs by 10 percent and manufacturing cycle time by 50 percent from 1985 levels. In another, they are investing in communications systems designed to link subsidiaries and customers via computer to process orders more quickly.[34]

Consider the increased appeal to energy efficiency. The low relative cost of fuel has justified developing many technologies that would otherwise have proved unaffordable. Cars were inexpensive to run until the 1973 oil embargo changed the economics of the auto industry. However, transportation efficiency has significantly improved since the Energy Policy and Conservation Act of 1975: By 1988, all U.S. cars averaged 19 miles to the gallon, compared with 13 mpg in 1973. New cars now deliver over 25 mpg in the United States and more than 30 mpg in Europe and Japan. Honda's latest model Civic now offers 55 mpg. And prototypes already exist for models at 60 to 100 mpg.

To further cut costs, many firms have taken significant steps to improve industrial energy efficiency: In OECD countries, energy intensity (the amount of energy required per unit of industrial production) has fallen by 30 percent since 1973. Today, full-time energy managers are required by law in all Japanese companies that use large amounts of energy.

Surprisingly, recycling now provides a major source of industrial efficiency. Not only does recyling scrap metals reduce waste, it also takes much less energy than producing new metals from ore. In the United States, the proportion of aluminum produced from recycled metals grew from 25 to 50 percent between 1970 and 1983.

Another peripheral source of efficiency some companies have found increasingly attractive is cogeneration of heat, electricity, and mechanical power. A utility plant producing only electricity is only about 32 percent efficient; a cogenerator using the same amount of fuel can approach 80 percent efficiency. The cost of cogeneration systems is usually less than half the cost of new coal or nuclear power plants.[35]

Eliminating redudant materials used in production also significantly reduces pollution and improves efficiency. 3M started a reduction program in 1975. By 1984 it had eliminated over 10,000 tons of water pollutants, 90,000 tons of air pollutants, and 140,000 tons of sludge from its discharges. It had also saved $192 million in costs in less than 10 years.[36]

Through these and other efficiency-oriented strategies, many firms are aggressively reducing their cost structures to reduce product prices.

Improving Quality

Some firms facing environmental discontinuities are investing heavily in improving product quality and providing unique design features. By giving consumers products of greater reliability, durability, or superior performance, they hope to develop reputations for quality and service. Although managers can influence consumers' perceptions through astute marketing, only production-based quality changes actually create successful advantage, particularly if repeat purchases are desired. As management scholar Henry Mintzberg put it, reputation "... is managed substantively not only by promoting it but also by providing the basis for it, believing in it, and carrying *every* function with an eye toward it."[37]

In many industries, managers choosing to emphasize quality have had to make wholesale changes in their relationships with employees. Hampered by union work rules, for instance, Ford, GM, and Chrysler have negotiated a new relationship with the powerful United Auto Workers, developing contracts that provide for automation, participation in quality circles, cooperative conflict resolution, flexible allocation of tasks, and a stronger voice for workers in corporate decisions.[38] Despite these changes, factories of Toyota, Nissan, and Honda transplants turn out as many cars as American plants, but with a work force some 15 to 20 percent smaller than those of the United States' Big Three.

In the early years of globalization, many U.S.-based firms had successfully penetrated foreign markets by exporting their successful domestic products.[39] The 1973 oil crisis and Japanese firms' subsequent invasion in consumer products caught U.S. managers unprepared to meet the value-creating attention to quality and the lean, low cost profile that these companies developed in earnest throughout the 1970s and 1980s.[40]

The gap in competitive outlook remains. At a meeting of the North American automobile parts makers in 1990, for instance, a Toyota Motor Company official pointed out that the quality of parts purchased domestically for Toyota showed defect rates 100 times higher for components supplied by 75 American and European firms than those supplied by 147 Japanese companies.[41]

In 1987, a comparison of three plants, one wholly run by GM in Massachussetts, one by Toyota in Japan, and the NUMMI joint venture between Toyota and GM located in Fremont, California showed how far behind U.S. quality has fallen. The GM car takes 31 assembly hours to complete, compared with 16 by Toyota and 19 by NUMMI. Assembly defects per car total 135 at GM, but only 45 at both others. Clearly, competing in globalized markets will increasingly require meeting the global standards of quality set by Japanese auto makers.[42]

Yet evidence of improvement is already here: In October 1990, GM's Cadillac Motor Division won the U.S. Commerce Department's Malcolm Baldridge National Quality Award for producing better cars and offering better service than other leading manufacturers. Indeed, estimates indicate that GM, Ford, and Chrysler have improved quality dramatically: Overall car defect rates have fallen from being 3 times higher than Japanese cars in 1980 to only 25 percent higher in 1990.[43]

Recall Motorola's aggressive catch-up strategy in semiconductors and communications. In addition to developing R&D, a critical aspect of implementing its first-mover strategy has also involved rethinking the manufacturing process in order to develop product quality to rival that of its Japanese competitors. It was Motorola that won the Baldridge Award for quality in 1988, and by 1992 its chairman Robert Galvin expects to the company to achieve "six sigma" quality, that is 3.4 defects per million products, a result rarely achieved by U.S. manufacturers, and then only in the production of simple products such as calculators. To support the quality thrust, Motorola also has built what is reputed to be one of the best customer service organizations in the semiconductor business and is anxious to anticipate and accommodate customer needs.[44]

As many firms like Motorola are demonstrating, quality and service go hand in hand. Firms that invest in producing better quality products also look for ways of improving the level of support and service provided to consumers. They prop up firms' products by bundling valuable complementary characteristics into every sale. The most common means of building a reputation for service involves providing special considerations such as credit terms, rapid delivery, user training, repairs, and instructional materials.

Although paying attention to the customer is hardly a new concept, it proved easy to neglect service in the booming postwar era. For many firms, competition largely revolved around either cost cutting or scale economies. As firms grew, *Business Week* notes, "chief executives turned to strategic planners for help. The MBAs helped create centralized bureaucracies that focused on winning market share—not on getting in touch with remote customers."[45] In the 1970s, the incursions into U.S. markets by Japanese firms like Honda and Toyota brought renewed attention to strategies centered on satisfying the customer. Popular books such as *In Search of Excellence* chastised American managers for their lack of attention to service and pointed to customer focus as the hallmark of Japanese managers' competitive outlook.

In addition to providing enhanced service, some of our firms recently have recognized the merit of developing a support infrastructure. In personal computers, for example, the battle for market share has been heavily influenced by firms' ability to provide compatible software. In the early years, competition stabilized only after IBM selected Microsoft Corporation's DOS as an operating system, promising that software support would be more abundant for DOS-based machines than for rivals. IBM's entry led to the demise of Osborne and other non-DOS-based PCs.

Since IBM and Microsoft parted ways, however, a flurry of activity has resulted over AT&T's more versatile operating system UNIX that is already offered by IBM, Compaq, Sun Microsystems, and NCR in open system PCs. With open system architecture a likely outcome, personal computer firms will be able to achieve a differentiated position only by bundling support and service to develop a reputation among consumers as being customer-focused.

But a strategy of improving quality is generally costly, while a strategy of cost reduction often drives down quality; hence, the recent surge of interest in *value marketing*, that is, developing a reputation for providing to the consumer a better ratio of quality to price by bundling guarantees, 800 numbers, and frequent buyer plans—that is, service—as key product features.[46]

Becoming Good Citizens

More visible recently as a veneer on more traditional sources of advantage have been managers' attempts to show that their companies are employee-friendly, that their products are environment-friendly, and that their practices are socially conscious. The more clairvoyant among them are recognizing that corporate publics now judge how well firms respond to their noneconomic agendas, and that their verdict affects market value.[47]

At Du Pont, for instance, CEO Edgar Woolard, Jr. has made concern for the environment one of the hallmarks of his administration, referring to himself as his firm's chief environmentalist. Once content simply to sell the basic resins used to make plastic bottles, Du Pont now spends some $1 billion a year in an effort to establish a reputation for being environmentally friendly. The company has created an environmental services division and set a target of reducing toxic emissions in 1993 to 60 percent of their 1987 levels and emissions of carcinogens by 90 percent by the year 2000.[48]

By acting in socially responsible ways, some managers are indicating aggressively that their companies have achieved a healthy relationship with their environments. Social and political involvement often relates directly to a firm's operations. Sometimes it represents a means of thwarting environmental challenges from powerful constituents.[49]

The auto industry, for instance, long an adversary of public demand for more environmentally friendly vehicles, appears to be changing its tune. With clean air acts proliferating both in the United States and in Europe, auto makers feel pressured to stamp out harmful exhaust emissions, and that means revamping the old internal combustion engine, even as oil companies try to come up with cleaner gasoline. A speculative frenzy is already under way as oil producers and auto makers vie to be the first to bring to market alternative cars powered by natural gas, methanol, hydrogen, or electricity.[50]

Or take 3M, the company best known for consumer products such as Scotch tape and Post-It notes. Environmental groups give the $13-billion company the highest rating on environmental issues, despite its continued emission of large quantities of toxic chemicals. In fact, cleaning up pollution is a centerpiece of both its corporate ethic and competitive strategy: Product design and manufacturing rely on processes that are as clean as possible; pollution control equipment is regularly introduced into older plants; and customers are provided help in disposing of polluting packaging.[51]

Typically, managers have sought to indicate their firms' social concern by contributing to charitable causes, developing nonpolluting products, achieving equal opportunity employment, creating foundations, placing women and minorities on boards, or adhering to codes of conduct such as the Sullivan principles. Responsiveness generates goodwill from employees, consumers, and other publics that enhances the long-run profitability and viability of firms, and the employment of incumbent managers.[52]

Since 1975, for example, the MacDonald's Corporation had packaged its hamburgers in what industry jargon called "clamshells"—square, hinged containers made of plastic foam. In November 1990, some 15 years later, the fast food chain's managers announced that it would do away with plastic foam and switch to back to paper packaging. The decision came largely as a result of pressure from the Environmental Defense Fund, a coalition of special interests that scrutinize firms' effects on the environment. McDonald's constitutes some 8 percent of the United States' 1-billion-pound annual consumption of foam packaging.[53]

In April 1990, managers of H.J. Heinz, the company that markets Starkist brand tuna, announced that they would no longer buy tuna from boats that imperiled dolphins. Later that same day, Bumble Bee's parent company, Unicord Inc., and Chicken of the Sea's parent company, Van Camp Seafood, followed suit. Marketing "dolphin-safe" tuna had become a competitive issue after the Earth Island Institute, an environmental group headquartered in San Francisco, urged a consumer boycott of canned tuna. In December 1990, the Institute initiated another media battle when it ran newspaper ads charging Bumble Bee with breaking its pledge to sell only dolphin-safe tuna. Bumble Bee countered with full-page ads accusing the group of false and misleading statements.[54]

Examples like these now abound—of firms trying to differentiate their products by their social responsiveness. Pressured by consumer groups, employees, and other stakeholders, managers are finding it advantageous, if not essential, to factor into their cost-benefit calculations the externalities they have traditionally ignored. Indeed, researchers calling themselves ecological economists have gained prominence recently by accusing traditional economists of underestimating pollution costs and ignoring society's responsibility to future generations. Members of the International Society of Ecological Economists, for instance, work to persuade governments to give sustainability of natural life support systems priority over conventionally measured economic growth.[55]

Both the United States and the European community are independently considering proposals to label consumer products for their effect on the environment. The "green" label would indicate how a product compares with those of competitors in their use of, say, toxic chemicals, recycled products, and energy efficiency—both in terms of their effects, and in terms of the inputs required to make them.[56] The consequences are clear: By making environmental performance a competitive dimension, managers are finding themselves forced to consider differentiation, not only on the basis of price, quality, or service, but also on the basis of social responsiveness.

Slicing Up the Business

As markets have grown more competitive, managers have increased either segmentation of their business activities or customization of their product offerings. To target buyers better, executives are developing products capable of meeting the needs of a narrower set of market segments either by customizing product features to targeted segments or by standardizing offerings across segments.[57] By fragmenting market segments, changing environments pressure managers both to target carefully their products and to customize product features to local needs.

For U.S. soda giant Coca-Cola, cutthroat competition with archrival Pepsico has meant that both firms have had to pursue aggressive strategies for building market share—introducing a wide range of new products targeted to ever narrower market segments—on the one hand, and, on the other, sponsoring extravagant promotions. Through its New Products group, formed in 1989, Coke hopes to snare various local markets from Pepsi with line extensions ranging from Fresca to New Coke and Caffeine Free Coca-Cola Classic.[58]

Changing demographics are creating narrower niches. As consumer markets exacerbated the split between haves and have-nots in the 1980s, many traditional retailers like Alexander's and Abraham and Strauss have found their middle-of-the-road strategies squeezed at both ends. On one side, they are nibbled at by discounters like Wal-Mart Stores and

K-Mart that appeal to the growing share of households with annual incomes less than $15,000. On the other side, their market is attacked by premium-priced outlets like Bergdorf Goodman and Bloomingdale's expanding downward from their market of upper income households, and by specialty chains such as the Limited directly targeting the middle income market.

The Segmenting Solution

Companies differ in whether they attack a broad sweep or narrow niche within a market. At one extreme are generalist firms whose managers target multiple markets by standardizing the components that go into their products. Most car and cigarette manufacturers, for instance, do so.[59] Pursuing such a comprehensive strategy in times of environmental change, however, requires access to large pools of capital and human resources: Products must be tailored to the demands of each segment, calling simultaneously for standardized production and for customized packaging, marketing campaigns, and support services.

Most firms respond to environmental upheavals by specializing: They target their firms' products to a limited number of segments. Geographical location often provides firms with such protected niches: The corner drugstore, dry cleaner, barber shop, or supermarket hold local monopolies that potential competitors find difficult to attack because of these firms' established relationships to consumers. Publishing houses specializing in low-volume academic treatises, for instance, occupy a narrow but profitable niche within the larger college, trade, and mass-market segments of the industry.[60] In television, Fox has emerged as the United States' fourth television network by targeting provocative, offbeat programming such as *Married with Children* and *The Simpsons* at kids, teens, and young adults—a market attractive to advertisers but relatively neglected by the three established networks.[61] In pianos, Steinway holds a near monopoly in the limited high-priced segment for concert grands. It is increasingly threatened, however, by standardized manufacturers such as Yamaha who rely on innovative technology and automation to lower price and capture market share. Steinway has been slow to capitalize on its reputation to build market share in neighboring segments.[62]

And look at Chemical Bank. Since 1983, under Walter Shipley's leadership, Chemical Bank has followed a strategy designed to differentiate it from its large New York rivals. Rather than emphasize lending to larger companies, a more congested niche, Chemical executives went after the middle market business, a group of 10,000 firms whose sales range from $10 to $250 million. Chemical now claims to have relationships with over 36 percent of those firms, a result that places it at the top of the heap in the middle-market segment, with Citicorp and National Westminster in second place[63]—and, not coincidentally, makes it an ideal merger partner for Manufacturer's Hanover.

As segments have proliferated, the niches within which firms compete have grown narrower and tighter. Throughout the 1980s, some firms with access to larger pools of resources found it attractive to broaden their scope by acquiring small-niche players. In book publishing, for example, McGraw-Hill purchased dozens of small businesses that provided access to specialized market segments. Integrating them into a coordinated whole, however, has proved to be a recurrent theme of McGraw-Hill's reorganizations in the last few years, and should prove to be its key challenge in the years to come.

Customizing

More than before, competition is driving companies to customize their offerings to consumers within market segments. Take the software industry. As competition has intensified, industry leaders such as Lotus and Microsoft, once content to mass market their successful spreadsheet packages 1-2-3 and Excel, now gear their programs to specific customers. However, tailoring products means hiring specialists who lavish weeks and months on specific customers—a costly departure from their traditional mass market strategy.

Similarly, although globalization significantly increases the market reach of firms, it has pit managers against strong rivals, many of whom are more closely attuned to the characteristics of local markets. Increasingly, both national and transnational marketing require more careful targeting of local consumers. Gone, then, are the mass markets of yesteryear for which manufacturers produced standard, single-brand-name, homogeneous products. In their place, *mass customized* markets are emerging.[64]

In recent years, Procter & Gamble, for example, has responded to globalization by revolutionizing its own operations and targeting local market segments. Recognizing cross-cultural diversity, they regularly customize products to individual tastes by linking consumer data to product characteristics. They introduce product line extensions to capitalize on brand names and advertise in new media such as schools or cable TV to reach target populations. In the intertwined but culturally disparate economies of the world, this kind of customized production and targeted marketing should be key to achieving competitive advantage in consumer products. P&G has already shown how applying these techniques globally can pay off: Between 1985 and 1989, P&G's earnings from foreign operations grew from 14 percent to 33 percent, on $8.4 billion in foreign sales.[65]

Although the prospect of scale economies encourages many firms to globalize, achieving these economies also calls for a degree of product standardization. In the airline industry, United and American have emerged from the long era of deregulation as head-to-head competitors, vying for air supremacy. Scale economies have proven critical as both airlines, equally strong in their domestic markets, expand their operations on a global basis. So, in October 1990 United agreed to buy troubled Pan Am's London routes in a deal valued at $400 million. Soon thereafter, American agreed to the purchase of TWA's London routes for $445 million, demonstrating their intent to provide an identical service.[66]

In many industries, however, scale economies have failed to materialize, partly because of pressure to customize, partly because of logistical barriers and transport costs associated with moving goods from centrally located plants to remote consumers and partly because efficient plant size precludes capturing additional scale economies. The washing machine industry in Europe, for instance, has demonstrated that local producers generally outdo competitors engaging in cross-border specialization because transport costs and management costs of larger factories seriously dampen the gains from scale they produce. In the apparel industry, competitive pressures make speed of delivery an important factor, encouraging production closer to end markets and making standardization difficult to achieve. Technological developments now offer some assistance. Computer controlled devices facilitate precise cutting of cloth, eliminating precious waste. Garment patterns, stored in computers, enable cost-effective production of small runs and even individual garment orders. And telecommunications can save time: A subsidiary of the Limited, a U.S. retail chain, now uses satellite transmission and high-definition television to transmit pictures of the latest designs to factories in southern China, delivering finished garments within 6 weeks to U.S. stores.[67]

Customizing also has become a familiar tune to airplane manufacturers like Boeing. Direct competition from McDonnell-Douglas and Europe's Airbus has made the industry more competitive, demanding flexibility and efficiency in the design of airplanes to customer specifications. In one bidding auction to fill a $20 billion United Airlines order, Boeing, Airbus, and McDonnell-Douglas teams were provided a wish list of 54 demands and hundreds of subdemands for customizing a new long-distance aircraft. Competition was fierce to see who could best meet United's needs.[68] Airbus won. Indeed, defeated by Airbus in one too many such auctions, McDonnell-Douglas has actively sought an infusion of cash that would enable it to strenghten its product development efforts. In November 1991, it petitioned Congress for authorization to pursue an equity joint venture with Taiwan Aerospace (a government-backed operation), who agreed to provide $2 billion in exchange for 40 percent of a new subsidiary. The aim of the joint venture is to produce and market aircraft for the rapidly growing Asian region.[69]

Contested Terrains

As Table 5.1 suggests, companies occupy distinct competitive positions based on their particular combinations of timing, differentiation, and scope. Compaq competes in personal computers as a first mover, but also holds a reputation for quality that differentiates it from clones and justifies the price premium it charges. Through a broad product line that encompasses portables, desktops, and work stations, Compaq also targets narrower markets within the industry. In contrast, clone makers such as Packard Bell go after consumers with a followership strategy backed by a low price position in every market niche.

Profiles of timing, differentiation, and scope define implicit groups of firms that compete more intensely because they pursue the same business-level strategies. Increasingly, these groups overlap as competition erodes established sources of advantage.* They force managers to contemplate making strategic changes within their business units.

By making systematic commitments to build a more aggressive strategic profile through changes in timing, differentiation, and scope, managers are reinventing unique capabilities for their firms. They are also working hard to create cognitive barriers in the minds of consumers and other corporate audiences. New competitors will hesitate to attack well-regarded firms on their own turf, partly for lack of skill, and partly for fear of retaliation. Solid reputations, they hope, can inhibit rivalry and protect their profitability.[70]

Early studies of the beer, pharmaceuticals, retail grocery, and banking industries supported the existence of distinct groups within which managers implemented similar combinations of business strategies contrasted according to timing, differentiation, and scope. These profiles placed firms on trajectories from which change proved difficult. They also built barriers that inhibited new rivals from making direct assaults on firms' markets.

In recent years, performance differences between groups, however, have proven to be less consistent than anticipated. Managers whose firms pursued similar strategies, and so belonged to the same groups, have not necessarily obtained similar profit levels, either because the *inputs* on which they relied were sold in imperfect markets, or because firms had differing levels of market power in *output* markets. On the input side, knowledge about manufacturing processes or organization of a new

---

*The term *strategic group* was originally coined to explain enduring differences in the observed performance of firms competing in the major appliances industry during the 1960s. Early empirical research, not only tried to show the existence of these groups, but sought to demonstrate the persistence of performance differences among groups. Many studies found profitability levels to be higher within groups characterized as leaders than within groups characterized as followers due to internal hurdles that separated leaders from followers. Researchers expected managers' strategic investments over time to create advantages that would prove difficult to imitate, and so erect barriers against rivals' intrusions.

Table 5.1. Changes in Business Strategy

Firms competing through:	Experiencing pressure to:
Timing	
First mover	Protect R&D
Imitator	Organize a more rapid response
Differentiation	
Price	Control costs
Quality	Improve quality and service
Responsiveness	Show social and environmental awareness
Scope	
Segmentation	Target narrower markets
Customization	Mass-customize

venture has proven more complex and difficult to obtain in many industries, hampering a firm from quickly imitating a rival. Similarly, on the output side, firms with greater market share often exercise local monopolies and thereby achieve greater returns than their rivals from competing in a market segment.[71]

A study of the British retail grocery industry between 1982 and 1986, for instance, identified the group structure of the industry on the basis of seven key dimensions of firms' business strategies, for example, number of stores, average size of stores, advertising expenditures, number of food lines, and number of private label lines. The analysts found that the strategic groups within the industry remained stable over time despite significant performance differences within groups.[72]

Or consider the banking community. To capitalize on opportunities resulting from deregulation and technological developments in the electronic transfer of funds in the late 1970s and early 1980s, firms that had historically specialized in offering a narrow range of these products began diversifying across industry lines. Nonbank intermediaries such as Sears Roebuck entered the fray, following Merril Lynch's attack on banking with the Cash Management Account. Banks and savings and loan associations retaliated by collectively petitioning legislators to rescind the Glass-Steagall and McFadden Acts, raising interest rates, and developing new products such as money market funds, interest-bearing checking accounts, annuities, and insurance policies.

As competition intensified, the search for higher returns to cover higher costs led banks and S&L's to make business-level strategic changes: They made riskier investments in commercial real estate, junk bonds, and foreign currency—one result of which was the S&L crisis whose cost, borne by taxpayers, could exceed $500 billion including interest. In flagrant disregard for the McFadden Act that restricted interstate banking, many of our largest banks also implemented a corporate-level strategic change: They diversified across state lines by purchasing regional banks. Institutions such as Citicorp, Chase, and BankAmerica broadened their business and product portfolios in anticipation of becoming one-stop financial supermarkets.

Financial service firms made familiar strategic responses to the community-level convergence provoked by deregulation: New products proliferated, mergers were consummated, and interfirm alliances formed. One study showed that although the pattern of strategic changes to which managers committed varied, the community progressively congealed into three strategic groupings: (1) one-stop financial supermarkets, particularly among the largest money center banks and brokerage firms; (2) regional financial service firms emphasizing customer service; (3) specialized institutions offering in-house expertise to clients, particularly prevalent among smaller, local firms in the United States' Northeast.[73]

Despite these early attempts at strategic change, by the end of the 1980s the Glass Steagall Act still officially separated financial services delivery in the United States between the 14,000 commercial money center, regional, and local banks, and the 6,308 securities firms. Of these, the seven leading investment banks were by far the most aggressive. By the 1980s, for instance, investment banks had diversified extensively through consolidations and innovations, reducing their dependency on commissions and dramatically increasing their advisory services, particularly in mergers and acquisitions.

Between 1982 and 1988, investment banks proliferated financial products, increasing in number from some 62 in 1982 to over 253 in 1988. Competition swelled, and the close relationships on which investment banking historically had been based foundered. Clients developed ties to multiple banks, and bankers became more transaction oriented, battling for every deal.

By the late 1980s, four clusters were evident: (1) a lead cluster constituted by Salomon Brothers, First Boston, Goldman Sachs, and Merrill Lynch, catering primarily to very active users of investment banking services; (2) a more highly diversified group consisting of Shearson-Lehman and Morgan-Stanley; (3) a second tier of less diversified banks serving middle-market customers, including Bear, Stearns; Dean Witter; Drexel Burnham Lambert; E.F. Hutton; Kidder, Peabody; Paine Webber; Prudential-Bache Securities; and Smith Barney; and, finally, (4) a fourth cluster consisting of niche players with little diversification but strong specialties in either mergers and acquisitions, individual placements, or common stock offerings, and comprised of Alex Brown; Dillon, Read; Donaldson, Lufkin & Jenrette; L.F. Rotschild; and Lazard Frères.[74]

Because investment banks compete most heavily within clusters to attract particular types of clients, a strategic concern of firms across clusters, then, has become their relative strength within a group, and the implications that continued convergence between banking and securities segments will have for each group's ability to retain competitive advantage in the enlarged but insecure community of firms delivering financial services. Take Smith Barney. The company has benefited dramatically from events that have decimated its cluster rivals. Drexel, Burnham Lambert unraveled following the insider trading charges brought by the SEC. Kidder, Peabody was similarly tripped up by SEC charges, and caught up in merger trauma after its purchase by General Electric. E.F. Hutton disappeared into Shearson Lehman and the American Express empire. The reduced cluster therefore pits Smith Barney against arch-rivals Bear Sterns and Paine Webber, and promises an intensification of competition for the middle market through timing, differentiation, and scope.

Outrunning the Red Queen

In Lewis Carroll's *Alice through the Looking Glass*, the Red Queen tells Alice that, even though they are all running at top speed, they really should not expect to get anywhere. This is because inhabitants of Looking Glass Land are obliged to run as fast as they can just to stay where they are. To get anywhere, they have to run ever so much faster.

Environments are compelling managers to do much the same. Increasing rivalry has eroded many firms' traditional sources of advantage, forcing managers to instigate strategic changes within business units. Timing is proving more critical than ever: Maintaining first-mover status is difficult, as imitators run faster to catch up. There are distinct gains to having well-differentiated reputations; however, the traditional advantages of image also appear more easily eroded. Where narrower scope used to provide firms with a sense of invulnerability, managers of even the largest firms now seek to mass-customize their products to meet the needs of niche markets.

To compete in the revolutionary marketplace of the late twentieth century, managers are implementing strategic changes designed to increase their firms' aggressiveness. Those too small to maintain a credible and determined presence through timing, differentiation, or scope are unlikely to survive. In part, success in maintaining competitiveness will depend on how adept managers prove to be at inspiring employees to implement changes in their firms' traditional profiles. As the next chapter indicates, corporate-level consolidations are also likely to result as companies in historically sheltered industries get beaten up by more aggressive global players.

6
Cultivating Synergy

*We must all hang together or assuredly we
shall hang separately.*

BENJAMIN FRANKLIN

While divisional managers struggled to carry out strategic changes designed to make their business units more agggressive in terms of timing,
differentiation, and scope, many top executives at headquarters were
busily manipulating the portfolio of businesses under their firms' corporate umbrellas. Some held divergent views of how they could create
synergy among business units. Many also felt an allegiance to different
stakeholders.

Consider Kohlberg Kravis Roberts & Co (KKR). In 1986, they engineered one of the most successful leveraged buyouts of all time, that of
Beatrice Foods. Structured as a $7-billion "breakup deal," the branded-
products conglomerate was quickly split up to pay off the $6.5 billion of
debt incurred to take the firm private. By year end 1986, Beatrice had
divested Avis, Coca-Cola Bottlers, and its dairy, cold storage, and printing
businesses and, within a year, its international businesses and bottled
water operations would be gone. Remaining businesses were pooled into
two groups: Beatrice, the food products group, and E-II, the consumer
products group. Beatrice managers subsequently took E-II public and
sold their holdings to American Brands. In 1988, Beatrice sold Tropica-
na, by which time only three businesses remained: Swift Meats, Hunt-
Wesson Foods, and a cheese operation. By 1991, the company, now
known as TLC Beatrice, consisted of less than half the original.[1]

Some favored the breakup. After all, they argued, it was impossible for
managers to produce enough real value from so diverse a conglomerate.

115

Since the breakup, TLC Beatrice has demonstrated greater profitability and seems poised to capitalize on its foothold in the European ice cream and snack food markets. Skeptics, however, point to the far greater skill demonstrated by a company like Philip-Morris in exploiting a portfolio of branded-goods comparable to that of Beatrice. Not only did Philip-Morris originally acquire the Miller Brewery where it applied its marketing acumen to redefine competition in the conservative beer industry, but later it again made back-to-back acquisitions of General Foods and Kraft to capitalize on related synergies with the marketing-driven food business. Where Beatrice disintegrated, cry the skeptics, Philip-Morris continues to search, define, and mine a very profitable source of synergy across its businesses.

Beatrice and Philip-Morris exemplify two quite different corporate-level strategic changes that managers relied on to respond to environmental turbulence since the 1970s. The first consisted of *financial restructurings*, in which managers and raiders scrutinized firms' financial profiles for hidden market value, often leveraging their companies right out of the equity markets. The second were *synergistic restructurings*, in which managers identified operating benefits from adding, combining, or eliminating entire lines of business.[2]

Time has favored the latter. Indeed, the recent collapse of many financially motivated deals of the 1980s suggests that, in the coming years, managers will be looking more actively to derive benefit from developing corporate-level synergies. In an environment characterized by ever more rapidly changing technologies and competitive incursions by aggressive rivals, top managers are pressured to scrutinize the sources of synergy they spurned in better times, and to restructure their firms in ways that permit capitalizing on the latent sources of advantage that related diversifications offer. Increasingly, competing involves tapping the secret reservoir of efficiencies that lies hidden in the vast array of products and businesses many large firms have brought under their corporate portfolios during the diversification binge of the 1970s and 1980s.

Looking for Quick Payoffs

Managers initiate strategic changes at the corporate level to reap economic benefits from holding multiple businesses. Throughout the 1980s however, many corporate initiatives involved manipulating balance sheets and designing tactical gambits whose principal purpose later proved to be monetary gain for a small class of privileged shareholders and incumbent managers. Although some observers staunchly defend these financial maneuvers as a vehicle for increasing corporate efficiency, a larger group asserts that unbridled greed dominated the implementation of these financially motivated corporate strategies, many of which subsequently went awry.

Mergers, spin-offs, and leveraged buyouts: These, then, were the corporate bywords of the 1980s as U.S. industry underwent its most radical restructuring since the turn of the century when, spurred by innovations in transportation (the railroad) and communication (the telephone), John D. Rockefeller, Andrew Carnegie, and J. Pierpont Morgan built such monolithic firms as Standard Oil and U.S. Steel by aggressively combining smaller competitors.[3] Over 50 percent of all large firms were involved in restructurings in the 1980s, often provoked by such swashbuckling raiders as T. Boone Pickens and Carl Icahn, who loudly accused incumbent managements of inefficiency and threatened their firms with takeover. Managers scrambled to reconfigure corporate assets to ward off these menacing suitors.

Table 6.1 demonstrates the boom in merger, spin-off, and LBO transactions since 1979. To finance these asset movements, combined corporate borrowing ballooned from a low of $835 million in 1979 to over $2 trillion in 1988.[4]

The Defensive Buy and Sell

This was not the first burst of corporate-level strategic change. In the 1960s and 1970s, newly minted portfolio views of the corporate role justified financial juggling of firms' assets in order to diversify risk.

Table 6.1. Mergers, Spin-offs, and LBOs

	Acquisitions		Leveraged buyouts*		Divisional buyouts†	
Year	Number	Value ($ millions)	Number	Value ($ millions)	Number	Value ($ millions)
1979	2128	43,500	16	636.0	59	318.6
1980	1889	44,300	13	967.4	47	621.5
1981	2395	82,600	17	2,338.5	83	1,742.0
1982	2346	53,700	31	2,836.7	115	4,680.5
1983	2533	73,100	36	7,145.4	139	8,089.8
1984	2543	122,200	57	10,805.9	122	12,688.0
1985	3001	179,800	76	24,139.8	132	14,533.2
1986	3336	173,100	76	20,232.4	144	26,020.8
1987	2032	163,700	47	22,057.1	90	12,978.0
1988	2258	246,900	125	60,920.6	89	16,135.7

SOURCE: W.T. Grimm & Co., Mergerstat Review, Chicago, IL.
*Involves only buyouts of public companies.
†Where managers take divisions private.

Consistent with these principles, successful managers like James Ling at LTV, Royal Little at Textron, Harold Geneen at ITT, and Charles Bludhorn at Gulf & Western acquired firms in unprecedented numbers, diversifying into far-flung businesses, both domestically and abroad. In contrast to the vertically integrated, core-business focus of most large U.S. firms, they built portfolios of businesses, introducing into managerial parlance the concept of the conglomerate structure in which corporate staff remain aloof from operating decisions and act as aggressive monitors of decentralized divisions. In 1982, over 300 of the Fortune 1000 relied on portfolio-planning techniques.

What made the 1980s interesting was the appearance of a new breed of deal-making raiders who astutely identified the lack of productivity underlying many previous acquisitions. Spurred by a buoyant stock market and Reagan entrepreneurial rhetoric, portfolio firms suddenly found themselves under attack. Managers chose either to prune their portfolios, sloughing off peripheral businesses, or to use innovative financial tools to restructure corporate assets.

Rather than sell off core businesses, some managers called out for white knights who would agree to retain incumbent managers and maintain a hands-off policy on operations. In January 1988, for instance, Hoff-mann–La Roche & Co, the Swiss pharmaceutical firm, extended a $4.2-billion takeover bid for Sterling Drug, the maker of Bayer aspirins and Phillips Milk of Magnesia, among other household products. Sterling's managers declined the offer and began holding discussions with other potential buyers. Photo and chemicals giant Eastman Kodak moved quickly to seal a deal by accepting an option on Sterling's attractive Glenbrook Laboratories business, and making a $5.1 billion offer. As a friendly owner, Kodak promised to keep Sterling's operations intact.

Many white knights contributed to corporate-level reorientations by agreeing to combine operations or explore sources of synergy. At Sterling/Kodak, for instance, both parties viewed the link as potentially fruitful on an operational level: Kodak had already committed to diversifying into the pharmaceutical industry, and both companies stood to benefit from their respective research, marketing, and sales expertise in related product lines.

Some divestitures and acquisitions also provoked strategic reorientations that revived many firms' commitments to their core businesses. Others, like those at American Can and U.S. Steel, led managers to jettison their seemingly sterile core businesses and change identities: Container manufacturer American Can turned into financial services provider Primerica, and steelmaker U.S. Steel metamorphosed into diversified USX. In those years most tobacco firms diversified into other lines of business in response to antismoking pressure. Challenged by health reports linking smoking to cancer, barred from mass advertising, lobbied by consumer health groups, sued by victims, firms like Philip-Morris sought out businesses such as Miller Beer, General Foods, and Kraft to which they could apply their skill in consumer marketing.[5]

In the final analysis, raiders' tenacious attacks on corporate portfolios highlighted some managers' inabilities to capture the full value of their firms' diversified assets. Coveting for themselves the gains raiders were making, many of our most aggressive managers chose neither to divest assets nor to diversify, but committed their firms to leveraged buyouts.

Leveraging Corporate Assets

Following a hostile takeover bid of $1.8 billion from Black & Decker Corp. in March 1988, American Standard Inc. went private for $2.5 billion. Its market value before the tender offer had been $1.2 billion. As is typical with most LBOs, the deal involved about 7 percent equity and 93 percent debt in the form of loans from bank syndicates. The debt was used to purchase firms' outstanding shares. The new owners relied on estimates of the LBOs' future cash flows to cover interest payments.

Similarly, when conglomerate LTV Corp., the number 2 integrated U.S. steel maker, sold off J&L Specialty Products Corp. in 1986, the $160-million management buyout was financed almost exclusively with bank debt and stock, and only $800,000 in cash by a group that included Drexel, Citicorp, and the Bass brothers. With only minimal reinvestment, the company was sold within three years to the world's second largest steel maker Usinor Sacilor for a whopping $270 million in cash, over $320 million in cash and bonuses having been extracted in the intervening years.[6]

Not all firms make such good prospects, however. We know that LBOs tend to have higher-than-industry-average cash flows and dividend payouts.[7] Lacking stable, recession-proof cash flows, few LBOs have been completed in high-tech, turbulent industries. Moreover, research suggests that firms whose shares were more concentrated in the hands of insiders and whose incumbent managers were younger were more likely to go private. Since many LBOs relied on employee stock ownership plans (ESOPs) and pension funds to raise debt and acquire firms' outstanding securities, firms whose operations were heavily unionized (and more likely to have such plans), were also more viable LBO candidates.[8]

At least some of these buyouts offered significant benefits. Empirical studies of postbuyout performance find that many did enhance efficiency without either massive layoffs or cuts in R&D. Efficiency gains and highly profitable asset sales built more efficient companies that benefited, not only prior shareholders who gained buyout premiums estimated at some 40 to 56 percent, but also LBO sponsors such as KKR and Kelso & Co.[9] By making owners out of managers and employees, taking firms private also appears to have enhanced the productivity of firms such as Wilson Sporting Goods, widely said to have suffered a stifling stint as a subsidiary of PepsiCo.

LBO structures also reduce the costs of complying with SEC reporting requirements imposed on public corporations; lessen firms' tax obligations, since interest paid on debt is deductible; and ensure that managers, as owners, act in their firms' best interests. A comparison of 65 firms taken private between 1980 and 1987 with an industry-matched group of 130 firms confirmed that firms that went private had higher levels of cash flow and lower levels of receivables and demonstrated higher growth rates in the 3 years preceding the buyout.[10]

When firms go private through LBOs, however, their indebtedness exposes them to higher levels of risk. Cash flows can prove insufficient in economic downturns, and managers are then forced to liquidate assets. The 1986 $1.3-billion leveraged buyout of Revco D.S., Inc., for instance, a 2000-unit drugstore chain, ended in disaster. In July 1988 it filed for Chapter 11 bankruptcy protection, a result of overly optimistic sales, earnings, and cash flow projections. Debt dealt a crushing blow to other leveraged buyouts, including Fruehauf, the United States' largest maker of truck trailers; Dart Drug Stores, which filed for Chapter 11 in August 1989; and Hilsborough Holdings, the largest LBO to file for bankruptcy protection. In 1991, famed retailer Macy's, taken private by management in 1988, itself would file for protection against its creditors.

Because the debt incurred in going private is also below investment grade, LBOs tend to increase the risk exposure of institutions extending the loans. Evidently one of the factors contributing to the debacle of the U.S. savings and loan industry has been these institutions' extensive investments in high-yielding but risky junk bonds. In *The S&L Debacle*, former Federal Home Loan Bank Board Chairman Larry White points to the highly leveraged nature of S&Ls in the early 1980s, and the incentive that low-interest debt provided to managers of these banks to make risky investments and conceal losses.

Recent events suggest that some of the egregious financial excesses of the 1980s may even come back to haunt participants. A report assembled by the Federal Bankruptcy Court intimates that some leveraged buyouts currently in Chapter 11 may have constituted fraudulent conveyance— an improper transfer of firms' corporate capital to investment banks, lawyers, and shareholders. If so, then many who worked on failed deals could be sued to return fees. In Revco's case, this amounted to some $80 million.[11]

Although the jury is still out the evidence on leveraged buyouts and other financially driven strategic changes of the 1980s is somewhat mixed, but weighs toward the negative. On the one hand, leveraged buyouts, particularly when units were divisions of larger firms, did generate increased entrepreneurship and productivity. The high levels of debt incurred appears to have encouraged managers to reassess all operations and internal controls, thereby fostering productivity gains. On the other hand, many of these buyouts also created hardship for employees, families, and communities because of layoffs induced by divestitures, plant closings, and consolidations. Overall financial benefits seem skewed to a relatively limited group, principally buyout managers and the shareholders of the acquired firms who collected gains from repurchased shares— at the expense of remaining shareholders, employees, banks, and other institutions.

Since most firms and investors have become phobic about debt, even buyout lords Kohlberg Kravis Roberts & Co. have had to modify their strategy, taking minority stakes in businesses such as First Interstate Bancorp and working to manage the assets under its portfolio more aggressively. For instance, in a departure from the customary LBO tack, KKR managers invested heavily in upgrading and promoting the budget chain Motel 6, an effort that paid off with a $1.3 billion sale to France's Accor in April 1990.[12] Similarly, after engineering the $26 billion buyout of RJR Nabisco, KKR focused its energies on quickly improving RJR's profits by slashing expenses, laying off staff, and dumping excess inventories. Strategically, they emphasized competing with Philip-Morris by concentrating on building RJR's core brands Winston, Salem, and Camel and pruning peripheral investments.[13]

In the end, many of the corporate strategies that involved financial maneuvering constituted a kind of paper entrepreneurialism through which wealth was principally redistributed among stakeholders; little wealth was actually created. Firms that came out stronger at the end of the decade were more likely to have pursued strategies designed to capitalize on core capabilities: namely, internal sources of synergy among employees and products, obtained by forging stronger links among research, production, marketing, and sales across their different businesses.

Exploiting Relatedness

Corporate historians tell us that large U.S. firms such as General Motors and Dupont grew in two principal stages at the turn of the century— beginning with a systematic acquisition of direct competitors, then through backward and forward integration into sources of supply and into distribution as transportation and communication systems consolidated local markets into national mass markets.[14] Within their own industries, firms protected themselves from all-out competition by pursuing business-level strategies that called for investments in advertising and in product development that effectively differentiated their products, making them noncompetitive with those of rivals.*

Once business-level profits saturated, managers sought profits by diversifying into other industries. By extending their corporate umbrellas, managers could, in one fell swoop, increase their firms' market power, diffuse the risks of operating in a single business, smooth over cyclical downturns, and capitalize on dormant synergies with neighboring firms. The enthusiasm for building empires like those of Andrew Carnegie, John Rockefeller, and J.P. Morgan returned in the 1960s as managers discovered the financial conglomerate, run purely by the numbers and principally by decentralizing and delegating operating decisions to division managers.

Lost in the exuberant media accounts of ever larger merger deals, leveraged buyouts, and corporate raids, however, were the far more significant attempts by some visionary executives to capitalize on what had been undervalued latent synergies among businesses. In fact, the best-remembered firms of the 1980s will likely be those whose managers actively reshaped corporate portfolios to exploit dormant sources of synergy among businesses. Not surprisingly, the record already suggests that the most successful LBOs may be those in which managers concentrated on attaining operating efficiencies in core businesses.[15]

Consider the contrast between May Department Stores and Campeau Corp., two of the decade's most aggressive acquirers. Under Chairman David Farrell, May forged a larger and healthier retailer by combining its operations with less-efficient firms, such as Associated Dry Goods, and improving their productivity. In contrast, Robert Campeau's highly leveraged takeovers threw firms such as Federated into disarray, strangling them with debt. Both firms came out of the deal decade singing significantly different tunes, and, as *Business Week* concluded, "success favored the strategist over the financial engineer."[16]

In fact, few characteristics of firms have proven so elusive as *synergy*—the seemingly sensible idea that managers could increase their firms' competitiveness by combining businesses in different industries. A plethora of studies have strained to show that some diversification patterns realize synergies by reducing firms' exposure to risk—increasing their ability to capitalize on the relatedness of their end markets or to exploit common technologies and distribution channels. Conceptual work and empirical research to date, however, provide only limited input to our understanding of the factors that contribute to observed performance differences between more- or less-diversified firms.[17] They suggest

---

*The original model of monopolistic competition relied solely on advertising as the principal source of differentiation among rivals [See Carlton, D. and J. Perloff, *Modern Industrial Organization* (Glenview, IL: Scott, Foresman, 1990).]

two dimensions of corporate diversification that warrant further elaboration: (1) whether diversification is more or less related to firms' core businesses, and (2) whether managers diversify by acquiring established businesses or by internal development.

Building Synergy

Royal Little taught corporate America about unrelated diversification by transforming Textron from a flabby, cyclical textile corporation into the first modern conglomerate. Between 1955 and 1962 Little designed a unique corporate structure consisting of a small management team that decentralized, allowing responsibility to devolve to the presidents of operating companies, insisting only on a minimal 20 percent rate of return. By judiciously acquiring privately held companies in growing industries, Textron grew to number 47 on the *Fortune* 500 list for 1968, with revenues of $1.7 billion and earnings of $76 million.[18]

During the 1960s, conglomeration took Wall Street by storm. Litton Industries under Charles "Tex" Thornton, LTV under James Ling, Gulf & Western under Charles Bludhorn, and ITT under Harold Geneen, all left the cocoon of their core businesses to metamorphose as portfolios of unrelated operations. The rise to prominence of the Puerto Rican telephone company ITT under Harold Geneen's leadership demonstrated how financial synergies could produce significant shareholder gains in two ways: (1) By combining businesses whose returns were not highly correlated, conglomerates could reduce shareholder risk; and (2) by establishing careful financial planning and controls, conglomerate managers could make better-informed capital allocations across divisions than could outside investors.[19] The resulting financial conglomerate or holding-company structure centralized finance, accounting, planning, and legal functions, while delegating all other decisions to divisions.[20]

In fact, in 1963 ITT's CEO Harold Geneen provided a blueprint for what was to become the quintessential conglomerate strategy.[21]

1. To diversify into industries and markets that have good prospects for above-average long-term growth and profitability

2. To balance foreign earnings and domestic earnings

3. To balance high-risk, capital-intensive manufacturing operations and less risky service operations

4. To balance high-risk, engineering-labor-intensive electronics manufacturing and less risky commercial and industrial manufacturing

5. To achieve a sound ratio between commercial-industrial products and services and consumer products and services

6. To balance cyclical products and services

After being heralded as a managerial phenomenon, by the early 1980s, unrelated diversifiers seemed frayed around the edges as corporate raiders pointed to the undervalued assets they managed, and as researchers asserted that there were higher pay-offs to be had from investing in related diversifiers. In a path-breaking analysis, a doctoral student at Harvard had shown that managers who implemented unrelated diversifications, not only reduced their businesses' underlying competitiveness by depleting operating funds, but also produced lower economic returns. The more successful corporate strategy, he suggested, was to diversify into related businesses, thereby capturing the benefits of synergy.[22] Numerous replications and extensions have reinforced his findings. A recent study of 218 mergers between 1962 and 1983, for instance, found that strategic fits, in fact, were critical in determining the economic gains created in an acquisition: Acquisitions that permit expansion in the same industry or into related markets yield the greatest value.[23]

In May 1991, after 5 months of public resistance, the National Cash Register Company (NCR), the fifth largest computer maker in the United States, agreed to be acquired by AT&T for $7.4 billion. The merger opened a new chapter in AT&T's continuing evolution toward the computer business. It also marked a clear break from the era of takeovers for gain to the era of mergers for synergy.[24]

In fact, studies conducted in the United States, Britain, and Canada show that firms tend to diversify more into industries similar to their primary industry in terms of advertising intensity, research intensity, and relationships with suppliers and consumers.[25] Indeed, many U.S. acquisitions and spin-offs of the 1980s were driven by managers who recognized that they had previously extended their firms in too many directions, and now sought to refocus their activities in strategically related areas. An examination of the diversification patterns of 82 conglomerates between 1974 and 1984, for instance, shows that managers decreased their firms' portfolios from a peak in 1977 to a low in 1980, presumably to capitalize on latent synergies.[26]

What then is synergy, and how have managers recognized and tried to exploit relatedness among businesses to yield economic benefits in recent years?

Synergy implies that the combined performance of several entities can be greater than the algebraic sum of their independent contributions—that 2 plus 2 can make 5, so to speak. For managers, it means that careful coordination of businesses enables cross-pollination of ideas, products, resources, and skills and achievement of benefits greater than those that division managers could achieve on their own.

Harvard's Michael Porter calls synergy "perhaps the most critical item on the strategic agenda facing a diversified firm."[27] The principal means through which firms tap latent synergy is by sharing activities among businesses. A common sales force and shared advertising, promotion, and distribution enable managers to lower marketing costs for the firm as a whole. Cross-fertilization of technologies can lower design costs and create production efficiencies. Central purchasing can reduce procurement costs and increase quality of common supplies. Finally, an active management team can identify intangible similarities in the types of buyers, competitive profiles, and success factors in their different businesses, enabling a transfer of know-how and managerial skill. Firms shifting from a portfolio profile to a related strategy appear to pursue these sources of effiency in order to generate financial synergy, operational synergy, or managerial synergy.[28]

Take Textron. Since its birth as a widely diversified conglomerate, Textron's managers have progressively consolidated the firm's activities into three areas: aerospace technology, commercial products, and financial services. Under Chairman Beverly Dolan's leadership, its managers have attempted to capitalize on both diversifying risk and generating managerial synergies. As the Cold War ends and military expenditures decline, Textron's strategic posture, with only 28 percent of its revenues from military sources, appears stronger than the postures of either General Dynamics or Northrop, with, respectively, 85 percent and 91 percent dependence on the military.[29]

At the corporate level, managers typically take on three critical functions: allocating resources among businesses, formulating and coordinating those business-units' strategies, and setting and monitoring performance targets. Table 6.2 suggests some of the strategic similarities managers have been trying to exploit to concretize the relatedness of their different businesses.[30]

What the table suggests is that diversification involves both conceiving how to fuse the disjoint capabilities of separate businesses and exploiting the fusion through the design of appropriate corporate-level controls and cultures.

Table 6.2

Corporate management function	Building strategic similarity in:
Allocating resources	Time spans of projects
	Sources of risk
	Management skills required
Planning	Key success factors
	Stage of industry life cycle
	Competitive positions
Control	Performance variables
	Time horizons of targets
	Measurement systems

Marital Problems

Unfortunately, as I pointed out in Chap. 4, naturally occuring biases impede managers' attempts both to conceive and to exploit relatedness. After all, synergy is partly perceptual: Managers define a logical relationship by interpreting commonalities among products, consumers, technologies, and businesses.[31] So Exxon's failure to diversify successfully into high-tech electronic businesses in the 1970s was based partly on an inability to effectively conceive the differences between its core petroleum business and the kinds of people, structures, and practices valued by the entrepreneurial businesses it lumped into its Exxon Enterprises division.

Characteristics of the management team involved in the planning process also influence the kinds of relationships among businesses that managers notice and pursue. Senior executives whose backgrounds and specialties are similar easily agree on a course of action but tend to lack the cognitive breadth necessary to identify intangible sources of relatedness. In more diverse management teams, conflict abounds, more ideas are generated and processed, and managers conceive more creative ways of relating businesses.[32]

Even when managers recognize complex sources of relatedness, to realize the mutualistic benefits of relatedness has often proved difficult. Merging operations is partly a political process that creates *winners* and *losers*. When Louis Vuitton merged with Moét-Hennessy in 1987 to form LVMH, it became the world's largest luxury goods company, a conglomerate of some of France's best-known products. The portfolio encompasses a collection of best-selling champagnes that includes Moet & Chandon; Dom Perignon; and Veuve Clicquot, the best-selling Hennessy cognac, and the Louis Vuitton leather goods empire. Although the logic of building a diversified firm whose operations are related principally on the basis of external image and niche seemed viable to both sides, it quickly ran up against the sticky problem of actual consolidation. Corporate infighting between the two firms resulted as Bernard Arnault, LMVH's 40-year-old chairman locked heads with Henry Racamier, the 77-year-old head of the Louis Vuitton group. The French press dubbed the battle, "The Young Wolf versus the Old Lion."[33]

To capitalize on relatedness necessitates managers skilled, not only in identifying latent synergies and in finessing political infighting, but in the design of administrative controls that can actually exploit these dormant sources of synergy. The kinds of financial controls needed to operate a conglomerate efficiently, for instance, are quite different from the administrative controls required for coordinating related operations.

Moreover, firms previously committed to a strategy of unrelated diversification often lack, at both the corporate and business levels, the managerial talent to successfully coordinate businesses. At ITT, for instance, a skeletal corporate staff inherited from the Geneen era exercised strict financial control over otherwise autonomous businesses. When ITT began consolidating its operations after Rand Araskog took over from Geneen in 1979, neither corporate staff nor division presidents were prepared to cope with the complex information flows required to manage a related diversifier. Managing by the numbers does not produce an integration of operations, an exchange of information, or a judicious application of skills across divisions. The company sold off $9 billion in assets and was recast into nine groups, dominated by ITT Hartford financial services and the Sheraton chain of hotels. Increasingly, its corporate managers are involving themselves in managing business unit operations.[34]

Many other previously diversified firms have chosen to pare down the breadth of their diversification. Under Jack Welch, for instance, General Electric divested $9 billion worth of businesses, while acquiring some $16 billion in more focused businesses. Over 25 percent of its 400,000 jobs were eliminated, with remaining employees allocated to a simplified structure consisting of 14 business groups.[35] Similarly, since founder Armand Hammer's death, Occidental Petroleum has launched a massive $3-billion sell-off of unrelated businesses designed to slash the company's debt burden and refocus on its core oil, natural gas, and chemical operations.[36]

Most mergers produce large layoffs. Managers reduce expenses and boost profits by consolidating redundant operations across business units, eliminating duplication, fusing suppliers, and combining distribution channels. When two groups of employees are brought together, each with its characteristic interaction patterns, organizational outlook, and history, blending operations dictates harmonizing social relationships between employees of the two companies, and that means linking promotion ladders, rationalizing lopsided compensation systems, and attending to the philosophical and cultural differences that made each company distinctive.

Recently, commercial banks have taken to consolidating with a vengeance. In 1991 alone, BankAmerica agreed to purchase archrival Security Pacific, Chemical Bank merged with Manufacturer's Hanover, and NCNB joined with C&S/Sovran in the southeast—creating three banking powerhouses to rival Citicorp. If managers of the merged firms succeed in overcoming internal barriers and capitalize on the latent sources of synergy, these mergers should provide the combined firms with increased market clout against Japanese and European rivals. They also are likely to reduce banking overcapacity and increase efficiency by permitting teller layoffs and branch consolidations.[37]

Observers of mergers regularly point to the difficulties managers face when trying to integrate the operations of business units. More than half of all acquisitions by major U.S. companies fail, although one in four involve the merger of related operations. Trucker Consolidated Freightways' purchase of Emery Air Freight in April 1990 was intended to provide CF with a global reach that could compete with Federal Express and UPS. Unfortunately, Emery itself had yet to fully absorb its earlier purchase of Purolator, and integrating the three firms' disparate systems has proved far more difficult than anticipated.[38]

One prominent exception comes in the case of pharmaceuticals, a turbulent industry in which Bristol-Myers and Squibb Co. agreed to merge in 1989 to improve their competitive position vis-à-vis industry leader Merck & Co. Chairman Richard Gelb compared the tensions of combining the two firms to putting two bee colonies together in one hive. "Do it too quickly," he said, "and the two sets of bees will sting one another to death. Do it right, and the two colonies settle down and produce more honey." The merged firm exploits the traditional strengths of Brystol-Myers in over-the-counter and consumer products with Squibb's success in cardiovascular drugs. The company's consolidated sales force is now the largest in the world.[39]

Eastman Kodak has not been nearly so fortunate with its aggressive $5.1-billion purchase of Sterling Drug in 1988. After installing Kodak managers at the helm, cutting costs, and expanding R&D, Sterling has few products in the pipeline likely to generate new revenues in the near future. Critics contend that the Kodak-Sterling merger offers too little synergy to benefit either firm. In contrast to the Bristol-Myers–Squibb merger that built a strong portfolio of new drugs, Sterling drags Kodak down. Moreover, Kodak lacks experience in the drug business, and its early managers may have axed valuable, albeit marginal, projects in an effort to cut costs.[40]

Numerous glitches have turned up as Chemical Bank and Manufacturers Hanover struggled to join forces. The $135-billion merger has been hampered by incompatible accounting systems, uncertainty about layoffs, conflicts over ongoing practices within branches, and which automatic teller system to use. Vested interests within each bank encourage managers to defend fervently their home-grown systems. Few expect a resolution before Manufacturers' boss Walter Shipley takes over the merged firm following the planned retirement of Chemical's John McGillicuddy in 1993.[41] At that time, achieving synergy will require drastic slashing of overhead and aggressive consolidation of operations.

A general analysis of the acquisition of related firms suggests that integration is typically hampered by four factors that inhere in the process of analyzing, negotiating with, and acquiring a firm:[42]

1. *The segmentation of activities:* The technical complexity of combining two firms leads to compartmentalizing necessary tasks. Specialization discourages dialogue between groups, and turns attention away from issues involving the structural correspondences that need to be estab-

lished. Lower-status personnel get assigned to postacquisition tasks than those involved in the phase prefacing the acquisition, signaling to employees that integration is of lesser importance.

2. *Escalating momentum:* The process of acquiring firms takes on a life of its own, with participants accepting premature solutions and foreclosing careful consideration of integration issues. Everyone wants to close the deal.

3. *Ambiguity and conflict:* Ambiguous agreements arrived at early during the negotiation phase lead to differences in interpretation after the acquisition, which escalates into outright conflicts between employees of the merged firms.

4. *Communication breakdowns:* Lacking familiarity with each other's operations, both parties fail to exchange information about competencies and capabilities. Thus, acquiring firms implement systems and controls designed to correspond to their own, without realizing that they alienate employees of acquired firms. Arrogance and defensiveness on the part of both parent and subsidiary lead to an inappropriate infrastructure for the merged entity.

To mitigate problems that derive from combining firms, it becomes particularly critical to attend to the culture of the merged firm. Achieving coordination may require exchanging a number of significant managers between firms. To build synergy dictates, not only a marriage of products and technologies, but a blend of firms' unique combinations of cultural attributes, controls, and capabilities. Ultimately, it means developing a shared spirit among the employees of both firms and providing a common core around which they can gather and from which they can recreate a corporate culture that is rooted in neither parent but is *unique* to the merged entity. And that is rare indeed.

To Innovate or "Exnovate"?

Managers differ in opting to drive their firms' corporate reorientations through internal growth or external acquisitions. In the United States of old, firms diversified principally through internal growth. The institutional environment frowned on takeovers almost as much as they do in Japan today. Prominent companies like AT&T, RCA, and IBM committed large sums to research and development in order to generate a stream of related products, which they marketed principally to existing consumers. Line extensions of this sort were common throughout industrial history. Products built on firms' existing strengths, and managers made only incremental adjustments to accommodate developments.

Historically, managers have often misconstrued innovations that significantly departed from their core skills, and, rather than develop them internally, chose to license them out for rivals to market. Indeed, a study of innovations in the cement, airline, and minicomputer industries showed that firms that grew from within tended overwhelmingly to develop innovations that enhanced their existing capabilities, and actively resisted revolutionary innovations that challenged their capabilities. These firms belong to corporate communities anchored around technological guideposts that hamper internal diversification into rival technologies. For them, the only solution is the takeover of innovating competitors.

In the 1970s, the escalating cost of product development and the shortened life cycles of many products occasioned by rapid technological change made acquisition-based corporate strategies increasingly appealing. Growth by merger seemed to offer a more efficient alternative to internal development, one that did not require the careful buildup of skilled employees, or the long-term investments that innovative firms make in cutting-edge technologies and in strong internal cultures. By buying an established firm, managers could muscle their way through the entry barriers that sheltered many attractive industries.[43]

Take Time-Warner. No one doubts its clout in launching a magazine... except perhaps the media giant itself. Time's well-publicized failure in starting a cable television magazine may have given it second thoughts about the future: In April 1990, in trying to addresss the growing market of young upscale parents, it elected to scratch its own project and buy an entrepreneurial start-up called *Parenting*. Its managers' rationale? The acquisition gave it a jump start in the marketplace and leapfrogged the company's self-doubts about internal development.[44]

The failed integration of many widely publicized acquisitions, however, has turned back the clock and forced increased attention to the merits of internal development achieved through the design of corporate systems that encourage "intrapreneurship"—the process of generating and capitalizing on entrepreneurship within large firms.[45] Studies of firms that diversified through internal growth suggest that their managers dwelled far more heavily on sharing resources across functions and divisions than did managers of firms that opted for acquisition-oriented growth.[46] So internal diversifiers appear better to exploit relatedness, which may be one reason why they are more successful.

There is good reason to believe that in coming years managers will aggressively pursue both internal and external sources of diversification. Internal development takes time, and timing is frequently the leading success factor in industries experiencing significant upheaval. Firms caught unprepared have little choice but to leapfrog entry barriers by acquiring key players. The acquisitions of Columbia Pictures and CBS

Records by Sony for a total of $5.6 billion, and MCA by Matsushita for $6.3 billion suggest that Japanese firms recognize the enormous hurdles they will have to overcome in order to single-handedly develop comparable capability in the kind of entertainment software that should prove key to competitiveness in electronic consumer goods. By combining hardware and software, both MCA and Sony extend their battle in consumer electronics and entertainment on a global scale.[47]

Some managers favor acquisitions because they recognize that corporate ventures typically take eight years to achieve profitability and over 12 years to generate adequate cash flows. Some 88 percent of innovations developed within firms fail ever to achieve adequate returns on investment, making internal development a high-risk strategy.[48] Ventures begun by established firms have showed a surprisingly poor track record. A study of ventures by major companies showed that of 47 ventures started, only 18 showed a profit after 4 years, while the median return for 61 businesses in their fifth and sixth years was minus 8 percent.[49] Other studies report even lower success rates, suggesting that large firms may have only a 10 to 20 percent success rate at launching new ventures.

Firms that gear up for external diversification also appear to invest less in research and development than do firms that grow from within. Such findings suggest that acquisitions serve as a substitute for innovation. Moreover, external expansion increases the employment opportunities available to firms' top managers. So risk-averse managers and firms facing liquidity problems naturally favor acquisition-based corporate strategies over internal development.[50]

Early observers of diversified companies proposed the creation of new venture divisions to house development and commercialization of innovations. The political and cultural problems managers encountered with internal growth led to widespread disillusionment about large firms' abilities to innovate. A detailed study of how a related diversifier transformed cutting-edge research into new businesses demonstrated that successful firms do not build walls between their ongoing businesses and their innovations. Instead, innovation managers skillfully weave execution and innovation into a dynamic process that encourages the autonomous initiatives of individuals dispersed throughout the firm.[51] Product champions assist by husbanding resources and shepherding pet projects up through the hierarchy.[52]

In the 1970s, Texas Instruments was justly acclaimed for recognizing the complexity of the innovation process and building a creative control structure to manage it. At TI, many employees wore two hats: an operational hat for execution of ongoing business, and a strategic hat for developing new business. Employees were expected to account for actual time spent in fulfilling each of these functions, and managers tied performance goals and incentives to their completion. Many of TI's most successful innovations in those years were ascribed to its excellent managerial process. Subsequently, the company floundered as it tried to build on its internal innovations to diversify out of semiconductors and into computers and consumer electronics. By developing consumer products around its microprocessors, TI managers had hoped to straddle bigger and higher-margin markets. Heightened competition in semiconductors and a declining share against aggressive rival Motorola prompted TI to announce recently a return to its roots in semiconductor technology.[53]

As environments continue to pose to managers the dual challenge of maintaining both efficiency and innovation, they are tasked to push their firms toward more focused acquisitions and toward more targeted internal development. Fewer domestic acquisitions should occur because of a resurgence of antitrust activity following the laissez-faire years of Reaganism.[54] Naturally, related diversification is nowhere more evident today than on the global battlefield.

Pursuing Global Synergies

The close ties among nations fostered by increased travel, capital flows, trade, and the homogenization of global tastes, has encouraged managers to find ways of quickly penetrating foreign markets to claim a beachhead against later entrants. Since internal growth takes time and frequently taxes the know-how and managerial talent of the expanding firm, related acquisitions offer many firms a quick route to achieving competitive positions abroad.

Interpenetration of transnational firms and nation-states through mergers has been facilitated by privatization movements in both developed and developing economies. Leading examples are France's privatization drive under the government of 1986; privatization of NTT and Japan Tobacco in Japan in 1985; the Tory government's privatizations of prominent U.K. firms including British Aerospace; British Telecom, Cable and Wireless; Enterprise Oil; British Gas; and Jaguar and the aggressive privatization of public firms in Argentina, Brazil, Chile, and Mexico—to name only a few.

Figure 6.1 shows that between 1982 and 1990, U.S. companies spent over $54 billion to acquire some 1758 foreign companies. In those same years, foreign firms consummated over 3109 acquisitions of U.S. firms valued at over $265 billion.[55] Throughout the 1980s, the United States was clearly a prime target of foreign acquisitions. As the regional communities of Europe and Asia-Pacific materialize, however, we expect to see a changing pattern of takeovers directed more heavily at these markets.

Of the 1000 most highly valued firms in the world in 1989, the United

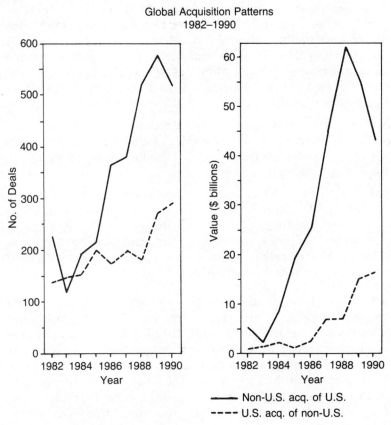

Figure 6.1. Global takeovers, 1982–1990. (*Source:* Mergers & Acquisitions, *May/June 1991*)

States was home to about 353 firms, Japan accounted for 345, and Europe claimed 214, representing respectively 33 percent, 47 percent, and 17 percent of total equity. Much of the increased market values of U.S. and European firms throughout 1989 resulted from takeovers, such as British whiskey and food producer Grand Met's acquisition of U.S. food giant Pillsbury for $5.8 billion; Nestle's $3.9 billion acquisition of British chocolate maker Rowntree PLC; French aluminum maker Pechiney's $1.2 billion purchase of American Can Co. from Triangle Industries; and French cement company Lafarge Coppee's $770 million purchase of the Swiss holding company Cementia.

Many of these cross-border mergers were spurred heavily by the prospect of Europe 1992, and are changing competitive dynamics in many industries; witness:

- *In telecommunications:* France's Compagnie Generale d'Electricite purchased ITT Corp.'s telecommunications division to become number 1 in Europe and number 2 in the world after AT&T. In 1987, France's Thomson purchased GE/RCA's TV operations in the United States for $800 million. Recently, Sweden's Asea and Switzerland's Brown Boveri merged to form a global giant in power-generating equipment. Siemens of West Germany spent $2 billion to acquire Britain's Plessey PLC, the Electronics division of Bendix, and France's IN2 computer manufacturer.

■ *In banking:* In 1986 West Germany's Deutsche Bank, Europe's fifth largest bank, purchased Bank of America's Italian operations for $603 million and by 1989 had taken control of leading banks in Italy, Spain, Portugal, the Netherlands, and Austria.

■ *In public relations:* British agency Shandwick's launched a buying spree of smaller PR firms in Europe. Large equity positions have been taken in foreign agencies by MSL Worldwide, the PR subsidiary of D'Arcy Benton & Bowles. In contrast, U.S. agencies Hill & Knowlton and Burson-Marsteller have elected an aggressive pattern of global growth through internal development.

Clearly the search for global competitive positioning in response to the increasing coherence of the large regional markets of North America and Europe is encouraging managers to speed their firms' entry into multiple national markets through takeovers and mergers with local firms. As German unification proceeds, as Eastern Europe's fate clarifies, more related acquisitions can be expected by U.S., European, and Japanese firms in their respective markets. Capitalizing on the latent synergies among regions should constitute a major preoccupation of managers for years to come.

In packaged consumer goods, for instance, P&G and Philip-Morris have both mounted aggressive campaigns in Europe, attacking Anglo-Dutch giant Unilever. To parry their thrust, Unilever has demonstrated increased willingness to undertake high-risk ventures in the United States through its Lever Brothers subsidiaries. Its managers have also committed to building market share in cosmetics by acquiring for $1.8 billion a range of prestige brands including Fabergé, Elizabeth Arden, and Calvin Klein. Shortly thereafter P&G purchased, for $1.3 billion, Noxell Corp., makers of Cover Girl cosmetics.[56]

From the Asian economies of neighboring Japan, a group of aggressive conglomerates are also growing rapidly by capitalizing on synergies within their portfolios. Some are majority-owned by governments, such as Singapore Airlines. Others, such as CP Group in Thailand, are groups of companies founded and controlled by overseas Chinese families. Others are privately held conglomerates like Samsung, a South Korean *chaebol*, a leading producer of electronics, food products, pharmaceuticals, and paper. Some of these Asian behemoths already dominate many global markets and are gearing up to exploit growth opportunities in Europe and America over the next decade.

Trimming the Fat

Strategic changes at the corporate level permit managers to redeploy firms' resources across multiple businesses. The unrelated diversifications of the 1970s and the financially driven strategies of the early 1980s have recently stimulated extensive divestitures by firms whose managers had failed to capture the mutualistic benefits that shared facilities, technologies, products, and skills could provide. The persistent attacks of raiders contributed to stimulating a reshaping of corporate portfolios toward increased relatedness, both in the conceptualization and the exploitation of synergies across businesses.

Integrating acquisitions invariably proves more challenging than anticipated. Inherent biases impede the blending of firms' operations, making all too frequent the subsequent divestiture of acquisitions that proved unproductive. Given the reality of acquisitions, internal growth may be more attractive than anticipated. Although slower and perhaps riskier, internal diversification capitalizes on firms' existing strengths and is simpler to relate to ongoing operations.

The interpenetration of nations fostered by increased travel, capital flows, trade, and the collapse of the Soviet empire is also encouraging firms to find ways of quickly penetrating foreign markets. In coming years, managers are likely to continue making acquisitions that more quickly overleap national hurdles and place them in the field of action—if only to worry deeply about integration after the fact.

7
Strategic Networks

I not only use all the brains I have but all I can borrow.

WOODROW WILSON

In 1982, a group of six computer makers led by Control Data defied existing antitrust laws by forming the Microelectronics & Computer Technology Corporation, the first research consortium between competitors. Between 1982 and 1989, corporate membership in the consortium grew from 14 to 38, with contributions amounting to some $60 million in 1989. Created in response to Japan's launching of the Fifth Generation Computer Project, the consortium funds research on software, high temperature superconductors, computer-aided integrated circuit design, chip packaging, and information technologies that member companies can then license and commercialize.[1] A wave of research consortia soon followed, cresting in July 1988, when 14 firms from the U.S. semiconductor and computer industries formed Sematech, a research consortium with a 5-year goal to develop technology that would permit U.S. companies to manufacture a chip capable of storing 64 million bits of information, that is, 64 times more than the most advanced chip on the market. On the premise that semiconductors are vital to national security, Sematech's $200-million annual budget was funded 50:50 by federal aid and member contributions.*

In September 1989, pharmaceutical high-flyer Merck & Co. traded

---

*For example, see *New York Times:* 28 July 1988. Debates about Sematech's merits have been around for some time, however. Some claim that the consortium benefits primarily large companies. Others contend that companies could do better by forging strategic alliances on their own.

136

distribution rights for some of its drugs for rights to develop Du Pont Co.'s heart drugs—a deal that could give Merck a significant share of an estimated $7 billion market by the mid-1990s. Earlier in March, Merck had formed a joint venture with Johnson & Johnson to develop and market nonprescription drugs. In October, both firms agreed to buy ICI's U.S. over-the-counter business for $450 million, in exchange for which Merck gave ICI its Elavil antidepressant, a drug with $25 million a year in sales. Later that month, Merck signed a 5-year, $20-million research agreement with Immulogic Pharmaceutical Corp. to develop drugs for arthritis and diabetes.*

In April 1991 a dozen computer companies announced the formation of an alliance—the Advanced Computing Environment (ACE)—to promote a microprocessor made by MIPS Computer Systems, a small company in Sunnyvale, California. Leading the alliance are Compaq Computer, Digital Equipment, and Microsoft. By banding together, they hoped to present a viable alternative to the chips designed by Sun, Motorola, Intel, Hewlett-Packard, and IBM.[2]

Strategic alliances like these represent extraordinary departures from more traditional self-reliant forms of reorientation at the business and corporate levels. As environmental changes have swept across the industrial landscape, managers have been quick to recognize their firms' mutual interests by signing licensing agreements, forming joint ventures, and participating in research consortia. Since strategic alliances constitute cooperative relationships between competitors, however, they also have been frought with tension: Firms mistrust one another's "true" objectives; they fear being taken advantage of by partners; they experience disdain for appearing "too weak" to act alone; they incur scrutiny from antitrust monitors concerned that alliances reduce competition.

Despite government skepticism, alliances constituted an important vehicle for effective strategic change throughout the 1980s. They placed firms at the heart of increasingly integrated networks, the epicenter of business communities. Where firms once competed in isolation, now more than ever they now compete as constellations of suppliers, distributors, franchisers, and alliance partners.

Consider mighty IBM, the original solo strategist if ever there was one. In recent years, the computer maker has struck deals with a diverse set of partners that includes GO, Metaphor, Novell, Borland, Wang, and Lotus. None was as portentous, however, as its announced alliance with archrival Apple Computer in July 1991. In an attempt to break market share erosion and boost stagnating revenues, IBM has agreed to engage in

---

*Cf. Markoff, J., "New Computer Alliance Forms," *New York Times:* 8 April 1991, D1, D4. Delays and competition have since placed some doubts on the potential success of the alliance, if not on the strategy itself.

extensive technology sharing with Apple. Jointly, the two firms intend to develop new software that will ease tie-ins between their computers and to produce new operating system code with which to target IBM's former partner turned rival, Microsoft.[3]

In fragmented industries and among smaller firms, interfirm networks have been common practice for a long time.[4] Silicon Valley in Northern California, for example, is known as a crucible of research and development, a global center for technical innovation. It brings together a critical mass of highly talented engineers who work in hundreds of spontaneous and informal research networks linking established firms to a host of start-ups born out of every new generation of semiconductor technology.

Network competition does not happen solely in the high-tech industries. Take the garment industry. Economists like to draw attention to the levels of competition between firms in, say, four-digit SIC code groupings: mens and boys shirts, trousers, work clothing; womens blouses, dresses, suits, or underwear. In fact, anyone familiar with textiles and apparel knows that the social structure of the industry is quite poorly described by these standard groupings. Even the narrowest industries are themselves fragmented into firms specialized along the value chain, each one delivering a component part or service—whether in garment design, sample making, marking, grading, sewing, production, and distribution. Competition develops, not so much within the broadly defined industries, but among networks that form around particular designers. Networks overlap, and each network is governed by a complex set of mostly informal handshake agreements.

Similar informal relationships tie manufacturers to an even more diverse network of suppliers and distributors in most industries. MIT professors Michael Piore and Charles Sabel described the important function these networks play in coordinating the many small, specialized firms that constitute a textile community in the Italian district of Prato, a group of towns near Florence and Pistoia in central Italy. While member firms do compete, their rivalry is limited by the overarching need for interfirm cooperation between designers and a bevy of cloth, trim, and apparel manufacturers.[5] Recent trends toward the disintegration of industries historically dominated by large firms in the United States suggest that such networks will continue to play a prominent role in affecting industrial profitability and competitiveness.

Even among large firms, however, participation in far-flung networks is redefining the meaning of competitiveness. In the concentrated U.S. automobile industry, for instance, the true locus of competition now lies less in the internal dynamics of General Motors, Ford, and Chrysler than in their managers' relative ability to develop more efficient and effective networks of parts suppliers, dealers, credit companies, computer service, advertising companies, joint ventures, and research consortia. Much as the legendary competitiveness of the Japanese *keiretsu* and its application of *kanban* (just-in-time) practices derives from the carefully orchestrated activities of its member firms, so, too, have U.S. firms become more aware that future gains in performance are likely to come, not from solitary combat, but from developing more effective modes of interfirm alliance—more successful collective-level strategies.

Moreover, interfirm cooperation has made more evident the link between firms' actions and national outcomes such as productivity, unemployment, and growth. The business communities that crystallize from these cooperative links constitute an ever more visible context for the growing competition between nations in the development, production, and distribution of goods and services.[6] Because many of these interfirm linkages also cross national boundaries, they actually bind firms into transnational business communities.

Throughout the 1980s the U.S. government insisted heavily that competition unfolds on a global level, and so relaxed enforcement of antitrust regulations that had outlawed horizontal mergers and interfirm cooperation throughout the century. Under the Bush administration, however, and following the debacle of the savings and loan and airline industries, the United States appears to be returning to a more severe stance regarding the regulation of anticompetitive takeovers, making alliances more attractive.[7]

Table 7.1 outlines the collective strategies that managers increasingly rely on to coordinate their actions with competitors and to counter the pressures placed on them by turbulent environments. These strategies appear in varying degrees: In some sectors of the economy, for instance, strategic targeting featured prominently throughout the 1980s; in others, coordination has been largely emergent, an unsystematic ebb and flow of personnel and information among firms.

During revolutions it is risky to act alone. Because of rising complexity, managers have found networking to be an invaluable means of effecting strategic change. As financially driven mergers and acquisitions wane, as

Table 7.1. Types of Collective Strategies

	Strategic coordination	Strategic targeting	Strategic alliances
Capabilities	Intelligence gathering	Contributions and donations	Licenses and contracts
Controls	Contracts and exchanges	Interlocking boards and trade associations	Shared equity and joint ventures
Culture	Similarity of backgrounds	Lobbying and propaganda	Consortia and cartels

global companies find themselves locked in mortal combat, alliances constitute a vital and complementary means by which managers are overcoming internal resistance and altering their firms' trajectories.

Networking Informally

Economists like to refer us to Adam Smith when they want to champion the merits of competition for producing industrial efficiency. Like him, they insist that firms act myopically and have no sense of their common fate. They assume that managers are locked in atomistic firms, with only arm's-length relationships to their counterparts in other firms. So they conceive and implement strategic changes in relative isolation.

Powerful results derive from these simple assumptions, of course, and most views of business and corporate strategy owe a significant debt to this narrow-minded world view. Ideological adherence to an atomistic grasp of competition is evident in legislative initiatives that date back to the Sherman Act of 1890 and the Clayton Act of 1914, both of which condemn relationships among firms and treat interfirm coordination as an illegitimate distortion of the economy.[8]

Although competition depicts a fundamental way in which firms do, in fact, interact, they also distort or overlook how the social environment of our companies influences managers to develop particular strategies.[9] Competition among firms is encapsulated by many rules and constraints: Limits are set on the kinds of actions firms can take, prohibiting, for instance, outright sabotage, violence, exploitation of children, or espionage.[10] Firms' managers attend the same schools, participate in the same labor markets, and belong to the same clubs and associations.[11]

It is not hard to see that managers themselves pursue strategies designed to shield their firms from competition by shaping institutional environments favorable to their activities: A large body of research confirms how managers actively strive to coopt or capture regulators, to lobby legislators, and to influence court decisions in litigation.[12] Government cooperates with firms in creating sheltered environments by allotting patents; by recognizing natural monopolies (such as AT&T until 1983); by providing tax credits for research and depreciation, which erect barriers to new businesses; by pursuing protectionist trade policies; by granting direct loans, loan guarantees, subsidies, grants, and military contracts to established firms. Moreover, in supporting or neglecting skill building, institutions like schools and governments also shape national productivity and so affect firms' abilities to compete internationally.[13]

A degree of informal, albeit strategic, coordination therefore increasingly characterizes the relationships among managers in competing firms and constitutes an aspect of firms' collective-level strategies designed to improve their competitive positions.

Chatting Up Rivals

The competitive struggle to gain customers pits firms operating in the same domain against one another, making information and know-how key resources. To informally acquire competitive information, managers have sought to establish stronger linkages between their firms. Prominent among these have been forms of competitive espionage, exchange of personnel, and overlapping memberships on boards.[14]

Various popular books have outlined archival and legal techniques for intelligence gathering. The abundance of court cases charging rivals with illegal espionage suggests, however, that the legal line is frequently crossed in gathering intelligence data. One investigation demonstrated the prevalence of industrial espionage in competitive markets: Through a study of court filings, the analysts found that more intense competitive rivalry fostered greater efforts on the part of rival firms to access trade secrets, research in progress, strategic plans, and other privileged information.[15]

The more rapidly the environment changes, the more managers prize up-to-date information about rivals' activities. Competitive advantage in such industries is short lived, and the recurrent search for advantage promotes cycles of intense opposition and so encourages corporate spying. The heavy fines imposed on Hitachi in 1989, when its executives were caught trying to buy proprietary information about new computers and software from IBM, however, point out the need for managers to assess carefully the ethical consequences and real costs of particular types of information gathering. Some of Japan's biggest industrial manufacturers, including Mitsubishi Heavy Industries and members of the Hitachi and Toyota groups, were recently charged with industrial espionage involving payments to spies for information about Komatsu and the joint venture Shin Caterpillar Mitsubishi.[16]

Managers differ as to whether they choose to centralize information gathering into intelligence departments (for instance, Motorola and McDonnell-Douglas) or to bring all their employees into the intelligence network (for example, Corning or Ameritech). All have the same goal, however: to provide top managers with an early warning of external events that might impact their businesses. Now that the Cold War is over, some have suggested (only half jokingly) that the United States' Central Intelligence Agency might be given the job of corporate espionage.[17]

Managers also heavily fund trade associations as a way of obtaining competitive information on rivals' products and prices. Associations help to stabilize rivalry by narrowing the range of uncertainty managers feel about competitors' actions. In the United States for some time the Tobacco Institute has actively coordinated the public positions of firms in the tobacco industry. The Petroleum Institute performs a similar function for oil producers and refiners.

Another important source of strategic coordination that is favored by managers involves industry-wide agreements over product standards. In the United States, almost 80 percent of all standards are set by a unique voluntary system that relies on cooperation among rivals. A set of more than 400 independent standard-setting associations exists, coordinated by the American National Standards Institute, whose legitimacy as a clearinghouse derives largely from its official role as U.S. representative in global standardization activity. The record suggests that standardization achieved through collective action creates a public good that benefits all market participants: Indeed, it appears that a greater level of involvement of firms in standardization activity is associated with more innovation within the industry—an indication that information flows among rivals have beneficial effects.

In the high-tech sector, investors, inventors, and managers of high-tech ventures meet regularly through clearinghouses through which they exchange informational cues about the state of the art. Sometimes these pools act as incubators for new businesses, but, perhaps more significantly, they provide a venue for propagating information about the cutting edge. In California's Silicon Valley and Boston's Route 128, for instance, rivalry within the industry is often exacerbated by firms themselves: Established firms spawn new ventures when former employees leave to start their own businesses—frequently drawing on intangible experience and information gained as employees.

More generally, managers benefit from personnel flows into and out of rival firms, which surreptitiously facilitate information transfer among them. The more competitive an industry is, the greater is the number of personnel exchanged. Flows of people between firms also help disseminate a common set of values, a shared language, and a convergence of product standards among competitors.[18]

Personnel transfers have unforeseen consequences, however. By enhancing information diffusion, managerial mobility tends to heighten rivalry: Imitation of nonpatented knowledge occurs more quickly. Because managers naturally hire on a strategic basis those employees whose prior experience will help them acquire competitive advantage, they often demand that their managers sign noncompetition agreements that limit their ability to work for competitors for at least a year. Corporate histories amply document how firms contemplating strategic changes frequently seek out from competing firms managers with desirable experience, skills, and outlooks.

Finally, we cannot discount the fact that managers are themselves social products: They attend common schools, form friendships, and participate in overlapping social circles.[19] A recent survey of 1891 present and former CEOs of leading U.S. firms by (*Fortune:* June 18, 1990) showed that 86 percent of all CEOs with MBAs graduated from one of the top 10 schools. Social bonds naturally form between managers as a result of these shared experiences. In fact, the prevalence of social bonds in particular industries should heavily influence competition: In industries with few social bonds, all-out competition results, leading to widespread conflict; whereas in industries with extensive social bonds, rivalry tends to be suppressed.[20]

As a result, and despite abundant propaganda to the contrary, in many industries competition itself is increasingly limited. The threat of rivalry has driven firms to develop more sophisticated ways for collecting, processing, and disseminating information. Managers have developed relationships across corporate boundaries to provide their firms with greater means for informally coordinating their actions and dampening competition. Many historical studies of industries document how managers struggled to reduce competition in order to secure stability and produce above-normal profits. A close examination by two Harvard professors of the steel, auto, and coal industries, as well as hospitals, agriculture, housing, and telecommunications, demonstrated how managers succeeded in creating industries with very little competition indeed.[21] In the dynamic, globalizing environment of the 1990s, these savvy managers doubtless will continue to take full advantage of their collective options.

Targeting Institutions

In addition to coordinating their activities with competitors, managers aggressively are tapping more their firms' economic resources to influence their environments strategically: In the 1980s, they targeted ever larger contributions to universities, foundations, charities, and political campaigns in an effort to promote their firms' interests.*

Economic contributions to external institutions buy a degree of cooperation and goodwill that can provide firms a slight advantage over competitors. For instance, Mobil's highly visible advertisements and support of public television after the 1973 oil embargo were credited with significantly dampening the ill will felt toward oil firms for price gouging. A similar concern was evident in the actions taken in the United States by large oil firms following Iraq's invasion of Kuwait in 1990: Managers struggled to convey the message, through extensive media presentations,

---

*Paul Lawrence and Davis Dyer, in *Renewing American Industry* (NY: Free Press, 1983), argued that moderate, but vigorous competition tends to improve overall economic strength: too little competition reduces growth and innovation, while excessive competition—the Hobbesian war of all against all—creates chaos. See also Dennis Carlton and Jeffrey Perloff, *Modern Industrial Organization* (Glenview, IL: Scott, Foresman, 1990), as well as Fred Scherer, *Industrial Market Structure and Economic Performance* (2nd ed.) (Boston: Houghton, Mifflin, 1980).

that price increases were justified and that the sudden surge in oil firms'
profitability was transient.

How have managers influenced their firms' environments? The record
suggests that companies increasingly shape how consumers, investors,
reporters—how all of us, in fact—see the world, by strategically directing
money, forming relationships, and distributing corporate propaganda to
four key cultural institutions: the mass media, schools and universities,
government, and the financial markets.

The Business of Giving

Capital flows from companies into cultural settings through debt and
equity investments, advertising, political contributions, and educational
donations. The financial markets account for most of the capital our firms
raise. In 1986, the New York Stock Exchange listed firms' shares valued at
$2.2 trillion, and firms' debt totaling $1.5 trillion. Not surprisingly, managers carefully allocate capital resources to stabilize and maximize the
value of their firms in the markets.

The media have been a significant target of companies' advertising
efforts: The billions spent on media advertising in any one year normally
represent 100 percent of broadcast firms' revenues, 75 percent of newspaper revenues, and 57 percent of magazine revenues.[22] Since corporate
advertising budgets frequently make up the lion's share of media firms'
revenues, firms that advertise heavily implicitly (and sometimes explicitly) pressure media managers either to provide favorable coverage or risk
losing the account. Occasionally, insistence on biased coverage is so high
that reporters appeal to constitutional rights guaranteeing freedom of
the press to decouple themselves from the business priorities of their
media managers.

Government also has become a very visible target of managers' efforts
to influence their firms' environments: Between 1974 and 1983, spending by political action committees (PACs) increased from $21 million to
$190 million, of which 43 percent of these were business PACs, represent-
ing the largest single source of election funds.[23] Chief executive officers
view PAC contributions as an important aspect of firms' political
strategies. In one study of 243 firms, each firm was found to contribute to
more than 80 candidates through its PAC.[24]

A comprehensive analysis by the Center for Responsive Politics, a
nonpartisan research group, documents how lawmakers are increasingly
dependent on these PACs. Business, it turns out, contributed more than
65 percent of all funds that were channeled to congressional candidates in
the 1988 race, while labor and single-issue groups gave, respectively, only
24 percent and 11 percent, for a total of $160 million. The study con-
cludes that PACs are quite pragmatic in doling out money, principally to
incumbents who sit on a Congressional committee that can help them.[25]

Finally, companies have recently contributed more heavily to education, particularly to private schools and universities.[26] Total corporate philanthropy amounts to more than $2 billion a year in the United States. A recent poll of 1000 large U.S. firms by *Fortune* magazine found that 78 percent of these firms contribute money to help public education. In these companies, 70 percent of top executives claim to be actively involved in educational efforts. A total of 18 percent give over $1 million or more, while another 28 percent give betweeen $100,000 and $500,000 a year. In 1986, business contributions to private universities in the United States became their leading source of revenue, surpassing the contributions of alumni for the first time. The largest donor to education was IBM, with worldwide contributions totaling $81 million in 1988, $135 million in 1989, and $150 million in 1990. Consumer products giant Procter & Gamble took second place, followed closely by General Electric and AT&T. The funds they expended were targeted to programs that ranged from scholarships, dropout prevention, and literacy enhancement to school reform, teacher development, and management training.[27]

Leading firms like General Electric, Chase Manhattan, IBM, Arthur Anderson, and General Motors also maintain full-time staff and facilities to teach in proprietary management development programs, and firms spend large sums on consultants who provide specialized training. Often these training centers act as boot camps for other firms unable to afford such expenditures: Smaller firms subsequently hire away graduates of leading firms' programs.[28] Moroever, since 1982 auto makers Ford and GM, in partnership with the United Auto Wokers, have offered employee education courses to workers. The program has been so successful that the companies agreed to extend it to workers' spouses in 1989.[29] Although their monetary totals are hard to estimate and their effects difficult to quantify, such programs constitute an important means by which managers influence their firms' external environments and build goodwill internally.

Well-heeled American companies such as American Express, Du Pont, and Alcoa have recently created formal programs of international philanthropy tied into their global business strategies. As one business weekly put it: "The goals are as business-oriented as they are humanitarian. With foreign markets playing a greater role in the earnings outlook of U.S. multinationals, companies are taking pains to project a positive image abroad."[30]

It's Whom You Know

Not to be forgotten is the fact that managers also nominate personal friends and prominent individuals to serve on their firms' boards. Extensive analyses of interlocking directorates have found that overlapping memberships create many opportunities for coordination among competitors: Most of these interlocks, in fact, occur between interdependent firms.[31] Although no study has documented concretely the transfer of intelligence data among competing firms through boards (for obvious reasons), most observers agree that directorates indirectly influence the informational inputs into firms' decision making. Financial institutions, for instance, serve on many corporate boards in which they have significant loans.[32] However, the resulting network has unexpected consequences. One study showed how the lending practices of banks were influenced by their connections to large corporations: Banks tended to direct their loans in ways that best met the capital needs of the leading corporations, avoiding loans (e.g., mortgages) that would more broadly distribute capital.[33] Another investigation contrasted airline interlocks in 1970 and 1982, and found that indirect interlocks were concentrated among competing airlines, and increased as the industry deregulated.[34] Through judicious selection of boards, then, it appears that firms indirectly coordinate their actions, reduce uncertainty, and limit rivalry.

The financial sector often features prominently in corporate networks because of its control over capital flows. Managers appear to rely heavily on social relationships to improve their ability to access capital. Various sociologists have taken pains to document the location of financial firms in the network of board interlocks among large industrial firms, and conclude that capital acquisition in the United States is highly centralized.[35]

Interlocking directorates are one means by which managers have ensured access to capital. One detailed investigation demonstrated that network ties can have important consequences for the behaviors of firms: It showed that business lending patterns by a set of commercial banks in St. Louis tended to mirror the relative centrality of these banks in a network of directorships that tied them to large local corporations.[36] These interlocks actually placed banks at the heart of business decision making: The allocation of resources to strategic uses.

Financial donations also engender social relationships. Contributions to political campaigns, for instance, are heavily influenced by the indirect relationships companies have with major banks and by those banks' shared ownership of companies in an industry. Different studies have shown how the pattern of interlocks predicts, on the one hand, the similarity of political contributions that firms make and, on the other hand, the level and type of charitable contributions.[37]

More generally, managers have linked up with members of cultural institutions to co-opt them and help produce favorable conditions. These interlocks have involved firms in extended networks that increased managerial cohesion across business communities and enhanced managers' ability to control threatening elements of their environment. One study of managers found that the business elite in the United States is dominated by an inner circle with extensive ties to leading nongovernmental and nonprofit institutions.[38] Centrally located managers clearly demonstrated a sense of unity, and groups such as the Business Roundtable in the United States acted principally to promote the general interests of business as a whole.

And What You're Known For

In recent years, managers have become far more aware that what people know about their firms profoundly affects how firms function. They invest heavily in public relations, issue advertising, and reputational management, and actively promote favorable images to relevant publics.[39] They use annual reports strategically to influence readers: A study of 18 firms over a 17-year period showed that managers of unstable firms claimed more attempts to control their environments than did managers of stable firms.[40]

Executives try to sway the business press and mass media by sending position papers and sponsored reports free of charge to reporters. Company representatives often testify before congressional subcommittees. Managers also distribute information and business propaganda to the educational system and routinely supply valued executives to universities and governmental agencies for internships.[41]

Finally, everyone tries to co-opt government in order to diffuse its power to influence their competitiveness. Many studies document how often regulatory agencies have become captives of the industries they monitor. Regulators rely on information provided by the industry to make decisions, and agency personnel frequently move in and out of line positions in the industry.[42]

In the booming 1980s, managers also conducted extensive public relations campaigns. Recent mergers indicate that public relations firms themselves are not unaware of their need to develop a presence in government: In 1986, public relations giant Hill & Knowlton acquired a Washington-based lobbying company. Within weeks, the world's second largest public relations agency, Burston-Marsteller, announced that it too was acquiring a Washington lobbying firm.

Not surprisingly, firms invest considerable sums on legal staffs to represent them to government regulators and in the courts. Corporate lawyers regularly prepare *amicus curiae* (friend of the court) briefs to influence judges' opinions. Senior managers directly lobby legislators and executive staff on behalf of their firms, their industries, or sectors of the business community.

If the prolonged court attack on the tobacco companies has nearly always ended in dismissal, it is undoubtedly because tobacco firms have made vast investments in legal and medical research, in countertestimony at court trials, and in adroit congressional maneuvering.[43] Declining domestic sales recently catapulted exports by U.S. cigarette makers and shifted the playing field to Europe and Asia. The proindustry Asian Tobacco Council, for instance, has helped companies lobby foreign governments to prevent them from adopting measures as strict as Thailand's, with its high import duties, cumbersome customs clearance procedures, and ban on cigarette advertising. Already, exports of U.S. cigarettes to East Asia have grown from 18.4 billion in 1985 to 75 billion in 1990.[44]

To an extent, savvy managers manipulate public opinion through deliberate, albeit veiled, relationships with trade press, public relations advisors, management consultants, investment advisors, and lawyers. By assisting competing firms and communicating through elaborate networks within industries, they enhance the spread of information about firms' activities, problems, discoveries, new product ideas, and innovations. They also help both to build up and tear down firms' reputations in their industries. One investigation of *Fortune* 500 firms found that the financial markets and the media relied on quite different kinds of information in assessing firms: The stock market and institutional investors assessed firms principally on the basis of profitability and risk, while the media were more attentive to large firms and firms donating more to charitable causes.[45]

To maintain their firms' reputations (and, frequently, the stock's price on an exchange), managers have become more involved in negotiating with their stakeholders over the impact of firms' activities on their welfare. Special interest associations representing labor, consumers, communities, or issues increasingly challenge managerial prerogatives and question the legitimacy of firms' activities. So firms in highly visible domains face higher levels of stakeholder conflict, whether because they deal with contested product-market domains (tobacco, biotechnology), raise questions of national public policy (aerospace, defense, oil), or rely on risky technologies (nuclear power, chemicals).

The more power a stakeholder group can marshall to draw attention to its concerns, the more likely companies are to incorporate stakeholder objectives into their decisions.[46] More than ever managers are seeking to appear socially responsive and environment-friendly, whether through charitable contributions, affirmative action, recycling, following the Sullivan principles, or promoting representative stakeholders to positions of influence, for instance to their boards of directors.

Building Strategic Alliances

Although coordination and targeting constitute important means by which managers are, in part, engineering their firms' environments, they are difficult to alter in the short run: Rules of thumb guide managers' advertising budgets and charitable and political contributions; it takes time for students to absorb information; forming relationships and systematically influencing regulators, judges, and legislators can pay off only in the long run. Strategic coordination and targeting, although valuable in coping with competition, prove less useful in contending with short-run environmental changes. For faster operational benefits, managers forging strategic alliances with competitors.

In the last decade, we witnessed an explosive increase in the frequency and volume of direct collaborative deals being struck by firms in many U.S. industries. Cooperation was eased by the Reagan administration's inclination to follow the early lead set by postwar Japan and many European countries in recognizing that competition unfolds on a global level. With antitrust laws out of favor, U.S. regulators found themselves supporting the formation of strategic alliances, particularly evident in the deregulated airline, financial services, and telecommunications communities.

In contrast to informal agreements and other forms of cooperation among competitors, alliances consist of formal contractual relationships that managers form to manage heightened competition and uncertainty and acquire capabilities at minimal expense.

Choosing Allies

Firms experience two principal forms of interdependence: horizontal and vertical. *Horizontal interdependence* binds competing firms into an industry: All managers in the industry perceive a sense of shared fate because the actions of any of their firms directly and negatively impinges on either the market share, the product, or the prices of its rivals. Increases in car sales at General Motors generally mean decreases at Ford and Chrysler, so auto manufacturers are horizontally interdependent. Much like competition between sports teams, horizontal interdependence produces in managers perceptions that their firms' fates are negatively linked, that they should act to obstruct competitors' effective actions and resist providing assistance.

In contrast, *vertical interdependence* is a form of mutualism. Firms whose activities are vertically related share an interest in each others' actions: Both perceive gains and losses in similar ways. So environmental developments that threaten the market of U.S. auto manufacturers, for instance, also endanger firms in vertically related industries, be they safety glass and mirror manufacturers, parts suppliers, or tire makers. More akin to partners in a relay race, vertically related firms' managers strive for mutual benefit, focus on their long-term interests, provide mutual assistance, and often act to prevent each other from making

ineffective actions. The fashionable marriages of suppliers to their manufacturers and distributors forces a convergence of interests that translates
into a common world view among managers.

Historically stable horizontal and vertical linkages can change suddenly
as firms experience rivalry from industries producing increasingly close
substitutes. In the late 60s, the once placid metal canning industry faced
dramatic increases in horizontal and vertical interdependence due to
technological developments in the production of styrofoam, glass, plastic,
and paper containers. Similarly, synthetic fabrics developed by chemical
companies such as Du Pont represented diagonal intrusions that increased horizontal and vertical interdependence in the textile industry in
the late 1950s, disrupting relationships between weaving mills and their
cotton and wool suppliers.

Table 7.2 outlines a typology of strategic alliances based on the type of
interdependence that concerns managers and the number of firms
affected. As managers have detected increasing horizontal and vertical
interdependence, they began by forging *bilateral alliances,* the two most
common forms of which were licensing and joint venture agreements.

Managers licensed rivals' technologies when they proved too difficult
either to imitate or supersede. Licensing provides a low cost means of
filling customers' demands, and frequently occurs between horizontal
competitors operating in different markets: In 1982, for instance, over
31,000 overseas firms held licensing agreements with U.S. firms. Licensing has been the preferred mode of interfacing around mature and
peripheral technologies in which firms faced little threat from rivals'
knowledge acquisition. More critically, licensing has featured prominently as a competitive tool in recent cutting-edge technologies where managers license widely to promote a product standard and dominate a market.

Sony's failure to license Betamax technology, for instance, ultimately
led to its defeat by the alliance of firms forged in 1975 by JVC and
Matsushita with Hitachi, Sharp, and Mitsubishi, which was centered

Table 7.2. Strategic Alliances

| | | Form of Alliance | |
		Bilateral	Multilateral
Form of Interdependence	Horizontal	License	Shared Equity
	Vertical	Joint Venture	Consortium

around the alternative VHS technology. AT&T's managers gambled on the competitive advantage licensing could provide when it decided to compete with IBM's proprietary operating system for personal computers by licensing its UNIX operating system to an alliance of rival manufacturers.

While joint ventures enabled firms to tap a competitor's technology, distribution system, or market, they were also beneficial to managers whose firms had complementary skills or assets. Although joint ventures occurred between direct competitors, they were more likely to result between vertically related firms.[47] Conservative estimates by the U.S. Department of Commerce, for instance, place the number of joint ventures involving foreign companies in 1982 at 16,000. In most of these ventures, managers sought to combine the market or distributional knowledge of a competitor with their firms' complementary knowledge about products or technologies.

Selection of joint ventures appears strongly influenced by the specificity of the assets managers were required to commit to the transaction. The more specialized the commitment managers had to make, the more likely they were to fear that their partners in the transaction would behave opportunistically, and the more they insisted on a joint venture rather than a contract. The joint venture created a superior framework for monitoring and enforcing partners' gains from the transaction than did a simple contract.[48]

Moreover, joint ventures could be either symmetrical or asymmetrical: Symmetrical joint ventures link partners horizontally; assymetrical joint ventures bind firms vertically. Many symmetrical joint ventures occurred between European banks interested in penetrating the U.S. market; Philips/Du Pont Optical, however, is an asymmetric joint venture between both firms established to manufacture and sell compact disks—a horizontal investment for European disk manufacturer Philips, and a diversification into consumer electronics for Du Pont.[49]

As interdependence intensified further in the 1980s, managers participated in more *multilateral alliances*. Trade associations are one such form of multilateral link. However, trade associations could seldom alter the strategic positions of their member firms. Take the highly competitive TV networks. In election years, each has traditionally spent millions of dollars in conducting independent voter surveys. In a much-criticized break with tradition, ABC, NBC, CBS, and CNN formed a multilateral alliance to conduct voter surveys in 1990 and produce vote projections across the country. Since each network based its projections on the same information, their artificial competition was eliminated, with no network gaining an advantage over the others.[50]

The National Cooperative Research Act of 1984 officially authorized U.S. competitors to pool resources into research consortia. Most notable has been the successful chip making consortium Sematech, funded jointly by member companies and $500 million from the U.S. Pentagon. In the 1980s, managers formed a number of such consortia because interdependence required more than the simple centralization and coordination of information that could be obtained through traditional trade associations. Consortia can enhance firms' competitive strength by enabling them to capitalize on economies of scale and reduce risk, frequently in research.[51] In recent years, managers have relied heavily on research consortia to keep up with new developments, to acquire new technologies, and to cultivate industry-wide product standards and prototype technologies. The latest round of U.S. budget proposals has spawned renewed debate about government's role in boosting R&D spending to create a level playing field for American firms competing with European and Japanese rivals whose governments actively nurture domestic industries.[52]

Finally, many managers in the 1980s committed their firms to complex shared equity arrangements. Multilateral equity ownership in a newly created firm is justified principally when specialized assets must be dedicated to the activity, when transactions between all the firms are likely to recur, and when uncertainty is high. In complex spider-web shared equity ventures, for instance, a large number of firms network around a single pivotal equity partner.

In 1990, entrepreneurial biotech specialist Genentech was swallowed up by cash-rich Roche Holdings, parent of pharmaceuticals giant Hoffman-La Roche. It thereafter turned away from its historically self-reliant posture and formed diverse alliances. To capitalize more quickly on technological developments in related areas, the company invested minority stakes in a network of start-ups. Recent accounts suggest that its managers are considering setting up an in-house venture capital fund of its own to actively search and promote these kinds of collaborations.[53]

To Network or Not?

Yet not all firms jumped into strategic alliances in the 1980s, nor are they likely to in the future. Some managers elected a solitary course for their firms, opting for internal development of technology, vertical integration into component manufacturing and distribution, and wholly owned subsidiaries in remote markets. Others participated in multiple bilateral and multilateral partnerships, forging a network of allies within and across industry groupings.

In fact, in many industries, increasing globalization, technological convergence, and competitive rivalry have encouraged a Janus-like splintering of corporate communities into two sectors, each with a distinct collective-strategy profile: on one hand, a proliferation of specialized niche players offering boutique-like products and services to narrow segments of an industry pursuing alliances; on the other hand, increased consolidation of smaller firms into behemoths as firms incorporate horizontal and vertical sources of rivalry. To compete with the giant firms produced by these consolidations, the more specialized firms negotiate bilateral and multilateral collaborative arrangements that fuse them into strategic constellations. Like Gulliver facing the Lilliputians, then, Goliath companies increasingly find themselves competing, not with isolated firms, but with the elaborate networks these firms construct.

Which firms act alone and which ones forge alliances? As environmental circumstances continue to disrupt traditional sources of competitive advantage, economies of scale are less significant and centralized coordination within large firms can prove detrimental, making alliances more attractive. Larger firms suffer from sluggishness and inflexibility when they act alone, so small is often better. Globalization creates markets that overwhelm even the largest firms, so alliances can enable firms to penetrate distant markets more quickly.

Firms pursue one of two collective strategies, either: (1) an alliance strategy, or (2) a fortress strategy. Alliance strategies place firms in strategic constellations of consortia, licenses, joint ventures, and shared equity arrangements. Fortress strategies involve firms in purely majority-owned equity joint ventures, or direct acquisitions of firms in diagonally related markets. (See Table 7.3.)

Take Scandinavian Airlines System. Since 1987, under the leadership of Jan Carlzon, SAS has fashioned a broad network of alliances and minority ownership positions in Inter-Continental Hotels and in other airlines such as Thai Airways, Texas Air, and Swissair in an attempt to build a global competitive position. As Europe's trade barriers fall, Carlzon has bet that SAS's alliance strategy will prove key to rivalry with the likes of European adversaries British Airways and Lufthansa who, like

Table 7.3. Fortress and Alliance Strategies

Key factors	Fortress strategy	Alliance strategy
Rate of environmental change	Low/moderate	High
Prevailing standards	Extensive	Few
Cost of capital	Low	High
Corporate strategy	Related	Unrelated
Business strategy	Innovation	Imitation
R&D capability	High	Low

U.S. airlines American and United, have steadfastly pursued a single-minded strategy of internal expansion.

Various conditions explain which firms prefer to address changing environmental conditions through alliance strategies, and which ones elect to pursue fortress strategies to cope with heightening globalization and competitive rivalry.

The Rate of Environmental Change

Recently, globalization, technological convergence, and deregulation have created enormous environmental change. Many large firms find themselves held back by the combination of momentum and inertia that keeps them moving along historical trajectories. When the rate of environmental change exceeds firms' capacities to adapt, fortress strategies prove less effective than alliance strategies.[54] Mergers, acquisitions, and majority stakes in equity ventures only increase the complexity with which managers must contend, and therefore increase the likelihood of sluggishness in adapting to the new environmental circumstances. Consolidating new businesses and incorporating alien products into existing businesses take time and energy, neither of which firms have as they struggle to maintain parity with competitors. Moreover, consolidations invariably heighten the internal variety of the firm, exposing managers to new sources of unfamiliarity (new employees, new facilities) and therefore increase the conflicts to be resolved.

In contrast, alliance strategies offer significant advantages. By grafting external relationships at the firm's periphery, managers contain the complexity they add to existing operations. External ties also provide added flexibility: Should environmental conditions change again, alliances are easily disolved and new ones formed, without disrupting core activities.[55]

The Cost of Capital

To cope with changing conditions, firms often must contemplate making large capital outlays for which they issue either equity or debt. Because alliances require a less substantial commitment of scarce capital, firms facing a relatively high cost of capital find alliance strategies more attractive than fortress strategies.

Lenders charge a higher cost of capital to firms heavily burdened with debt and to firms with lower profitability. A high debt indicates to banks an increased probability of default on payments. Similarly, low earnings reduce firms' ability to bear interest payments. So high leverage and low profitability should increase the likelihood that firms will pursue alliance strategies. In fact, firms may be motivated to form alliances in order to remedy declining profitability.[56] A colleague and I conducted a longitudinal study of the global telecommunications community between 1984 and 1987. In it, we confirmed that joint ventures were far less likely among more leveraged and less profitable firms.[57]

Since the cost of capital is generally higher for smaller firms, it is probable that they too will favor alliances. In fact, scholars often contend that small, R&D-intensive firms use significantly more joint ventures because partnering with larger firms enables them to pursue projects that they could not get funded on their own through the capital markets.

The Company's R&D Capability

Because technology drives many environmental changes that firms face, internal R&D capability looms large as a factor influencing the selection of collective strategy. Despite dramatic environmental turmoil, firms with extensive R&D capability are more likely to pursue self-contained fortress strategies: Built-in capacity is itself a source of competitive advantage facilitating adaptation. Empirical studies have found that firms pursuing joint ventures tend to lower their R&D expenditures, supporting the idea that these alliances substitute for internal development.[58]

Moreover, firms already committing extensive funding to R&D resist forming relationships that could involve sharing technological breakthroughs: Alliances are difficult to seal off, and knowledge developed from cooperating with close rivals is difficult to protect. So, where the probability is great that alliance partners could exploit a venture's R&D without sharing equitably in economic gains, managers are more likely to opt for a fortress strategy. My study of the telecommunications community between 1984 and 1987 supported the idea that larger firms and firms with greater R&D intensity were more likely to resist forming alliances and to go solo.[59]

The Company's Corporate Strategy

Managers' propensities to favor a fortress strategy over an alliance strategy is also influenced by their firms' corporate posture: Unrelated diversification weakens the ability to grow through internal development of products and technologies. Because corporate staff evaluate diversified businesses on the basis of divisional rates of return, division managers are pressured to maintain lean profiles, frequently cutting back on long-run investments like R&D and advertising.[60]

Highly diversified firms also appear to carry higher percentages of debt, which raises their cost of capital, and reduces their ability to fund R&D internally.[61] Lacking the capacity to pursue a fortress strategy at the division level, managers forge broad-based alliances in order to compete against more powerful integrated firms. A study of Japanese firms' entry into the United States found that they too favored an alliance strategy with U.S. partners when they were diversifying outside their main industries and needed complementary inputs, knowledge, or resources from firms already active in the target industry.

In contrast, firms that anchor their diversification in related arenas, be they technological or market based, tend to pursue integrating operations across businesses, and search for synergies from which to extend products and markets.[62] A corporate posture of relatedness therefore incites managers to rely on a self-contained fortress strategy.

An Existing Competitive Advantage

Firms' business unit strategies also affect whether managers favor alliances: In businesses that compete heavily through timing, managers are more likely to rely heavily on internal product development—favoring a fortress strategy. In contrast, managers of businesses accustomed to imitating established innovators are more likely to favor alliance strategies, partly because they lack the R&D capability with which to tackle industry leaders and partly because alliances allow them to retain their smaller size and flexibility, which provides them a cost advantage over first movers.

Moreover, evidence suggests that leading firms in a competitive market have less incentive to cannibalize their own products by introducing innovations: Waiting for rivals to challenge them and responding aggressively through deeper R&D may heighten profitability.[63] Managers therefore eschew alliances for fear of dissipating their advantage, preferring fortress strategies for both product development and subsequent retaliation to competitors' innovations. A study of 278 start-up firms involved in the commercialization of biotechnology found that larger firms, and thus firms with greater internal manufacturing and marketing capability, were more likely to pursue an alliance strategy.[64]

Product Standards

Industry-wide standards play an important role in facilitating the diffusion of new products and technologies. Managers can develop competitive advantages for their firms by successfully imposing their preferred standard on an industry. Where a number of standards compete, where voluntary standards have not been widely adopted, or where regulations have not imposed broad parameters around technological configurations and product features, even the largest firms find it difficult to dominate through fortress strategies. Despite Sony's technological lead and marketing might, for instance, its solo efforts to impose the Betamax format in videocassette recorders was outdone by JVC's alliance strategy with Matsushita to promote the competing VHS technology. AT&T's recent alliance with a group of computer manufacturers to promote UNIX as a universal operating system for office computers successfully challenged the proprietary operating system standard IBM sought to impose. Another powerful alliance of over 40 companies led by Microsoft, Compaq, and Digital Equipment is gambling that it can create a standard for an advanced desktop computer built around the RISC chip that is simpler and faster than the chips used in similar machines offered by IBM, Apple, and Sun Microsystems.[65] The message seems to be that where competing standards exist, firms that mobilize alliances have better chances of prevailing than firms committed to a fortress strategy.

Early in the life cycle of a technology, firms committed to fortress strategies have difficulty reaping the benefits of their innovations: The large investments required to establish a technological trajectory drain the firm, opening up opportunities for early followers. So a higher level of alliance activity in the technology's early stages increases the likelihood that first movers rather than imitators will reap the benefits of innovating.

Cooperating to Better Compete

In small towns throughout the United States, the nation's largest retailer, Wal-Mart, is known as "the merchant of death." As one study showed, when Wal-Mart established operations in 15 towns in Iowa, it caused sales by specialty retailers to drop by 12.1 percent. To survive the onslaught, businesses in many small towns have formed grass-roots networks of veterans from other Wal-Mart towns in an effort to develop combat strategies for collectively meeting the challenge.[66]

Interfirm agreements binding firms into global communities have become the norm in a surprising number of industries. The United Nations Centre on Transnational Corporations identified France, the United States, and the United Kingdom as the leading initiators of some 618 interfirm agreements occurring around information technology in selected countries between 1984 and 1986. Over 1200 foreign companies were involved in operating joint ventures in the different republics of the former Soviet Union. Networking of this kind presents managers with an alternative means for changing their strategic positions during periods of revolutionary change. They either substitute or supplement changes made at the business and corporate levels of strategy. The principal strength of networking lies in the speed with which change can be implemented, and the limited resources required of firms to form global networks. Smaller firms seeking competitive positioning in globalizing markets find it particularly attractive because of its affordability. Larger firms welcome the flexibility that networking provides. In some industries, alliances define a differentiated sector in which networks of smaller competitors compete against behemoth firms. In other industries, large firms participate in alliances to capitalize more quickly on technological and market synergies.

The success of a networking effort, however, like strategic changes at the business and corporate levels, requires careful addressing of concerns about implementation: mobilizing employees behind a strategy, overcoming cultural impediments, and reshaping the structural controls managers rely on to drive their strategic visions—subjects to which we now turn.

Energizing
Strategic
Change

Having opted to revise their firms' strategic postures at the
business, corporate, and collective levels, managers face the most
daunting challenge of all: carrying out the wrenching
transformations that shifting to a new posture invariably entails.
Chapter 8 emphasizes the importance of leadership that inspires
and motivates participation and involvement. Transformational
leadership mobilizes support by envisaging and signaling the broad
outlines of a change effort and allowing it to self-actualize through
the multiple contributions of middle managers and employees
throughout the firm.

Chapter 9 points out how implementation invariably runs up
against entrenched cultural practices that are likely to discourage
change. Ultimately, to mobilize support is to sign on to a profound
reshaping of the cultural makeup of firms with the intension of
imprinting firms with new capabilities. Many managers today are
struggling to incorporate into their firms' cultures, not only
common concerns with efficiency and entrepreneurship, but also
shared commitments to promoting equity and ethics to respond to
institutional pressures.

Chapter 10 focuses on the structural implications of a strategic
change and shows how managers are: (1) revising their business
structures to facilitate competitiveness by decentralizing authority
and encouraging integration across functions and divisions; (2)

altering their corporate structures to exploit synergies across their portfolios of businesses; and (3) participating in collective administrative structures that enhance their ability to compete. Jointly, they speak to a systematic attack on bureaucracy and to the progressive dismemberment of structures that now more closely resemble internal markets and elaborate networks than hierarchies.

In the final chapter I suggest that the revolutionary circumstances driving strategic change in firms also have major implications for other social institutions. For the corporate sector to achieve strategic change requires parallel radical transformations of schools, universities, labor unions, professions, and the media. These institutions produce much of the raw material input—personnel, ideas, innovations—that firms rely on to compete. They constitute challenging sites for the application of some of these ideas in the years to come.

8
Mobilizing for Action

It had been a difficult year for Compaq Computers: In 1991, revenues dropped nearly 15 percent, and the company was expected to show a $70-million loss. Nonetheless, it still came as a surprise when, on October 25, 1991 local television news crews hovered over Compaq Computer's Houston headquarters in helicopters. They were there to videotape a formal announcement that a change of leadership was in the offing: Compaq's board of directors was firing its chief executive officer and founder, Rod Canion. Replacing him would be Chief Operating Officer Eckhard Pfeiffer, a leader the board regarded as more willing to embrace the drastic kinds of changes the company needed to carry out.[1]

Often corporate reorientations are tied to such changes in leadership. That's because leaders prove their mantle in times of turmoil: Bad ones encourage resistance, are slow to push for change, and so become obstacles their companies must overcome.

Students of political systems know well how critical leaders are to revolutions: Devoid of leadership, they point out, revolutions quickly turn into anarchy. Recall the August 1991 coup against then Soviet chief Mikhail Gorbachev by old-line communists. Russian president Boris Yeltsin demonstrated skillfully how leaders can act as catalysts in expressing mass discontent. By channeling opposition to the coup, the Russian leader gave the resistance a focal point that tripped up the insurgents and prompted their fall.

161

In remarkably similar ways, none prove more central to shaping perceptions during turbulent eras than chief executive officers and their top teams. In their key positions at the apex of corporate structures, they stand responsible for engineering firms' reorientations through business, corporate, and collective strategies.

Clearly they are idolized for it. Popular periodicals routinely portray large firms' chief executive officers as messianic heroes, ascribing to the most successful among them extraordinary intelligence, wisdom, and savvy. In a shrewd fusion of marketing and self-aggrandizement, many of these same CEOs have taken over the media as corporate symbols and household names.*

Of course, celebrity has its rewards. In the go-go decade of the 1980s, CEOs' compensation jumped by 212 percent while factory workers' increased by only 53 percent, engineers' by 73 percent, and teachers' by 95 percent. Yet in that same time period, earnings per share of the S&P 500 grew by less than 78 percent. Many question whether even extraordinary CEOs can truly be worth the average $2 million they got in 1990 and $2.4 million in 1991—compensation that amounts to well over 85 times what the average blue-collar worker makes—and cannot be explained either by the performance or size of their firms.[2] Given the privileges CEOs enjoy, it is not surprising that corporate critics describe CEOs as members of an exclusive fraternity, more akin to a feudal elite indulging its every whim.

There may be some truth to the accusation. After all, it was not so long ago that the goings on at Bendix under William Agee and Mary Cunningham topped the tabloids. More recently, consider the strange saga of Robert Schoellhorn, the former CEO of Abbott Laboratories. In 1990 he was summarily dismissed by Abbott's board. After filing suit, Abbott countercharged, and an out-of-court settlement cost Abbott $5.2 million in July 1991. In the process, embarrassing charges were brought to light concerning Schoellhorn's gross misuse of company assets and flagrant abuse of expense accounts. Pricey corporate jets were purchased while R&D budgets were being slashed. Personal interests were catered to while potential successors were forced to resign. As it turned out, Schoellhorn himself was actually away from the firm most of the time, being busy sitting on the boards of other firms. These ailments afflict all too many of our senior executives.[3]

So how much are top managers really worth? This proves difficult to answer. Global comparisons suggest that some are paid far in excess of value: Similarly qualified executives in Japan or Western Europe, for instance, make considerably less than their counterparts in the United

*Of course, when corporate emperors are finally deposed, their stories make for revealing anecdotes full of palace intrigues, conspiracies, poison pills, and golden parachutes. Having crowned them, the popular press relishes exposing their fall, fueling public anger over corporate excess.

States: Seldom does the ratio of the CEO's income to that of the lowest-paid worker in Japan exceed 10 to 1; in the United States it often tops 100 to 1.[4] The popularity of "golden parachutes" in American industry, and the astounding payouts that were subsequently tendered to outgoing executives of merged firms made the issue especially visible throughout the 1980s. Findings from one research study of 105 firms in nine industries suggest that CEOs may use their social influence on directors to induce boards to grant them golden parachutes and artifically inflate their compensation.[5]

While a minority of top managers doubtless indulge themselves, most top managers, in fact, are probably conscientious, hard-working, over-achievers who play a key role in negotiating strategic turning points in their firm's unfolding.[6] By encouraging celebrity-based views of top management jobs, therefore, we not only distort their jobs, but we underestimate the other roles that less visible members of the top management team, middle managers, and firms' employees play in conceiving and implementing a strategic change.

Throughout the 1980s, the press seemed remarkably adept at inflating already outsized egos, encouraging us to forget how vital to successful implementation were the daily interactions all employees have with customers, suppliers, and distributors. In unduly celebrating CEOs throughout the booming decade, the press encouraged us to overlook the fact that corporate performance results from superior execution of myriad microscopic jobs on assembly lines, in work groups, research labs, and retail outlets, and in factories, warehouses, and offices.

As environments shift, as greater demands are placed on firms to embark on strategic change through business, corporate, and collective actions, implementation requires senior managers to attend less to celebrity and more to leadership, less to appearances and more to actions. The task of coaxing firms through strategic turning points requires executives to mobilize rather than dictate, to inspire rather than repress, to lead rather than control. It asks top managers to embrace strategic change as a deep-seated transformation of their firms, one that entails company-wide involvement and the inclusion, participation, and commitment of all employees. It involves a catalytic role in the act of leadership—in helping employees to interpret the company's environment, to envision the impending transformation, and to channel their emotional reactions to the threats implicit in changing.

Leadership of this sort is still rare. Some who seem to have shown signs of inspired leadership during revolutionary periods have become household names. One readily thinks of Lee Iaccocca at Chrysler, Ray Kroc at MacDonald's, Jack Welch at General Electric. A less visible example, perhaps, is United Technologies. In his 10 years at the helm, former chairman Harry Gray built the company into a sprawling $18-billion conglomerate with products ranging from military helicopters to shopping-mall escalators—but one run purely by the numbers. When Robert Daniell took over as CEO in March 1986, he brought together his top managers and decided with them to level the conglomerate's top-down structure, tighten the relationship between the firm and its customers, and involve UTC's 186,800 employees more closely in decision making. Out of the divided, dictatorial, intolerant company he inherited, Daniell went on a campaign to cut bureaucratic approval processes, cultivate customers, train employees, and improve responsiveness. By 1989, customers were nodding their approval with increased orders, and major divisions like Pratt & Whitney and Otis Elevators were showing a resurgence. A transformational leader seemingly had been found, and United Technologies was reborn.[7]

Inspiring Leaders

To successfully execute strategic change requires considered attention to both process and timing: how decisions affect incumbents, what is communicated to uninformed employees, who is involved in the details of implementation, and when actions are taken. Central to the effectiveness of a strategic change, then, are acts of *leadership*.

Attempts to catalog the characteristics that distinguish effective and ineffective leaders have produced a voluminous, though not necessarily illuminating, bibliography. On one side are those analysts who assert the universal importance of key personality traits such as intelligence, dominance, and self-confidence in making great leaders. On the other side are those who emphasize the interpersonal skills effective leaders appear to demonstrate.[8]

Trait fans further distinguish between two basic styles of leadership: authoritarian and participative. Sadly, however, they conclude little beyond the simplistic fact that each one is appropriate under different circumstances. So managers, they advise us, should act authoritatively when tasks are easily broken down and decisions simple, but should welcome participation when decisions are complex and require creative solutions.[9] As two prominent observers note, "never have so many labored so long to say so little. Such prosaic conclusions, though useful in highlighting the importance of adapting style to circumstance, capture little of the charismatic and magnetic qualities that make for memorable leaders."[10]

Nonetheless, trait theories have shown something of a resurgence lately. Recent studies suggest a distinct difference between business leaders and the rest of us in at least four traits:[11]

1. *Drive:* Leaders show distinctly higher levels of motivation, ambition, energy, tenacity, and initiative.

2. *Desire to lead:* Leaders seek power, they want to lead.

3. *Self-confidence:* Leaders project self-confidence and inspire it in followers.

4. *Cognitive ability:* Leaders tend to have keen minds, capable of gathering and integrating vast amounts of information.

If these innate characteristics explain why some people might become leaders, it does not necessarily make of them the kinds of *effective* leaders firms call for during revolutionary periods. That requires asking: What is it that inspiring leaders do so well?

Those who have closely studied leaders who have proven effective during revolutions, crises, and other turning points in governments and firms offer contrasting views. Some contend that leaders are like performers, concerned with presenting themselves to audiences much as actors do on stage. Senior executives lead effectively when, like actors, they deliver a rousing performance, one that attends to the content of the play, its message, and the verbal and nonverbal means through which that message is communicated. Continuing the metaphor, effective leaders imbue a script with meaning, for which we must also have an active audience, the kind that reacts to the performance and charges it with electricity.[12]

Equally revealing have been historical efforts to induce the inspirational styles of great leaders from their biographies. Political scientist James McGregor Burns, for instance, drew on studies of Hitler, Mao Tse-Tung, and Churchill to show that a key quality of leaders is their ability to identify unmet needs and propose visions that garner followers. More critically, he suggests, we should differentiate self-serving forms of manipulative leadership from a more consequential form of *moral* leadership concerned with transforming a group in the pursuit of noble values.[13]

Political economist Charles Lindblom strikes a similar note in his recent book *Inquiry and Change*. He contends that our society and firms overemphasize conformity to prevailing norms. Yet the pressure to conform impairs independent thought, originality, and creative exploration. As social instruments, firms handicap employees by relying on hierarchies and controls to induce job performance. To overcome the dependency fostered by internal control structures calls for settings that encourage greater competition of ideas, free speech, and reduced inequality in influence and power. Our corporate leaders therefore have a moral responsibility to emancipate employees by nurturing open communication, encouraging participation, and lowering the inequalities in compensation, status, and privileges that attach to hierarchies.*

---

*Lindblom's (1990) book effectively reformulates Erich Fromm's thesis *Escape from Freedom* (NY: Avon Books 1941). It highlights the threat that conformity presents to individuality.

Strategic changes invariably challenge throughout firms privileges of power and resources arduously won over time.[14] Reorientations also provoke predictable emotional reactions: Employees panic because change threatens their jobs; managerial actions upset continuity; employees' moods swing wildly through varying cycles of optimism and pessimism. Not surprisingly, top managers' efforts are often blocked by employees who actively or passively sabotage them.

Strategic changes therefore compel *transformational leadership*, that is, symbolic acts through which senior executives unshackle employees from the familiar constraints of bureaucracy.* As some researchers argue, driven by grand passions, transformational leaders excel at articulating a new vision for their firms and mobilizing a critical mass of employees to commit to that vision. Unlike run-of-the-mill dictators, these transformational leaders both identify themselves as agents of change and act accordingly: They empower employees, insist on core values, foster learning, and welcome ambiguity. Not only do they have solid knowledge of the industry, but they also have strong networks; a positive reputation based on achievements, intelligence, skills, and integrity; as well as the drive required to attain power and hold on to it.[15]

A tall order—which may be why CEOs seem cut from a different cloth than other executives. A study of the backgrounds of 108 CEOs of large British firms, for instance, found that they were more likely than other managers to have been exposed to multiple experiences: A generalist degree, an entrepreneurial venture, different functions within firms, international exposure, and prior responsibility for a profit center.[16] Strong CEOs rely heavily on the force of their personalities, their visions, compulsions, passions, and anxieties to effect change. Examples easily come to mind of forward-looking leaders who presided over dramatic transformations in firms, whether Robert Crandall at American Airlines, John DeButts at AT&T, or Jack Welch at GE. On the other side of the coin, examples are forthcoming of leaders who are said to have retarded change, individuals like John Weinberg at Goldman Sachs, Robert Fomon at E.F. Hutton, or Ed Spoor at Pillsbury.

An analysis of 300 retiring CEOs distinguished four types: monarchs, generals, ambassadors, and governors. Monarchs ruled their firms with an iron glove, holding on to power until death or forcible departure—leaders like Edwin Land at Polaroid and Armand Hammer at Occidental Petroleum. Generals hand-picked successors to ensure the continuity of their battle plans—individualists like William Paley at CBS or Robert Woodruff at Coca-Cola. Ambassadors acted as external representatives of their firms, emphasizing statesmanship and stewardship—for instance

*Tichy, N. and M. Devanna, *Transformational Leadership* (NY: Wiley, 1986) contrast transformational leadership and transactional leadership, the more mundane, incrementalist, and authoritarian view of the role.

Reginald Jones at GE and Thomas Watson, Jr. at IBM. Finally, governors conducted themselves more like temporary keepers, inclined to move on once their tour of duty was completed—leaders like Royal Little at Textron or Thornton Bradshaw at ARCO. Differences in leaders' style help explain how firms managed change: Monarchs were more likely to resist, while governors were more likely to facilitate. Data showed that firms run by monarchs showed the highest increase in market value 2 years after their leaders' departure, while firms run by governors and ambassadors realized the greatest market gains during their leaders' terms.[17]

However, successful change requires more than the commitment of senior executives. It also compels attention to firms' other employees. A study of 90 senior executives concluded that at the heart of effective leadership lies an "ability to translate intention into reality and to sustain it."[18] To actualize the future, to improve competitiveness and achieve institutional effectiveness, corporate managers are asked increasingly to abandon traditional authoritarian models and recognize the merits of leadership that empowers employees to contribute to strategic change instead of emasculates their positions. Without transforming leadership, firms may miss the turn, and continue to limp along, outpaced by more visionary competitors.

Bringing Midlevel Managers Back In

In April 1991, a memo from IBM chief John Akers to a small group of managers leaked out to the press. In it, he vented his frustrations in no uncertain terms about the company's poor performance. A few months later, he confirmed his original point by electronic mail directly to the company's 370,000 employees: "While I know many IBMers have never worked as hard as they are working today, I am convinced that some of our people do not understand that they have a deeply personal stake in declining market share, revenue and profits." To redress complacency, he suggested that IBM's managers needed to improve direct communication across the firm. Commenting on the original leak, he pointed out: "When I asked a small group of managers to help get the message out, I got more help than I expected. I would have preferred that more managers communicate face to face with people. And I absolutely believe people should learn about what's going on in IBM within the company, rather than second-hand, through the media."[19]

While leaders interpret environments, create visions, and fuel strategic change, midlevel managers actually translate visions into reality. In their haste to carry out seemingly attractive strategic changes, senior executives occasionally overlook the key role middle managers play in actualizing change, and thereby sabotage reorientations.

Consider the decentralizing efforts of a large family-run firm such as

South Korea's Lucky-Goldstar Group. Since its start in 1947, members of the founding Koo family have dominated all corporate decision making. In that time, however, the company has diversified into a host of unrelated businesses, including shampoos, semiconductors, televisions, and solar power systems, and faced increasing competition from its Korean archrival, the Samsung Group. With over $25 billion in sales from 31 separate companies, in the mid-1980s innovation lagged and quality fell. Much of the blame was laid at the hierarchical, centralized decision-making style of Chairman Koo Cha-Kyung, so a strategic change was initiated to revitalize the company and push authority and accountability downward to middle managers.[20]

Similar attempts to push down decision making and involve lower-tier managers have become a commonplace in U.S. firms also. At General Electric since 1980 Chairman Jack Welch has spearheaded a program of ongoing company-wide town meetings in which GE's 291,000 employees from all levels are encouraged to contribute ideas that will make GE more competitive. As he put it: "We have the ultimate chance at GE during the 1990s to create a corporate atmosphere where it's culturally acceptable to speak out—where telling the truth is rewarded and where bosses who yell at people for speaking up are not."[21]

A program of research led by Harvard's Michael Beer documents the importance for senior managers of involving midlevel managers early on and allowing a nondirective process to unfold. In a 4-year study of change in six large firms, they found that the more successful programs were initiated by leaders who focused on creating a climate for change and outlined the general directions, without providing detailed solutions. By decentralizing the change effort, they encouraged a grass-roots effort.[22]

And for good reason. To carry out a strategic change is much like coping with a crisis: Studies of commercial airline crashes and other disasters show that effective coping requires: (1) extensive internal communication, especially of bad news, (2) handing decision making to those closest to the operations, and (3) making sure technology does not hamper employees' ability to size up a situation.[23] Applied to firms experiencing environmental turbulence approaching crisis proportions, it suggests that senior managers should act similarly to promote extensive communication throughout their firms, delegate problem-solving, and free employees from the superfluous constraints of bureaucracy.

Communication is central to success in galvanizing middle managers. Numerous observers point to middle managers' rancor over the political domination of strategic decision making by senior executives. Extensive surveys of midlevel executives—for instance those conducted by the American Management Association in 1967 and again in 1983—indicate extensive dissatisfaction with top management. The 1974 survey explicitly criticized top managers for their lack of responsiveness, while the 1983 survey accused senior executives of dishonesty in their dealings with middle managers.

Lacking trust in their leaders, many middle managers grow disaffected with their lot, and can easily sabotage implementation efforts.[24] Through their close contact with subordinates, customers, suppliers, and distributors, midlevel managers can either motivate or discourage cooperation with change efforts. Additionally, research suggests that middle managers are central to corporate innovation, and so their cooperation is necessary to realizing competitive parity in changing environments: They support initiatives from lower operating levels and thereby help senior executives' efforts to regenerate their firms' strategies.[25]

An analysis of 157 responses to a survey of top and middle managers in 20 firms provides support for a positive relationship between managers' involvement in strategic planning and corporate performance. As one manager put it, "since I have a better understanding of how decisions impact our customers, I could probably improve on what they're trying to do."[26]

Another observer has proposed that successful change depends in part on the quality of the strategic conversations top executives have with their middle managers. In these exchanges, juniors frequently experience exclusion from meaningful discussions of strategies themselves, thereby reducing their ownership and pride in the actions they are asked to take. Lacking opportunity to question the kinds of informational inputs relied on to justify change, middle managers are prevented from participating in the process of interpretation and so experience meaninglessness and isolation from the pivotal changes taking place.[27]

Top executives are often tempted to suppress strategic conversations with lower-level employees in order to consolidate their own power and status. Unfortunately they thereby reduce corporate effectiveness. Exclusion increases middle managers' apathy, reduces cooperation, and inadvertently promotes sabotage. In contrast, by engaging middle managers in more than nominal strategic conversations, senior executives expose key employees to the sense-making process through which strategic decisions are made, and so empower them to innovate creative solutions to corporate concerns.

To involve middle managers, however, is not to abdicate control. Top managers cross a fine line when they decentralize authority without retaining supervision of decisions made down the line. The disarray at Prudential-Bache Securities left behind by George Ball is a case in point. Known more as a cheerleader than a disciplinarian, during his 9-year tenure at Pru-Bache, Ball granted complete autonomy to profitable groups run by middle managers. When he resigned in 1991, he left behind more than $250 million in losses and a legal mess for parent Prudential Insurance Co. of America. Not coincidentally, his critics point out, he had also been E.F. Hutton's president when the firm was charged with overdrafting branch-office checking accounts around the country. Blaming itself for excessive decentralization, Hutton subsequently pleaded guilty to 2000 felony counts in 1985 and paid a $2-million fine. By then Ball had left for Pru-Bache, but the lack of oversight would cost Hutton both its reputation and its independence.[28]

Similarly, the debacle at First Boston in the late 1980s resulted in part from the rivalry between the Boston-based investment bank and the other subsidiaries of CS Holding, its Swiss parent. Under the leadership of Rainer Gut, Chairman of CS Holding, subsidiaries were granted complete autonomy and allowed to build self-contained empires, producing at First Boston stars like Bruce Wasserstein and Joseph Perella. Decentralization encouraged competition and squabbling between transatlantic subsidiaries that culminated in a house cleaning at First Boston and a shift in control from New York to Zurich.[29]

Effective leadership of a strategic change, therefore, involves defining a shared vision of how to compete, building consensus with midlevel managers about how to execute the vision, and encouraging local solutions to the problems that result as the change program is carried out—an ability to mobilize support and creativity from the firms as a whole.

Amassing Support

If carrying out a strategic change requires transformational leaders who recognize the importance of infecting middle managers with the enthusiasm necessary to carry out a vision without abdicating control, it also compels involvement of firms' lower-level employees, those individuals actually making products, delivering services, and interfacing with customers. Broad participation is particularly useful because strategic change heightens ambiguity, disrupts routines, and creates tension—all characteristics that call into question the effectiveness of authoritarian decision-making styles.[30]

Although we pay lip service to the notion of generating employee participation, most managers are raised on a hierarchical concept of organization, and so regard participation as an instrumental tool with which to achieve predefined ends. And, appropriately enough, cynical employees are well aware of this. Many refuse to get involved, resist change, and even actively sabotage managers' efforts.

In *The Critical Path*, Michael Beer and his colleagues emphasize the importance of creating an internal environment that allows *real* participation to develop. They find that successful leaders encourage a grass-roots level of participation that generates genuine enthusiasm, localized problem solving, and overcomes natural resistance to any imposed solution from top management.

More generally, research suggests that participative programs generally affect four critical aspects of firms: (1) decision-making and power, (2) information flows, (3) the rewards of work, and (4) the application of knowledge and skills. Participation decreases worker resistance to change because it induces managers to share power, information, rewards, and knowledge with lower-level employees.[31]

A recent comparison of 91 studies of employee participation contrasted different mechanisms that managers use to generate involvement. The analysts found that three forms of participation demonstrated consistently positive effects on performance and satisfaction: formal systems, informal exchanges, and employee ownership.[32]

Quality circles are one example of formal systems that some 2500 U.S. companies, enthused by so-called Japanese management practices, rely on increasingly to generate participation and mobilize support for change among lower-level employees. In the typical quality circle, groups of employees meet 1 hour a week on company time to discuss ways to make changes in operating procedures that will improve departmental performance. Westinghouse, for instance, maintains over 1600 quality circles in 200 locations, groups that involve, not only blue-collar, but also white-collar employees. In all, about 16,000 of its employees meet regularly in these groups to focus on product improvement possibilities, affording top managers a direct mechanism for communicating with employees and receiving feedback about the impact of its their efforts at strategic change.

Informal participation occurs through the interpersonal exchanges employees have with their supervisors. Like top managers' strategic conversations with middle managers, lower-level employees appear to welcome informal exchanges with superiors that empower them to provide input on work-related decisions. Research findings suggest that informal participation is associated with favorable self-reports of job satisfaction, and may therefore facilitate bringing employees on board when effecting strategic change.

A more radical solution to mobilizing lower-level employees has involved instituting employee stock ownership plans (ESOP). In 1976, there were only 1000 firms owned by employees in the United States. By 1989, an estimated 10,000 companies of all sizes had operational stock ownership plans to which they distributed yearly tax-exempt profits covering over 10 million workers. Studies of firms with ESOPs uniformly conclude that ownership enhances both productivity and satisfaction: Profits were 50 percent higher in a sample of 98 employee-owned firms, while a more recent analysis of 37 firms concluded that ownership increased employees' involvement with their work.[33]

Stock ownership generates favorable outcomes primarily because it produces psychological ownership, a result of using various formal tools (e.g., more meetings, voting of shares) to encourage participation in making work decisions. In firms with large blocks of shares in the hands of employees, managers share information more widely, which fosters interaction and feedback.[34] To get workers thinking like owners, more and more companies are adding stock option plans to their benefits. Pfizer has had one since the 1950s. PepsiCo revitalized the idea when it unveiled one in 1989. The PepsiCo plan gives workers the right to buy, 5 years hence, stock valued at up to 10 percent of their pay.[35]

So different mechanisms for enhancing participation prove useful in promoting efforts to adapt firms to changing environments. Formal systems such as quality circles, quality of work life programs, and employee stock ownership plans successfully mobilize workers behind a change program when they are tied to a shared philosophy that cuts through all levels of the firm. By increasing formal and informal participation, managers promote employees' psychological involvement, make their firms more flexible, creative, and innovative, and so facilitate strategic change.[36]

Recognize, however, that participation does not mean achieving complete harmony. As social psychologist William Foote Whyte observed many years ago, ". . . harmony is an undesirable goal for the functioning of a complex organization. The objective should not be to build a harmonious organization, but rather to build an organization capable of recognizing the problems it faces and of developing ways of solving these problems."[37]

Involving Stakeholders

Most firms abide by a tradition of arm's-length relationships that has limited the degree of trust stakeholders have in managers' motives. Lacking information about—and identification with—corporate objectives, suppliers and customers have tended to invest little in cooperative efforts with managers. Increasingly, managers recognize, however, that their firms' competitiveness depends on their ability to better coordinate the flows of goods and services to and from key suppliers and customers. Competition forces attention to the quality of firms' products, and highlights the deficiencies of traditional arm's-length relationships that discourage suppliers from close involvement with their customers.

Accounts of how managers in Japan closely coordinate activities with their firms' parts suppliers through the *kanban* (just-in-time) system illustrate how improvements result. Through the close ties Japanese firms have with their *keiretsu* partners, managers maintain extremely low inventory levels. Suppliers are encouraged to invest in technologies that enhance the quality of parts delivered, and participate in managers' strategic efforts to improve overall product quality. Since parts are delivered as needed, product design changes are more easily effected: No obsolete inventories result, and lower re-manufacturing costs are involved. Similarly, Japanese managers rely heavily on loyal customers who routinely provide feedback, consult on research, and participate in market assessments of firms' products.

Globalization is forcing American firms to forge similar partnerships. Corporate leaders look for ways of minimizing costs and enhancing quality by establishing close linkages with both suppliers and customers. Strategic change invariably affects firms' products, and so indirectly impacts corporate suppliers and customers. By involving their vertical partners early in the process of planning, managers can anticipate and counter unexpected bottlenecks and technical impediments that could impede implementation.[38]

Reaching out to customers can take many forms. Many managers looking to build stronger ties with customers cleverly involve them more closely in their firms' hiring and developmental activities. They remind us that, after all, focus groups need not be used solely in the context of developing feedback about products for marketing purposes. At GE, for instance, customers provide feedback about individual managers, which feeds into succession plans. Whirlpool incorporates into its own managers' training programs a module on Sears, a key account. Digital Equipment relies heavily on customer specifications to formulate product standards in its manufacturing operations. By involving customers, these firms dissolve traditional boundaries and so induce greater customer commitment.[39]

As Table 8.1 suggests, successful implementation of strategic changes in rapidly changing environments requires leaders committed to increasing involvement of all employees and stakeholders in the task of regenerating the competitiveness and effectiveness of firms.

A Leader for Every Strategy

Implementing strategic change requires a distinctive breed of senior executive at the helm, distinguished less by traits and more by background. In particular, having the right kind of prior experience appears

Table 8.1. Strategic Decision Making

	In stable environments	In changing environments
Leadership	Dictatorial	Transformational
Middle managers	Compliant	Empowered
Employees	Obedient	Participative
Stakeholders	Negotiated	Collaborative

to help executives to act as transformational leaders in inspiring and mobilizing employees, unions, suppliers, regulators, and other stakeholders to recognize the environmental pressures firms experience and to collaborate with attempts to implement strategic change. Research confirms some implications for the kinds of experiences valuable to top managers concerned about initiating and implementing strategic changes at the business, corporate, and collective levels.

Business Leaders as Experts

Changing environments push managers toward more aggressive business strategies and so call for a broad cross section of employees who pull together to extend firms' abilities to innovate, differentiate firms' products from competitors,' improve quality, or reduce operating costs. Effective leaders of business units that underwent change in recent years had characteristics appropriate to their firms' competitive strategies. For instance, a study of 58 business units of large firms found that better-performing growth businesses were run by executives with greater marketing and sales experience, willingness to take risks, and tolerance for ambiguity.[40]

A follow-up analysis of 121 business units concluded that different strategies did call for distinct managerial backgrounds.[41] Not surprisingly, functional experience in R&D, for instance, was more likely to contribute to the effectiveness of a business pursuing a differentiation strategy. Innovating businesses require leaders imbued with an understanding of the underlying technologies with which their firms compete. Renowned entrepreneurs like Ed Land at Polaroid, Steve Jobs at Apple, and Tom Watson, Sr. at IBM come to mind—pioneers whose commitment to the technological endeavor was unquestionably the driving force behind their firms' business-level strategies.

Investment banks have traditionally been led by two sorts of leaders: traders and bankers. The recent histories of prominent Wall Street firms describe the strengths and weaknesses that each brings to the leadership role: At Lehman Brothers, the traders gained ascendancy in the bull market of the 1970s, jeopardizing the old world banking culture of the firm, and forcing a merger with Shearson. More recently, at Salomon Brothers the aggressive trading culture was challenged explicitly by the Board's strategic decision to appoint a nontrader as chief operating officer following the crisis-driven departure of long-time CEO John Guttfreund.[42]

Research on leadership in high tech firms confirms the importance of involving junior managers when pursuing an innovation-based strategic change. Because technology so quickly renders products obsolete, senior managers in high-tech industries facilitate innovation by insisting on a free flow of ideas, opening up the decision-making process to junior managers, and encouraging strategic participation across the board in the selection of ideas. Since involvement is risky, empowerment of midlevel employees is eased by norms that encourage risk taking and recognize that failures are inevitable but tolerable.[43]

Provoked by change in either technology or regulation, many firms sought to implement radical change in their products and markets. Contrary to popular belief, preparation for radical change and its subsequent implementation were better achieved, not by traditional top-down command structures, but by a decision-making process that mobilized a broad coalition of middle managers, located an upper-level sponsor, and bypassed formal channels. A case study of a large high-tech company demonstrated that major innovations resulted when these "autonomous loops" were mobilized. Talented engineers bombarded key sponsors with initiatives and ideas, engaging them in strategic conversations. In firms where senior executives acknowledged the importance of these sidebars and actively participated in a political, bottom-up process of change, greater effectiveness resulted.[44]

In contrast, cost-based business strategies call for leaders more oriented to process engineering and operational tasks. Top managers with backgrounds in production tend to enhance the performance of firms competing on the basis of price. Leaders with prior experience in retrenchment settings, in businesses that required firms to pare down costs, carefully monitor expenditures, enforce rules, and minimize overhead, which enhances profitability and competitiveness. Because tasks are known and programmable, these managers tend to rely on more authoritarian hierarchies to direct their change programs. Controls are more systematic, quantitative, and routinized, and they incline their firms more toward bureaucratic procedures.

In the publishing industry, strategic change has meant a new kind of executive at the helm, more marketer than scholar. German media giant Bertelsmann A.G. paid $475 million for Doubleday & Company in 1986 and merged it with Bantam. Concerned about limp profits, in 1991 they appointed a former marketing executive from noted promoter Pepsico to the top spot as vice chairman of the publishing house. The move parallels changes at Random House and Simon & Schuster where both top jobs are held by marketing oriented managers rather than literary gurus.[45]

Corporate Leaders as Integrators

At the corporate level, building synergy across a portfolio of businesses requires overcoming the parochial interests of individual companies whose divergent histories, cultures, and practices pull the corporate parent in contrary directions. To effectively manage highly coupled businesses, corporate leaders need greater versatility and broader experience in multiple businesses, which can help elicit cooperation from division-level employees.

For instance, in a bold departure from tradition, a special committee of outside directors from Philip-Morris' board named Michael Miles, a non-smoking executive from its Kraft General Foods subsidiary, the new chairman, effective September 1991. The selection appears to signal the end of an era that saw the transformation of Philip Morris from a tobacco company to one whose portfolio is now dominated by food and consumer products. Clearly, the board felt that the company's corporate strategy of related diversification called for a leader whose background characteristics would both support and symbolize the reorientation.[46]

Or take American Express. In the early 1980s, Chairman James Robinson's visionary strategy of forging a financial service empire seemed eminently plausible. The firm would capitalize on selling its services across customer groups. To this end, Robinson embarked AmEx on strategic acquisitions of Fireman's Fund Insurance, broker Shearson Loeb Rhoades, investment banker Lehman Brothers, retail broker E.F. Hutton, Swiss private banker Trade Development Bank, and mass market investment advisor IDS. Unfortunately, synergy with "The Card" has proved elusive. Robinson decentralized decision making to subsidiary executives, each of which eventually bore the blame for failure to deliver bottom-line results, and then left AmEx. Did Robinson delegate inappropriately in trying to build a core diversifier? Might a team structure have produced greater integration?[47] Perhaps. In July 1991, Robinson created a more centralized "office of the chairman" by appointing the head of American Express' best-performing subsidiary, IDS Financial Services, to the presidency of the firm. He also took the opportunity to identify two principal strategic objectives: Restoring Shearson Lehman to "full profitability and stature" and capitalizing on the brand franchise of American Express.[48]

Extensive familiarity with both the firm and industry enhances the likelihood that a corporate executive will have the required credibility to implement strategic change in a firm trying to increase relatedness across its business portfolio Broad-based experience and limited industry specialization also reduce the likelihood that the top executive will be accused of bias and favoritism toward a particular business, and can help overcome political resistance to a change that commits the firm to a core competence.[49] At Amex, Robinson's background in investment banking at Morgan Guaranty Trust and his local experience rising up through the ranks of AmEx doubtless helped give him the credibility to commit the firm to the related diversification he sought throughout the 1980s.

In contrast, conglomerate strategies have been implemented more successfully by authoritarian senior managers whose backgrounds are primarily in accounting and finance. To treat firms as portfolios requires a willingness to acquire and divest businesses rapidly strictly on the basis of financial profitability and risk, without corporate involvement in their underlying operations or commitment to their employees. Conglomerator Harold Geneen demonstrated how an authoritarian leadership style and nimble juggling of businesses could produce corporate profitability for ITT in the 1970s.

Today, the kinds of revolutionary changes taking place in the environment force managers to identify and exploit synergies across businesses. As firms embark on programs to link their business units more closely, effective leadership at the corporate level increasingly calls for personable executives skilled in the fine art of communicating across boundaries, with backgrounds developed through multibusiness, multifunctional experience.

Collective Leaders as Statesmen

Shaping and maintaining strategic relationships with competitors, suppliers, unions, the media, government, and other stakeholders demands that senior executives act increasingly as institutional statesmen, recognizing not only their own objectives but those of partners in strategic alliances—defending not only their firms' interests, but also the wider concerns of society at large.

Take Alfred Herrhausen, the former chief executive of Germany's Deutsche Bank who was slain by terrorists in November 1989. He is the acknowledged catalyst of the 119-year-old Bank's strategic change toward a pan-European presence. He was also a pioneer in championing management philosophies that frowned on Germany's traditional emphasis on authoritarianism and recognized a role for executives as institutional statesmen, readily combining politics with business, and favoring more democratic input from firms' diverse constituents.[50]

As chairman and CEO of General Electric, Reginald Jones was applauded for his statesmanship in dealings with unions, regulators, and competitors. He also chaired the Business Roundtable in Washington, a key group that brings together the CEOs of the largest firms in the United States to develop a shared platform on the macroconcerns of business, with an eye to influencing legislators and politicians.[51]

Institutional pressures compel managers now to perform as diplomats in their dealings with vocal and powerful environmental actors. Diplomacy also proves necessary as managers cooperate with competitors in trade associations, in lobbying regulators, and in strategic alliances to share information, technology, and services.

More than ever, perhaps, corporate leaders also assume ambassadorial and institutional responsibilities. Media presentations and charitable activities have become routine aspects of executives' jobs, as are sponsorships of public schools, forays into vocational training in underprivileged areas, and programs for making corporate activities environment-friendly.

At Du Pont Co., for instance, over $1.5 million has been spent between 1989 and 1991 to build child care centers near its major work sites in the United States. Spurred by senior executives advocating profamily policies, the company is now at the forefront of developing policies designed to help employees balance family life and careers through generous benefits for birth, adoption, relatives' illness, flexible hours, job sharing for working mothers, and other family-friendly programs.[52]

Such initiatives suggest how deeply executives experience the environmental pressure to make firms relate to their social settings. At the collective level, transformational leadership compels managers' involvement, not only as organizational caretakers, but as moral guardians of the social fabric.

Improving Governance

What can inspire top managers to overcome inertia, to pursue rather than resist strategic change? Three factors appear to facilitate strategic leadership and change: (1) the nature of the top team surrounding the CEO; (2) the composition of the board of directors; and (3) the CEO's compensation package.

Building Top Teams

Although most forms of strategic change doubtless are spearheaded by CEOs, their success in conceiving and carrying out a transformation depends heavily on characteristics of the top management team, the key cabal that forms around the chief executive. Unfortunately, many CEOs favor teams of one. At over 80 percent of *Business Week*'s top 1000 firms, one person rules as both chairman of the board and chief executive. Not surprisingly, it encourages imperialism, and many critics suggest a separation of roles and a strengthening of the top team as a way of mitigating dictatorship and resistance to change.[53]

Top teams differ in bringing together managers who are more or less similar in age, background, experience, values, and attitudes.[54] Observations of top managers of 199 banks indicate that more innovative banks were managed by team members who were more educated and diverse in functional areas of expertise.[55] Similarly, an investigation of 100 firms showed that top teams whose managers were longer tenured demonstrated greater persistence in keeping their firms on historical strategies, as well as greater conformity to the typical strategies through which firms competed in their industries.[56]

A wealth of analysis by social psychologists insists that more homogeneous groups tend to reach agreement more quickly, to experience less internal conflict, and so to become more cohesive. Nonetheless, various observers have debated the merits for firms of homogeneity and consensus among upper-echelon managers. On one hand, they point out, homogeneity facilitates achieving consensus and so making more timely decisions. On the other hand, by suppressing conflict, homogeneity underexposes managers to information that might have altered the decisions taken. Following his takeover of Primerica in August 1988, for instance, Sandy Weill brought in two prominent Wall Street executives, Frank Zarb and Lew Glucksman, to run Smith Barney. The team was built on complementary strengths: Weill was the architect of Shearson Loeb Rhoades, the brokerage firm built from acquisitions; Zarb built the back office that became the backbone of Weill's Shearson; and Glucksman was the notorious trader and former CEO of Lehman Brothers that was swallowed up by American Express and folded into Shearson in 1984. Early on, the trio agreed to work in a consultative manner, with each one technically holding veto power over key decisions, but with Zarb, as Chairman and CEO of Smith Barney, in command.

So agreement among top managers cuts both ways.[57]

In fact, homogeneity and consensus in top teams appears to reduce corporate performance when firms are competing in turbulent environments. So, when contemplating strategic change, effective CEOs do not surround themselves with yes men. Greater diversity of opinions and lack of agreement force top managers to process more information during decision making, and so to consider more alternatives. To minimize premature closure, CEOs of better-performing firms, not only build coalitions with executives more likely to disagree, but also cultivate less structured interactions in meetings, less formalization of roles, and less reliance on bureaucratic procedures. They manage by opening up decisions to disagreement, by walking around, by listening to broad cross sections of employees, and by suppressing familiar status symbols like parking spots, corner offices, or executive dining rooms.[58]

Good Boards, Bad Boards

As representatives of stakeholders' interests, directors are responsible for actively monitoring and controlling the actions of managers. Abundant evidence suggests, however, that most boards fail in that role, having been made subservient by aggressive top managers to whom directors are indebted, on whom they rely for information about internal goings on, and who find it relatively easy to suppress dissent and cajole directors into complacency.

The fear that truly independent outside directors can inspire may never have been more visible than at Sears Roebuck & Co, whose CEO Ed

Brennan reportedly spent $5.6 million to deny shareholder activist Robert Monks a seat on the board. Monks campaigned on the claim that Sears had been stagnant in recent years, partly because of insider control of the board, and because of claims that those insiders formulate strategy for the company principally to perpetuate their own positions in the firm.[59] Win or lose, the claim is clearly stated: Board composition dramatically impacts firms' likelihood of favoring strategic change.

Despite formal support from institutions like the New York Stock Exchange, the Securities and Exchange Commission, and the American Law Institute for naming outsiders as directors, many corporate boards continue to be dominated by insiders, that is, executives who are also members of the top management team. Insiders are more likely to go along with CEO options, and so are unlikely to provide independent input into strategic decisions. Research suggests that even outsiders get coopted: Many owe their appointments to incumbent CEOs, and so support their opinions.[60] A more attractive option may be to insist that directors themselves be shareholders.

Firms that lack an independent board are more likely to succumb to inertial forces that favor the status quo. The more top teams dominate the board through insider appointments, the more likely they are to screen out information that might compel strategic change. Healthy boards bring breadth and diversity to firms, and a stronger representation of shareholder interests that compels managers to confront events, opinions, and possibilities they otherwise choose to bypass. A study of prominent firms incorporated in Delaware found that boards sued had a larger proportion of insiders than those not sued.[61]

Executives often opt to paper the board with independent but inactive directors—frequently celebrities who lend their cachet and little else to the firm. Nonetheless, in recent years the proportion of celebrity outsiders sitting on corporate boards has declined systematically, due partly to the increasing time commitment required of board members and the greater likelihood of lawsuits filed against directors.[62]

Aware that inertia leads incumbent executives to favor the status quo, many boards vote to recruit outsiders when faced with a crisis that requires their firms to change corporate trajectories. When the Salomon Brothers market-tampering charge became public in August 1991, the board replaced outgoing Chairman John Guttfreund with prominent investor and director Warren Buffett. Outside hires are unencumbered by internal commitments to the political hierarchy and are more likely to bring fresh enthusiasm to firms. They also signal greater credibility to external observers—witness the positive reception by regulators and the media to the Buffett selection.[63]

In fact, one study of restructurings found that incumbents were 3 times less likely to initiate "frame-breaking" changes than CEOs recruited externally.[64] Numerous examples come to mind: Lee Iacocca brought in from Ford to spearhead Chrysler's reorganization under government supervision in 1979 or John Sculley brought in from PepsiCo to reorient Apple in 1982. More recently, Rod Canion, Compaq's founder, was booted out of the CEO job by his directors—the motive? Knowledge that a strategic change was needed, and that Canion was too wedded to the status quo.[65]

One indication that directors are increasingly concerned about strategic change is the dramatic rise in turnover rates of CEOs. A study of 227 *Fortune* 1000 companies found that the rate of outsider CEOs tripled from 9 percent in the late 1960s to 27 percent in the 1980s, while an analysis of 667 position changes among 2500 public firms reported by the *Wall Street Journal* during 1978 and 1979 found a turnover rate of some 27 percent, or a CEO change on average once every 3 years.[66]

At the Goodyear Tire and Rubber Company, insider CEOs have been the norm. In 1991, the board selected Stanley Gault, former head of Rubbermaid, as its first outsider to the top post since 1926. Gault's reputation was built at Rubbermaid where he engineered a turnaround through cost cutting, work force reductions, and innovation, catapulting the company's earnings sixfold in his 11-year tenure. At Goodyear, the board clearly expects similar efforts to prune losses, reduce debt, and refocus the company around its core strength in tires.[67]

To introduce strategic change, firms whose boards bring in external CEOs typically move through five phases, what Harvard's John Gabarro labeled "taking hold," "immersion," "reshaping," "consolidation," and "refinement." Taking hold involves asserting control over the firm. Through immersion in firm-specific conditions, new executives establish competence and credibility. Reshaping involves building consensus, securing commitment to a particular direction, and designing suitable structures. Finally, by creating motivating systems, executives refine firms' movement toward strategic objectives.

Detailed observation of a $400-million U.S. distributor of liquefied propane gas suggests that, in fact, strategic change involves two sets of activities: (1) a plan for implementation of change that addresses both short- and long-run concerns, and (2) a plan for addressing political concerns that arise when change is called for. By engaging firms and their boards through these activities, new CEOs begin the process of reorienting firms and implementing strategic change.[68]

Pay for Performance

Concerned observers also point to the lack of a relationship between top managers' pay and corporate performance as evidence of boards' failure to control compensation setting. Insofar as CEOs set their own pay, they are more likely to be risk averse and so to favor guaranteed forms of compensation rather than pay that is tied to the profitability of their firms' stock price.[69]

A study by reformed-compensation consultant Graef Crystal found that CEOs at the largest American companies are paid 150 times more than the average U.S. worker. By comparison, the ratio is a lowly 17 in Japan. In dollars, the difference is staggering: The average American CEO brings home $2.8 million; the average Japanese CEO, $300,000.* Moreover, the data demonstrate a poor relationship between CEO pay and corporate performance.

Since compensation is a prime motivator, there is good reason to question whether top management pay practices encourage or retard efforts to produce strategic change. Tying managers' pay to short-run measures such as profitability appears to discourage what might be much needed investments in high-cost activities such as product development, which have longer-term pay-offs. Firms that compensate their CEOs with long-term contingent pay tend to have higher R&D expenditures.[70]

Compensation consultants suggest, in fact, that to capitalize on the motivational value of pay, compensation packages should consist of a balanced mix of salary, bonus tied to corporate profitability, and stock options whose value increases with stock price.[71] Goodyear's board, for one, seems to have recognized that fact when it appointed Stanley Gault to the top job in the company: The directors tied his compensation package directly to the stock's long-term performance.[72]

In addition to its motivational effect on top managers, pay also has value as a symbol. High pay signals to observers that firms have a secure competitive advantage, enjoy excess resources, and are able to afford waste. When Lee Iacocca cut his own salary to $1 in 1980, he symbolized his deep commitment to the strategic change and motivated employees to stay aboard. Pay also reflects the supply of well-regarded managers: Firms must pay dearly to get executives whose reputations precede them in the managerial labor market.[73]

Active boards of directors, therefore, can use pay as a tool for inducing managerial support for strategic change. By tying components of pay to both short term and long term, that is, to accounting and market measures of performance, they are more likely to encourage top managers to engage in the kind of balanced risk taking required to reorient their firms. By benchmarking executive pay to industry-wide norms, they also limit the potential for corporate excess and provide shareholders a clear-cut justification of the company's pay levels.

---

*Different authors make different estimates, depending on whether or not total pay includes or excludes stock options. *Business Week* estimates the ratio of pay from top to bottom in the United States to be 85, but that excludes stock distributions. Crystal's (1991) numbers include an estimate of the value of CEOs' unexercised stock options.

Lead the Way

Just as our popular culture thrives on celebrity, reveres reputation, and worships stardom, so too does our business culture tend to overidolize its corporate leaders. In that heady atmosphere it becomes all too easy to forget that successfully guiding a strategic change requires, not only visionary leaders, but also a strong top team, a cooperative middle stratum, and a mobilized work force.

Strategic change surely begins with a viable vision. But senior executives are credible agents of change only when their actions breed followers: Their ability to lead is inversely tied to their reliance on either authority or power to implement these changes. To command a revitalization from the top down is to short-circuit the necessary mobilization of all employees and stakeholders in the process of transformation.

Leadership, however, should be appropriate to the strategies firms pursue. Within businesses, competitive pressure requires leaders who understand success factors and can apply operational skills to ensure that firms' strategic postures are supported through the design of systems that mobilize employees behind them. At the corporate level, senior executives are pushed to help define core competencies and build stronger linkages across business units. Additionally, environmental turbulence pressures top managers to play an institutional role as statesmen and ambassadors to regulators, foreign governments, the media, the financial markets, and other key institutions.

Visionary executives recognize the effect that their top teams, boards of directors, and corporate pay practices have on their ability to stimulate strategic change. They welcome diversity instead of insularity, outsiders rather than insiders, and prefer to make pay contingent on multiple measures of performance. The few firms willing to show such internal restraint should also recognize the wholesale changes they will necessitate in the cultural features of their firms.

9

Reshaping Corporate Cultures

*If the rascals knew the advantages of virtue,
they would become honest men out of
rascality.*

BENJAMIN FRANKLIN

Leadership can mobilize attention to a new vision, but it is the corporate culture that ultimately confers legitimacy on that vision. Strategic change commands a commitment to articulating and communicating new world views, and careful attention to the cultural contradictions between the new world views and existing practices.

Take Salomon Brothers, the latest investment bank to have been caught bending the financial rules. After the resignation of Salomon's top team, well-known investor and board member Warren Buffett was named chairman and CEO. As he pointed out, the company's aggressive risk-taking culture had much to do with encouraging violations of securities laws on the government bond trading desk. It had the makings of "what some people might call macho and others, cavalier. I don't think the same thing would have happened in a monastery."[1]

In July 1991, the Bank of England led a seven-nation effort to seize the assets of the Bank of Credit and Commerce International. According to the governor of the Bank of England, for years BCCI was guided by a "criminal culture." Through a complex web of financial transactions, bribes were apparently paid, drug money laundered, dictators supported, and terrorists financed. Its success was partly predicated on strong relationships with high-profile statesmen and lobbyists around the

184

world. Incredible as it seems, few appear ever to have perceived the ethical transgressions that spurred an international investigation into the bank's global activities.[2]

It appears to have fooled even esteemed lobbyist Clark Clifford. As he told the U.S. House Banking Committee, despite many close contacts with BCCI as the chairman of First American Bankshares, he was unaware that BCCI held a controlling interest in First American. As he rationalized:

> ...in BCCI there were really two banks. There was this outside façade thing. That's the one we dealt with. In all these years, we didn't encounter a single suspicious circumstance. And I think the reason is because they had that second inside bank, and that's the one that was engaged in what we've read about so much in the paper... Apparently we were deceived. I don't know that it's any comfort, but the Bank of England was deceived. My judgment is questionable. I guess I should have in some way sensed it. I did not. Others perhaps should have sensed it... I want to know how it can be prevented in the future, and that is a main aim of mine.[3]

Corporate cultures mold the way employees see the world. Because what one sees depends on where one stands, environmental changes invariably are perceived differently by employees who belong to different national cultures, professional cultures, departments, and other corporate subcultures. Not only are top managers' favored responses to ongoing changes likely to differ, but so are employees' understandings likely to vary—and so are their abilities to conceive and their willingness to go along with a strategic change.

Revolutionary change challenges entrenched values held by employees. To reform established firms is therefore to run up against the practices, rituals, and norms to which employees have grown accustomed. That means managers must engineer the interpretations employees will make of their initiatives, and so pave the way for a new vision of how work should be done in the future.[4]

Various aspects of firms' cultures result partly from the unique histories of firms themselves, and partly from the particular administrative systems and structures with which senior managers choose to operate. Founders imprint a particular style onto their firms, which lingers long after they have departed. The folklore of most large firms abounds with many true stories—but also with tall tales—about the actions taken by visionary executives. Cultural histories are passed on by long-term employees to describe aspects of firms' unique experiences, interpretations of events, and sanctioned values. In firms with coherent internal cultures, shared worldviews also result from the kinds of controls and competencies firms have developed over time, which provide them with a source of advantage in the marketplace.

But the values to which employees adhere derive, not only from the features of the firms within which people work, but also from characteristics of the societies and business communities firms themselves inhabit. Societies provide the raw material of corporate cultures by infusing specific events and actions with shared meaning. For instance, expressing dissent might be welcomed as a creative input in a management meeting in more conflictually oriented U.S. firms. In consensus-oriented Japan, its expression tends to be viewed as disrespectful.

National cultures imbue a work force with particular value orientations, expectations about relationships, and interpretations of work. As firms cope with globalization by deploying assets across multiple cultures, their own internal cultures grow more diverse, increasing the complexity managers face as they try to integrate operations in which employees have differing sensitivities, attitudes, and understandings.

Moreover, aspects of firms' cultures derive from the institutional matrix of relationships that binds firms into business communities. Business communities bring together individuals with similar education and training, a shared understanding of their competitors, and common mind sets.[5] Individuals working within a community compete for the same jobs, attend the same social functions, and orbit around the same regulatory agencies and professional groups. Naturally, then, the values expressed within a firm are partly a reflection of these community-wide values and attitudes.

Given the multiple influences on corporate cultures, to alter intentionally a company's culture is a difficult endeavor, one likely to meet with considerable resistance. Cultures are not merely an assemblage of corporate features resembling organization charts. They constitute a means through which workers make sense of the technical and organizational worlds they inhabit. Because they are unique, they also comprise for firms assets that competitors find difficult to imitate. The challenge for managers embarking on strategic change is to apprehend the symbolic features of corporate life that are to some extent manipulable, and to explore avenues for reducing reactance and prodding change—without damaging those features that provide firms a degree of competitive advantage.

Moreover, as nations interpenetrate and as firms globalize, the cultural bonds that once tied employees closely to one another are weakening. Increasing diversity means firms' cultures are becoming more diluted and incoherent, less capable of providing firms with the internal glue that once shaped common interpretations of environments, strategies, and events. At the same time, environments are placing pressure on managers to make their internal cultures, not only more efficient and entrepreneurial, but also more equitable and ethical. In response, the more visionary are recognizing the merits of building within their firms "ownership cultures"—thin, lean cultures that cherish self-control, pay for performance, and deemphasize status differences. Future corporate leaders are

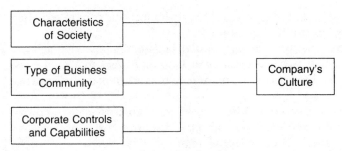

Figure 9.1. Determinants of a company's culture.

likely to rely simultaneously on cultural symbols that support efficiency, entrepreneurship, and ehtics to entice employees and other stakeholders, to participate in strategic change.

Cultural Barriers to Change

Employees' actions are governed by norms that express the content of firms' cultures and specify the boundaries of acceptable behavior.* (See Fig. 9.1.) To attempt a strategic change is invariably to run up hard against a wall of cultural codes that derive from firms' operations in multiple countries, firms' membership in multiple business communities, and firms' established self-image and identity.

Barriers to Globalization

Corporate cultures are partly rooted in the national cultures of their countries of origin. So long as a firm's operations were circumscribed to the domestic scene, and insofar as employees were homegrown, few cultural stresses were ever diagnosed. The study of corporate culture, in fact, began in earnest in the 1960s as U.S. firms expanded abroad and found themselves struggling to absorb a managerial cast whose members manifested increasing diversity, and as firms from other countries (espe-

---

*As two researchers have put it:

> Any organizational culture consists broadly of longstanding rules of thumb, a somewhat special language, an ideology that helps edit a member's everyday experience, shared standards of relevance as to the critical aspects of the work that is being accomplished, matter-of-fact prejudices, models for social etiquette and demeanor, certain customs and rituals suggestive of how members are to relate to colleagues, subordinates, superiors, and outsiders and a sort of residual category of some rather plain 'horse sense' regarding what is appropriate and 'smart' behavior within the organization and what is not.[6]

cially Japan) demonstrated considerably greater internal coherence when they set up shop in the United States.

In the last decade, a number of popular best-sellers have detailed the features of Japanese firms. They urged U.S. managers to emulate the unique controls and practices of Japanese managers in order to improve productivity.[7]

Yet there are good reasons to be skeptical of such cross-cultural transplants. Transferring seemingly valuable but disparate corporate features proves difficult partly because those features make sense only in the context of their own environments. As some analysts stress, it is impossible to divorce the firm from the cultural milieu from which it derives. Japan's consensus-based management practices are rooted in a distinct cultural context that espouses harmony rather than conflict, favors collectivism rather than individualism, and fosters dependency rather than autonomy.

Students of multinationals indicate the difficulties that Japanese firms themselves continue to face in applying group-oriented decision making in an alien environment like the United States. Of the three principal approaches relied on by Japanese firms operating American subsidiaries, only *imperialist* firms—principally large trading companies such as Sumitomo, Mitsui, and C. Itoh—have opted to transplant wholesale their Japanese practices, thereby severely limiting local hires and treating them as outsiders. Firms such as Honda and Nissan, recognizing the difficulty of operating with their unique management styles in densely populated settings, chose to set up their operations in isolated areas where they could exert power over local communities and act like army barracks to socialize local employees.[8] Aware of the difficulties involved in inducing urban employees to operate under consensual approaches, firms like Matsushita, Sanyo, Sharp, and Sony elected to apply Japanese practices quite selectively and with minimal fanfare.

A number of U.S. firms attempting to import Japanese practices appear to have failed. The records of firms that have chosen a piecemeal approach, mimicking only selected features of Japanese firms, suggest that their innovations have proven "largely cosmetic and exploitative, confined to employee participation at the lower level, and discarded when pressures mounted from management to follow through."[9]

Anthropologists often describe how societies differ and point to the influence of cultural characteristics on the managerial practices of firms in Japan, Europe, South America, and the United States. An early analysis of American managers, for instance, concluded that they demonstrated distinct and enduring values that differed from those revealed by managers from Japan, Australia, India, and Korea.[10] An examination of a prominent U.S. multinational also showed that the values of its employees were influenced by the local cultures in which they worked.[11]

Subsequent studies amplified that fact by suggesting how distinct groupings of countries (such as Latin American, Anglo, Latin European, and Germanic) could be distinguished by language, religion, and geography. Within these country groupings, employees demonstrate greater similarity of basic values and attitudes to work.[12] Local differences originate, not only in historical cultural commonalities, but also in the particular educational, governmental, and economic conditions peculiar to countries of the region. These enduring cultural differences often present significant impediments to firms struggling to globalize their operations.

Community-Wide Barriers

Insofar as strategic change involves attacking values and norms rooted deeply within a business community, they prove more difficult to change. Business communities set norms of conduct for all employees. Many communities are anchored around core technologies that delineate firms' capabilities, and thus the backgrounds, skills, and training of employees; their work values; and much of the content of firms' cultures. Shared beliefs emerge from the constant exchange among these firms of personnel and information, which creates a common stock of knowledge that employees rely on to solve work problems. In Silicon Valley, for instance, careers are built as entrepreneurs, engineers, scientists, managers, and clerical workers jump from firm to firm in the wider high tech corporate communities within these regions.[13] Internally, these firms demonstrate seemingly contradictory characteristics that are widely shared by all rapidly growing firms in the region, whether in pursuing both efficiency and innovation; centralizing decision making while encouraging professional autonomy; or allowing political fiefdoms while insisting on the importance of intensive coordination.[14]

Features of communities trickle down to individual employees and help to shape their understandings of work and of the environment. For instance, business communities differ in being more or less homogeneous, that is, in the extent to which employee attitudes are more similar among member firms. Communities whose employees belong to large professional associations, who are heavily unionized, or who are heavily regulated, tend to display greater internal homogeneity; and their employees demonstrate greater conformity to shared professional codes of conduct.[15] For instance, the heavily regulated and professionalized commercial, investment banking, and insurance communities are more homogenous than, say, the motion picture, music recording, or mass media communities. The heterogeneous composition of the motion picture industry is visible in the latter's more overt forms of conflict and varied displays of creativity in language, styles of dress, and products.[16]

When managers try to carry out a strategic change that attacks core values in tighter, more homogeneous corporate communities, they threaten the essence of the community itself, and so face greater resistance. Efforts to implement change must overcome, not only local corporate resistance, but the organized resistance of community-wide interests such as unions, professional groups, and other groups with a stake in the _status quo_. When the _Chicago Tribune_ attempted to introduce new printing technology into the operations of its subsidiary the _New York Daily News_, it ran smack into the unions, concerned with the layoff implications of the new technologies. The prolonged strike mobilized community-wide attention and culminated in the sale of the paper to British media king Robert Maxwell early in 1991. How the new management team deals with the mandatory shift to a more competitive operating technology remains to be seen. Similarly, when in 1991 U.S. railroads insisted on renegotiating century-old work rules that have kept staffing levels on freight trains at arbitrarily high levels, they attacked community-wide values. The result? Eleven unions chose to strike, paralyzing the economy for 2 days and forcing congressional intervention.[17]

Developing Cultural Strategies

To carry out a strategic change is to attack the configuration of internal features that is at the heart of a firm's "identity." Managers rely on three sets of corporate controls to reshape their firms' cultural environments: (1) reward systems, (2) educational systems, and (3) socialization systems. Implementing strategic change requires adapting all three systems to new realities.

Reward Systems. People do what they are rewarded to do. Managers motivate employees by tying bonuses and other forms of incentive compensation to completing specific objectives. Because strategic change redefines corporate and business objectives, it requires managers to rethink the criteria according to which they distribute attractive rewards, particularly incentive compensation. At Salomon Brothers, for instance, a recent change in the compensation systems removed caps on annual bonuses, arousing resentments and building incentives to emphasize short term profits at all cost. Since there are few better ways to make big profits than to corner a market, it created an internal environment that encouraged ethical infractions and doubtless eased the firm into its recent debacle.[18]

Educational Systems. Firms hire individuals with varying skills and subsequently provide them with learning opportunities—whether on the job, through training programs, or by funding part-time study, conferences, and professional growth. Training affords senior managers an opportunity to convey to employees the firm's strategic priorities; core competencies; dominant values; and interpretations about competitors, the environment, and the future. The more extensive and integrated the training experiences to which employees are subjected, the more likely they are to develop a shared understanding of where their firms are headed. Strategic change can be facilitated by the kind of ongoing training offered on corporate campuses like GE's in Crotonville or IBM's in Armonk.

Socialization Systems. Employees are socialized into firms' cultures through a wide range of informal practices. Often casual encounters with peers are a key vehicle for conveying corporate folklore, stories, and legends involving founders and corporate heroes or for recounting informative failures. Rituals describe in nonverbal ways managers' seriousness about the values that motivate the ceremonial. Executives can signal strategic change through their symbolic management of food, dress codes, and recreation. Shared meals communicate a friendly, familial culture, whereas cafeterias and dining rooms segregated by rank (as in the insurance industry) signify a culture in which interests and values do not overlap. Dress codes implicitly identify the positions employees occupy and so signal the behaviors deemed acceptable by incumbents. Managers who routinely support picnics and sports teams clearly encourage solidarity. By merging leisure time with work, they convey a specific message: that work is a lifestyle commitment.

The net effect of these systems for rewarding, training, and socializing employees is to produce company cultures that vary along three key dimensions:

1. Transparency
2. Strength
3. Coherence[19]

A strategic change typically affects all these dimensions.

Corporate cultures differ in their *transparency* to external observers. The more permeable firms' boundaries are, the more consistent will be stakeholders' expectations of firms' actions. In transparent firms, customers, analysts, suppliers, and shareholders all know what the firm's priorities are and how their employees are likely to act. Transparency is obviously heightened when managers and employees communicate extensively across corporate boundaries.

Strength describes the density of unwritten rules guiding workers' behaviors. Practices that systematically socialize employees into the ways of a firm provide managers an alternative to the more direct form of control evident in written rules and standard operating procedures. As employees internalize expectations, less overt forms of control are required to ensure coordinated action: Adherence to cultural guidelines removes ambiguity in behavior.[20]

A greater or lesser degree of internal *coherence* also distinguishes firms' cultures. Firms' histories may have produced diverse cultural rules that now send conflicting signals to employees and cancel each other out. Strong leaders tend to foster greater cultural coherence by seducing employees into sharing a vision of the future and mobilizing their efforts to that end.

Over time, cultures tend to thicken and become more internally consistent.[21] Expectations shared internally among employees are diffused outward by job-hopping personal contacts, the press, analysts, and other observers, making corporate cultures more transparent. Insofar as these cultures are appropriate to firms' competitive strategies, they enhance performance. However, strong, coherent transparent cultures generate inertia. When environments change, thick cultures constrain adaptation, while thin cultures demonstrate far greater flexibility.

Table 9.1 illustrates how all firms can, in fact, be arrayed along a continuum ranging from thin to thick cultures—two polar opposites that typify how, in different firms, business units, and functional areas, managers opt to control employees. In thick cultures, managers place principal emphasis on training and socialization. During training programs and through informal activities, core competencies and values are carefully communicated to all employees. As they become well understood and as common standards are internalized, fewer direct controls prove necessary. Reward systems reinforce observance of shared cultural values by tying incentives to performance consistent with those values. Naturally, then, most thick cultures are led by paternalistic figures who reward seniority: The company increasingly takes on the characteristics of an extended family.

Table 9.1. Types of Corporate Culture

	Thin culture	Thick culture
Reward Systems	Mostly $$$ Tied to bottom-line No job security	Extensive social support Tied to core competencies and to seniority
Educational Systems	Limited technical training, mostly on the job	Extensive training and communication Emphasis on shared values
Socialization Systems	Limited social interaction Low integration of work with family and leisure	Extensive interaction Psychological contract

To support these family values, managers encourage a blending of work and leisure: They provide facilities for communal eating and exercising, invite participation in sports teams and Christmas parties, and advocate closer ties with employees' families through company picnics, outings, and other forms of socializing. In thick cultures, close contacts heighten employee identification with the firm, increase involvement, and, research suggests, reduce turnover: A psychological contract ties employees to their jobs and elicits their loyalty, making of the firm an internal labor market.

In contrast, firms with thin cultures place far less emphasis on the systems and practices that induce loyalty in employees. Few values are shared by all employees, and firms are better described by multiple subcultures. Managers emphasize adherence, not to explicit rules, but to core competencies. Performance tends to be unidimensional, involves the bottom line, and rewards are principally monetary. Work dominates corporate life, and little attention is paid to building bonds with employees' families or to leisure-time commitments. By maintaining a spartan infrastructure and emphasizing performance above all else, managers stimulate productivity but reduce loyalty. Lacking a psychological commitment to firms, employees easily move from job to job, company to company, gain in flexibility and in ability to respond to threats.

In a study that compared two companies' cultures, one thick, one thin, employees of the thick culture shared far more stories about their firms than in the thin culture of the more bureaucratic firm.[21] In fact, the characteristics that distinguish thick cultures from thin cultures parallel the contrast made by many observers between Japanese firms and American firms.[22] In Japan, employees of large firms—the *keiretsu* in particular—commit themselves life and soul to their firms' welfare. In return, their companies provide membership in a communal system of social benefits that guarantees income, job security, and health care, and treats employees like members of an extended family. Such thick cultures, although highly touted in the media today, could prove inflexible and costly in the future. They are also inconsistent with management styles that emphasize individualism, job performance, and minimal social benefits—values consistent with the prevailing ethic of Western capitalist democracies.[23]*

So corporate cultures are more or less appropriate to different national and competitive conditions. Strategic change requires senior managers to rethink the configuration of controls and capabilities developed to sup-

---

*Exceptions exist, however. Recognizing the psychological benefits of inducing loyalty, some large U.S. companies, the so-called "excellent" or theory-Z type firms, also operate as internal labor markets, stimulating productivity by early hiring, extensive training, and encouraging employee commitment in return for job security. It is unclear how successful they really have been.

port cultural features consistent with obsolete strategies. Firms within cultures are "leaner and meaner." They probably make better takeover candidates than firms with thick cultures when a complete merger is desired: They are easier to absorb by a strong parent. Thick cultures are slower to move and have difficulty accomodating differing points of view. They are therefore less likely to welcome mergers, better at remaining autonomous divisions, and more likely to resist change.

Aligning Culture with Strategy

Corporate cultures develop historically as firms grow. From their embryonic beginnings as single functions, be they sales staffs, a manufacturing plant, or a research lab, most firms metamorphose into businesses that heavily emphasize the principal departmental culture from which they originated. Polaroid's early commitment to R&D resulted from founder Edwin Land's emphasis on innovation. The innovation thrust has been perpetuated over the years by selecting reward systems, educational programs, and socialization practices that support innovation as a core competency. Similarly, AT&T's early commitment to the dominant value of universal service adopted by founder Theodore Vail came to permeate the telephone giant's internal culture. Insofar as the core capabilities undergirding these cultural features actually strengthened firms' competitiveness, it was natural for subsequent managers to perpetuate them. When they later proved to be at odds with firms' strategies, managers struggled to amend them.

Managers implement strategic change principally by modifying internal controls to realign features of subcultures and support redefined corporate values and outlooks.[24] Table 9.2 describes the relationships

Table 9.2. Strategy, Culture, and Controls

Type of strategy	Core capability	Rewards based on	Education emphasizes	Socialization encourages
Business Strategy:				
Timing	Innovation	Speed	Research	Creativity
Differentiation	Value	Market Share	Engineering	Productivity
Segmentation	Targeting	Profits	Marketing	Entrepreneurship
Corporate Strategy:				
Related	Synergy	Reputation	Management	Integration
Unrelated	Risk	Growth	Finance	Control
Collective Strategy:				
Alliance	Cooperation	Meet goals	Negotiation	Compromise
Fortress	Independence	Profits	Planning	Conformity

among the principal administrative controls managers use to implement strategies and the cultural overlays they produce within firms at the business, corporate, and collective levels.

Business Cultures

Business units compete either on the basis of timing, differentiation, or segmentation. The core capabilities consistent with these strategies signal employees about dominant values. Managers reinforce these values by designing reward systems, offering training programs, and encouraging socialization practices that make these values explicit.

Competing businesses shape their corporate cultures by tailoring administrative systems to their strategies.[25] In the early personal computer industry, for instance, advantage depended on timing, so managers fostered innovation-driven cultures. Selection and training emphasized technical skills; extensive socialization took place as managers tried to shape cohesive teams; and peer recognition was a crucial motivater. Tracy Kidder's popular book *The Soul of the New Machine* described well how the internal culture of innovation at Data General was driven by technical skills, team dynamics, and the will to beat the competition above all.[26]

Managers stressing competition through differentiation insist on developing a "value equation" that trades off price against quality and service. Customers perceive value when product prices correspond to product image, quality, and service—compared with rival products. Consumer electronics firms such as Matsushita and GE, for instance, compete at multiple points on the value continuum, differentiating themselves through branded offerings like Panasonic, Technics, and RCA.

Business units competing through market segmentation generally underscore their skill at targeting customer groups. Employees are hired for their marketing outlook, and training programs drive an awareness of competitivess as an outgrowth of product strategies and market research. To achieve successful positioning against rivals, managers often decentralize decision making into autonomous groups within which employees are expected to act entrepreneurially in developing and maintaining market share.

Business cultures consist of an overlay over the basic functional cultures of the sales, research, and production departments. Managers of research departments, for instance, are more likely to demand intensive team cooperation than are managers of production plants. Insofar as functional heads control a limited portfolio of incentives, they insist on values that support departmental activities. Business managers attend to the net effect produced by the mix of incentives provided up and down the hierarchy and across functional areas.

Corporate Cultures

By diversifying, firms evolve into one of two types of company cultures: synergistic or conglomerate. In conglomerate cultures, top managers shun relationships across businesses, buying and discarding businesses solely on the basis of their profitability and cyclicality. Not suprisingly, holding companies have weak, undeveloped corporate cultures, with few company-wide norms and values disseminated into firms' business units. Since the corporate umbrella is principally concerned with allocating capital, employees have financial backgrounds, experience little shared training or socialization, and are rewarded principally on the bottom line.

Empirical studies support the idea that successful financial conglomerates keep minimal corporate staffs and act principally as internal capital markets, shifting funds to their most promising uses.[27] A comparative study of six firms, of which four were conglomerates and two were synergistic diversifiers, found that the corporate staffs of successful conglomerates performed far fewer functions and tried less to integrate divisions than did those from synergistic cultures.[28]

Conglomerate diversification forces managers to abandon their firms' historical centers of gravity. However, changing centers of gravity proves difficult because it means dismantling the existing power structure, rejecting parts of the old culture, and establishing new management systems.[29] This helps explain why diversification may have proved difficult for money center banks in the 1980s because the combination of technological change and deregulation called for dramatic change in banks' centers of gravity.

In contrast, managers whose firms compete through a corporate strategy of related diversification search for ways to cement bonds across business units in a portfolio. Coca-Cola supports its globalizing efforts by encouraging employees to think "one world": The distinctions *foreign* and *domestic* are banned from the corporate lingo; overseas managers are promoted through Atlanta and into upper levels.

To integrate operations, managers can encourage the development of synergistic cultures by: (1) hiring on the basis of the core competency they hope to build around; (2) rewarding key employees for overall corporate performance; (3) developing educational and socialization programs that provide employees with a sense of shared understanding of the corporate culture; and (4) transferring personnel across business units to shape commonalities.

Take Sony. Its pursuit of a related diversification strategy has largely been implemented through acquisitions of established businesses such as CBS Records and Columbia Pictures. However, recent efforts to capitalize on the latent synergy between its entertainment and electronics businesses have been marred by tensions between the two groups. For instance, the hardware group's support for digital audio tape technologies (DAT) has been resisted by a software group fearful of widespread copying by bootleggers.[30] IBM's efforts to create synergies between its micro-, mini-, and mainframe divisions have been hampered in much the same way by cultural differences among the divisions.

Just as managers support cultural features at the business level that are an overlay on departmental cultures, so too are corporate-level features an overlay on business-unit cultures. Employees bear the burden of values, constraints, and norms imposed within departments and overlaid by cultural features from the business and corporate levels. Mergers, for instance, force attention to the complementarity of cultural features imposed by the firm's overarching diversification strategy.

When General Electric purchased venerable investment banker Kidder, Peabody & Company in 1986 for $600 million, the merger was carefully described as a conglomerate diversification, a marriage of GE's financial backbone with Kidder's proven brains. In the spring of 1987, however, after former advisory superstar Martin Siegel pleaded guilty to insider trading violations while at Kidder, GE's top managers, shocked by the news, did a turnabout: They centralized control and opted to imprint the investment bank's operations with GE's culture, provoking a clash between GE's more bureaucratic, risk-averse management systems and Kidder's entrepreneurial, risk-taking approach. Not surprisingly, employees left in droves, taking clients with them. It became yet another example of a marriage gone awry.[31]

Alliance Cultures

Alliances are two-edged swords. Managers initiate them in the hope of gaining valuable information and know-how, adding value to products, enhancing scale, or overcoming barriers to entry. However, alliances also threaten firms' core strengths since partners can spirit away sources of competitive advantage. To guard against compromising their strategic strengths, cooperating firms therefore develop unique cultural features. (See Table 9.3.)

Firms whose internal cultures are thick—that is, strong, consistent, and opaque—generally resist forming alliances, opting instead for internal

Table 9.3. Alliance Cultures

		Partner #2	
		Thin	Thick
Partner #1	Thin	Organic Alliance	Defensive Alliance
	Thick	Predatory Alliance	Bureaucratic Alliance

development and favoring fortress strategies. When they do form alliances, they are more likely to favor free-standing units such as joint ventures within which control is well delineated and potential friction between partners is contained. New United Motors Manufacturing (NUMMI), the highly publicized joint venture between General Motors and Toyota, is a prime example of two firms with thick corporate cultures forming a bureaucratic alliance to exchange technology and know-how.

Firms with thinner cultures, on the other hand, are more likely to pursue defensive alliance strategies involving multiple informal and formal contracts. Because they depend more heavily on cooperative relationships to maintain competitive advantage in their primary markets, the principal threat comes from being stripped of core strengths by partners pursuing predatory strategies. Where both partners have relatively thin internal cultures, alliances are more benign and the relationship more likely to be organic, with both firms forced to invest relatively less in designing defensive controls.

The combination of cultural features that derive from firms' collective, corporate, and business strategies shapes the cultural makeup of firms and defines the normative constraints that employees experience daily. To adapt to the kinds of revolutionary pressures on firms for increased competitiveness and institutional effectiveness, managers are placing increased stress on rejuvenating their corporate cultures to mobilize employees behind a strategic change.

Recasting Corporate Cultures

What, then, are changing environments doing to corporate cultures? By exposing firms to greater diversity, the pressures that derive from globalization, increased competition, and institutional considerations penalize firms with thick cultures and thin out the cultural features of established firms. They demand that managers pay more attention to the symbolic side of corporate life and communicate to employees symbols that support, on the one hand, efficiency and entrepreneurship, but that also recognize, on the other hand, the importance of equity and ethics.

Building Efficient Cultures

Environmental pressures to enhance efficiency and competitiveness are forcing managers to pursue strategies that build more integrative relationships within firms. They are also pushing managers to find ways of improving productivity.

Psychologists tell us that productivity is heavily influenced by employees' ability and effort. Employees' abilities depend on skills developed through education and training, while the amount of effort they devote to their work hinges on firms' compensation practices. In changing environments, managers therefore cultivate productivity by investing in training programs and tying pay more closely to individual contributions.

Efforts to improve employees' skills are evident as firms struggle to adapt to rapidly evolving technologies. High-tech systems are taking over in the office, the plant, and at the cash register, requiring more sophisticated skills from operators. Where typing and shorthand were once the principal skills expected of office workers, they must now show mastery of complex software packages for word processing, graphics, and spread sheets. Where assembly lines once broke tasks into repetitive routines, deskilling the content of work, manufacturing environments require workers to interface with robots and computers, compelling more skillful and alert personnel. To improve productivity, managers are devoting more resources to tooling and retooling employees. The surge in popularity of quality improvement programs indicates the intense interest managers have in rebuilding competitive strength in the production process.

To make cultures more productive compels managers to compensate according to employees' individual contributions rather than according to seniority and loyalty.[32] To pay for performance, however, requires appraisal systems capable of distinguishing among individuals whose results often depend on other team members. Evaluation calls for subjective assessments by superiors, thereby opening the door to political bias and favoritism, and provoking anger, resentment, and cynicism among employees who feel they have been unjustly rated. Encouraging efficiency and productivity mandates reliance on more objective performance measures, such as sales growth, market share, and costs of goods sold, whether in functional departments or for divisional managers.

Making individual distinctions fosters rivalry. As conflicts escalate, pitting employees, departments, and divisions one against the other, firms are finding that merit pay systems discourage cooperation and dampen corporate performance—an outcome that directly contradicts the strategic objective of enhancing company-wide integration.

To counter the potentially negative consequences of merit pay, while encouraging productivity, many firms are inducing employees to identify with company-wide performance by creating profit-sharing plans. Senior executives have long benefited from bonuses tied to corporate profits. In *The Share Economy*, economist Martin Weitzman proposed that we extend the opportunity to more employees. Paying employees on the basis of corporate profits, he argued, would eliminate built-in pressures that push up costs and dampen productivity.[33]

A variety of such gain-sharing plans—the best known of which are the Scanlon plan and the Rucker plans—involve employees in cost cutting and quality improvement and distribute financial gains monthly to all participating employees. One analysis of 33 such plans found that they occurred in both union and nonunion settings; in small, medium, and large firms—though predominately in manufacturing plants. Most firms experimenting with gain sharing, in fact, consistently report productivity improvements.[34] These successes suggest that the productivity gains from profit sharing may result partly from increased involvement in decision making, partly from the financial incentive, and partly from greater perceived equity within firms.

Finally, managers concerned about deriving efficiency from their corporate cultures are actively manipulating the training and reward systems to encourage employee productivity on three levels: (1) individual productivity; (2) business-unit productivity; and (3) company-wide productivity. To meet these objectives requires a complex training program that builds technical, administrative, and comunication skills. It also requires a stratified reward system that supports individual performance through merit pay; business-unit performance through profit-sharing bonuses; and corporate performance by distributing stock options. The highly visible Baldridge Awards instituted under the Reagan administration in the U.S. constitute a complementary recognition-based appraisal and reward system that motivates efficiency and quality throughout participating firms.

Making Cultures Entrepreneurial

In her popular book *Change Masters*, Harvard professor Rosabeth Kanter studied how large firms innovate.[36] Not surprisingly, she found that firms that routinely smothered innovations had segmentalist cultures, while innovative firms solved problems in an integrative fashion. With specialists in charge of projects, segmentalist firms compartmentalize ideas, reducing their probability of success. With a team orientation, employees of integrative firms share a family feeling that values individual initiatives, encourages involvement of middle managers, and equalizes power among all employees.

Kanter's subsequent book *When Giants Learn to Dance* explored in greater detail how some large firms are dismantling bureaucratic processes to become more nimble in competitive enronments.[36] The means: Exploring ways to induce synergy among individuals inside business units, across divisions within portfolios, and through complementary alliances with stakeholders.

Other observers also join in championing the importance of building within firms' structures a systematic process for self-renewal. Recognizing that companies easily succumb to advanced sclerosis due to inertia induced by prior successes, managers are advised to develop internal cultures that favor innovation. A study of 100 senior electronics executives involved in product development found multiple themes to characterize innovative firms; in particular: a core competency around which R&D

could focus; extensive cooperation among employees; and an "entrepreneurial culture." Key features of entrepreneurial cultures were the breakup of large bureaucracies into small divisions, a tolerance for failure that encouraged employees to take risks, and time to pursue outside projects.[37]

A detailed examination of one large high-tech firm found successful innovation to be heavily influenced by managers' willingness to build into their planning processes an "autonomous loop" for new venture development. Rather than completely decouple new ventures by isolating them in separate divisions, more successful entrepreneurial firms encourage employees through systems that reward, not only problem solving, but also problem finding and development of know-how.[38]

Since 1981, GE's maverick chairman Jack Welch has been systematically breaking up and decentralizing its 150 businesses to increase corporate responsiveness to competitiveness and make the firm more entrepreneurial.[39] In 1989, Welch created the position of productivity czar to back him up in preaching the gospel of productivity throughout the 271,000-person firm.[40] Similarly, General Motors' joint venture with Toyota and its launching of the Saturn plant constitute attempts to rekindle an entrepreneurial spirit at the outer periphery of its old-line bureaucracy.

Another example of a company struggling to establish and maintain a culture that prizes innovation is the NutraSweet Company, a subsidiary of G.D. Searle, itself acquired by chemical giant Monsanto in 1985. Dependent on a patent for aspartame (better known as NutraSweet), that expires in 1992, for some time the company has been actively researching innovative products (the latest in line is Simplesse, the fat substitute). One observer characterized the NutraSweet culture as "intensely focused" on the start-up's mentality of creativity and market positioning. As rivals rob the company of market share in the years ahead, managers face a dual threat: On the one hand, they ask, how can they become the low-cost producer of aspartame when their culture drives innovation? On the other hand, can they remain innovative if they become cost conscious?[41]

Encouraging Equitable Cultures

Changing environments have called managers' attention to the inequities created by the skewed distribution of bonuses, promotions, and power among employees throughout the 1980s. The widely publicized golden parachutes that enriched senior executives during corporate restructurings, the green mail collected by maverick raiders, and the large bonuses paid to incumbent managements alienated employees amd reduced productivity. Why try to work hard if all the gains produced by the many go only to the few?

Managers seeking to improve their firms' innovativeness and break down old cultural barriers try to generate more internal risk taking. But risks and rewards seldom coincide. On the upside, there are large, often implicit penalties for failure in large firms. While on the downside, new ideas that produce patents and commercialization generally mean large returns for firms, but very small awards for those individuals who innovated—an outcome widely perceived as unfair. To address inequity, many firms seeking to encourage innovation have offered idea generators the opportunity to share in the returns from commercializing their ideas.

AT&T is a case in point. To encourage innovation, the company offers new venture participants different pay options. Under the most conservative plan, new venture employees remain at their AT&T salaries pegged to existing job grades. A more risky option, selected by most of the participants to date, freezes salaries at the level of their last job until the venture shows a positive cash flow, at which point venture participants are eligible for a onetime bonus of up to 150 percent of their salary. The final option, favored by risk takers, allows venture participants to invest 10 to 15 percent of their salaries in the venture, in return for pay-offs of up to 8 times their investment.[42]

At the new Dupont-Merck Pharmaceutical Co., a joint venture funded by the two pharmaceutical titans, key researchers are given stock options for work that leads to products. Scientists advance in pay and status without having to leave the lab and take management jobs. The focus on fairness extends to the relationship between the two parent companies: Top executives of both parents sit on the board of the joint venture and match pay-offs to each side's contributions.[43]

Equity issues are becoming more salient as firms brace for increased global competition. Large disparities in the incomes earned by managers and employees are likely to grow less tolerable in slow growth environments. Implementing strategic change tends to be far easier in corporate environments whose managers are recognized for distributing both gains and losses equitably among groups and levels.

Devising Ethical Cultures

Institutional pressures are compelling managers to make their firms conform to commonly accepted ethical principles, and to incorporate them into their reward, education, and socialization programs. Impelled by cases of improper political contributions, illegal payments to foreign governments, insider trading, and espionage, U.S. companies increasingly spell out their codes of conduct explicitly. A study of 100 large firms by The Business Roundtable in 1988 suggested that "many executives believe that a culture in which ethical concern permeates the whole organization is necessary to the self-interest of the company."[44]

During the two incidents of Tylenol poisonings, Johnson & Johnson's 40-year-old credo (a statement of beliefs about the company's relationships to its customers, employees, shareholders, and community) was frequently credited for guiding the company's exemplary behavior. As chairman James Burke often has remarked, "The credo is the unifying force for our corporation. It guides us in everything we do. It represents an attempt to codify what we can all agree upon since we have highly independent managers."

To communicate these values, top managers of J&J have held regular credo challenge meetings since 1975 to explore managers' understanding of the principles it sets forth, and to explore its relevance to their businesses. In 1986, J&J began an annual credo survey to assess how well employees perceive the firm to be doing. Profiles are fed back to departments and reviewed by the executive committee.

In the wake of environmental disasters and criminal prosecution, many visionary executives have developed similar codes of conduct and sought to turn them into living documents by emphasizing those principles in all their communications to employees. Chemical Bank relies on a corporate values seminar to underscore the firm's commitment to corporate social responsibility. At Norton, an ethics committee of its board of directors conducts an annual ethics review to ensure ethical standards are adhered to domestically and abroad.

A number of companies have set up full-fledged ethics offices: Dow-Corning has had one since 1976 and Texas Instruments since 1987.* Since General Dynamics staffed its office with three employees in 1985, it has dealt with over 6000 contacts by employees. While these offices signal the importance of ethics throughout the firm, they sometimes also convey a mistrustful aura: Many regard them as "snitchlines," with all the pejorative connotations associated with being a whistle blower. Potentially, they function as systems for punishing transgressions rather than systems for rewarding ethical behavior. The danger is that good behavior is not internalized, and employees simply become more cautious in their trespasses.[45]

Currently under review in the U.S. Congress is a set of guidelines for sentencing corporations and other organizations, such as labor unions, trade associations, government agencies, and pension funds, that are convicted of federal criminal offenses, be they fraud, theft, or antitrust violations. Under the proposal, hundreds of millions of dollars in fines could be levied by judges. Fines would depend partly on how much effort the organization had made to prevent or detect illegal activities through

---

*Clearly setting up an office is not enough. In early 1992, Dow-Corning was appropriately chastized for failing to make public damaging information it had long ago gathered about its silicone breast implants.

in-house education and monitoring systems.[46] This clearly provides added impetus for executives to build ethical cultures.

Few ethical guidelines, however, are likely to prove more beneficial than the famous "sunshine test" adopted by IBM, a rule that simply requires asking of any action whether it can be fully disclosed without embarrassment. Neither insider trading, influence peddling by government lobbyists, nor bribery of officials—the most common of our recent corporate scandals—would have stood up to the full light of day.

The Strategic Content of Corporate Cultures

Because firms' cultural features derive from characteristics of the nations and corporate communities in which they thrive, as well as from firms' own unique histories, they are difficult to change. Through stories and rituals, as well as systematic programs that reward, educate, and socialize employees, managers can convey the new cultural characteristics needed for their firms to compete and thereby signal to outsiders the core competencies, strategic posture, and ethical stance of their firms. These symbolic pronouncements create the internal environment within which employees and managers can develop a common understanding about how their firms are changing to adapt to new sources of competition and new environments.

Insofar as existing cultural features support past strategies, they act as a constraint on change. To generate strategic change means redefining a corporate culture whose dominant values are more consistent with the new strategic vision. As technologies have accelerated and markets become globalized, however, corporate cultures are becoming thinner, less focused on conformity, and more capable of enhancing firms' flexibility. Into these thinner cultures, managers are struggling to incorporate features that support, not only greater efficiency and entrepreneurialism, but also more attention to equity and ethics. In many firms, managers are achieving cultural change by modifying the structures that channel interactions and coordinate employees' activities—a subject to which we now turn.

10
Reinventing Structures

Chaos often breeds life, when order breeds habit.

HENRY ADAMS

After Grand Metropolitan P.L.C. acquired the faltering Pillsbury for $5.7 billion early in 1989, the British conglomerate embarked on a program to prune Pillsbury's bureaucracy, rationalize its strategic posture, revive employee morale, increase risk taking, and prop up earnings. Within a year, Grand Met sold off nearly $1 billion of businesses viewed as unrelated to Pillsbury's core capabilities, including the chain S&A Restaurants and seafood producers Bumble Bee and Van de Kamps. Pillsbury's overburdened subsidiaries Burger King and Häagen-Dazs were made into free-standing operations and remaining brands were consolidated around packaged foods. To reduce overhead costs, 2600 employees were laid off, a number of plants were closed, and operations were streamlined to produce net savings of $183 million in 1989. At the same time, Pillsbury has been modernizing older plants and increasing advertising on most brands by 30 to 50 percent. The result: Higher morale among Pillsbury employees, renewed confidence, a burst of product innovations, higher earnings, and favorable appraisals by analysts.[1]

On October 30, 1990, Merrill Lynch & Company announced a sweeping reorganization that dissolved its two largest operating groups, Consumer Markets and Capital Markets, into six product divisions: private client (focused on retail businesses), asset management, insurance, investment banking, debt markets, and equity markets. The structural change effectively decentralized authority by removing a layer of management. It also economized on administrative overhead: By consolidating retail operations, the company eliminated hundreds of duplicate jobs across divisions.[2] These changes were matched by continued efforts to push accountability down the hierarchy and into the hands of the line managers who incur those costs.[3]

In the financial services community alone, similar layoffs at Chase Manhattan; Bear, Stearns & Company; First Boston; and Prudential-Bache Securities were announced throughout 1990 and 1991.[4] Managers held that these moves reflected long-term price cutting and consolidations, the necessity for which was invariably attributed to the inhospitable marketplace produced by the crash of October 1987, the savings and loan bankruptcies, the insider trading scandal, Drexel's bankruptcy filing, and the recessionary U.S. economy. Such measures constitute a collective *mea culpa* for the excesses of the 1980s, a turn away from the culture of spending that had led even financially troubled firms like the Shearson Lehman Hutton subsidiary of American Express to build a $24-million ski resort for the firm in Vail, Colorado.[5]

Finally, consider mighty IBM. During the 1980s, the company saw its world computer market share drop from 36 to 23 percent. Battered by intense competition in every one of its markets, in December 1991 the company long known for its centralized structure and paternalistic culture boldly announced that it was carrying out a radical restructuring of its operations. Spearheaded by Chairman John Akers, the strategic change intends to push product-based operations into nine autonomous subsidiaries, granting them profit/loss responsibility, and encouraging responsiveness to market pressures. Service-oriented operations are splitting up into five geographical regions, with support from three centralized corporate functions. The new IBM will therefore resemble a holding company more than a divisionalized structure. In tandem, Akers announced that IBM would institute new administrative controls designed to tie employee compensation more closely to performance. To increase accountability within businesses, the financial results of individual operating companies will be made public. Finally, Akers concluded with an ominous warning: Having already reduced staff by 65,000 between 1986 and 1991 through voluntary departures and retirements, he pointed out that Big Blue could no longer guarantee lifetime employment. Employees' jobs would depend on the health of the economy and the actions taken by the autonomous businesses as they evolved—a radical change indeed from historical practice.[6]

Structural reorganizations like these clearly represent attempts to follow through on the internal changes needed to make a new strategy work. Often they are aimed at cost cutting, but often they also intend to build greater responsiveness to competitive conditions by more closely tying firms' activities to external constituencies. Within individual business units, for instance, functional structures tend to overly compartmentalize activities. So managers look for ways to encourage lateral interactions by forming temporary teams and task forces. In related diversifiers, divisional structures sometimes invite too much autonomy; so managers try to create corporate synergy clusters within which key functions can be centralized. Finally, conglomerates often rely on holding company structures prove wasteful of human, technological, and capital resources, so that managers develop managerial pools that can facilitate the transfer of generic skills across firms' activity sectors.

Structural parameters prove useful in implementing strategic change. They permit new relationships and interactions to emerge among employees. As managers negotiate strategic turning points, they are inclined to manipulate: (1) the degree of specialization and grouping of activities; (2) the intensity of lateral contact among specialists; and (3) the centralization of decision making. To alter patterns of specialization, lateral contact, and authority in firms is to induce among employees new communication networks that can facilitate a reorientation.

Ongoing changes in business strategy, for instance, compel managers to redeploy resources to build new capabilities. Turnarounds designed to provide firms with a low-price position in an industry typically dictate cost cutting, obtained either by automating production or by employee skill building—involving questions of capability. They also invite a continued review of the productivity of the firm, the efficiency of its operations, and the quality of its products—questions of control. Finally, they tempt an analysis of how informal practices may be breeding complacency and inertia—questions of culture. Indeed, top managers' failure both to sufficiently finance the necessary changes and to maintain control over middle and lower levels of firms has led to many well-documented cases of failure to produce successful revitalizations.

Lasting changes in corporate strategy are also encouraging deep restructuring of firms' cost structures, management staffs, and decision-making processes. As the bonds of corporate culture weaken from exposure to the global arena, top managers worry more about generating involvement in their employees. Visionary firms increasingly experiment with restructuring their operations in ways that can produce cost savings, while at the same time pruning cumbersome bureaucracies and encouraging more entrepreneurial activism among employees.

Take Hewlett-Packard. Long held up as a shining example of a firm whose thick culture made it one of the best-managed and innovative companies in America, by the late 1980s the "HP way" had developed into an unwieldy, entrenched bureaucracy mired in a quicksand of committees. Innovation, though critical for competing with fast-moving Compaq Computer and Sun Microsytems, proved increasingly difficult as schedules lengthened to accommodate larger and larger groups of specialized employees in technical meetings. Under John Young's leadership, the company underwent a radical reorganization in the fall of 1990: The committee decision-making structure was eliminated, and two operating groups were created from the computer business—one for personal computers sold through dealers and one for work stations marketed to large users. Other previously centralized corporate functions such as marketing and sales were also decentralized into the separate divisions, providing greater proximity to end users. Although the results are not yet in, Hewlett-Packard, like many other firms coping with rapid change, is clearly trying hard to reinvent itself by moving decision making downward.[7]

Finally, globalization is challenging accepted principles about arm's-length relationships among competitors, particularly in the United States. Managers call into question the traditional role of government in frowning on cooperative relationships among firms. For instance, Japan and other nations of Asia support a complex intertwining of business and government, which facilitates collective action. The European community is the backbone of a range of joint research and manufacturing endeavors devoted to exploring and exploiting firms' shared interests. Even U.S. managers have come to rely on these collective structures to negotiate the quantum changes that are reshaping their firms' environments.

Revolutionary conditions invariably alter social relationships and so require new structural solutions. Perhaps nothing demonstrates this better than the continuing transformation of what was once the largest of all organizations, the Soviet Union. In the late 1980s, the evident inefficiency of central planning drove Mikhail Gorbachev to champion market reform, encourage local entrepreneurship, and form closer ties with Western economies. But freedoms do not come without a price. Demands for political autonomy by the 15 Soviet republics quickly followed, leaving Gorbachev struggling to find a structural solution to the problem of simultaneously emancipating the republics and maintaining the union. By the end of 1991, the tug-of-war had resolved itself in favor of decentralization: A Commonwealth of Independent States was created. Gorbachev was out; Russia's Boris Yeltsin was in.

Like Gorbachev and Yeltsin, many corporate managers and institutional leaders today, faced with revolutionary changes, are searching for structural solutions that can unshackle specialized units and businesses from bureaucratic inefficiency and simultaneously enable firms to capitalize on latent synergies across functions and divisions. In response, consolidation, decentralization, and networking now loom high on managers' priorities. By liberating employees and subsidiary units, by granting them greater control over their own performance, managers are reinventing firms' internal structures, making them more like loosely coupled networks of specialized profit centers—each one more entrepreneurial and efficient, yet the totality more flexible. At the same time, by encouraging relationships with rivals across corporate boundaries, managers are creating collective structures that bind firms into business communities filled with competitors, suppliers, distributors, schools, and publishers with common interests. These network structures constitute a revolutionary new form of organization, one that requires management controls radically different from those applied in our anachronistic bureaucracies.

Revising the Structural Menu

In his aptly titled epic *Scale and Scope*, historian Alfred Chandler documented the development of leading firms in Germany, the United States, and the United Kingdom in the twentieth century. He showed how managers shaped their firms by building key capabilities through investments in physical facilities and human skills.*

Just as those turn-of-the-century managers judiciously established vertically integrated production facilities, elaborate distribution systems, and state-of-the-art research incubators to assemble secure competitive positions in their industries, so many enlightened companies today are rethinking their firms' underlying capabilities and controls, with the goal of creating structures that improvise quicker responses to changing demands; that allow greater creativity and initiative to blossom as they do in start-up companies; and that better motivate employees to contribute beyond the call of duty.

Strengthening Capabilities

Routine deployments of money and people, when apportioned across functions and divisions, build distinct capabilities that provide firms with a center of gravity—an anchor around which to organize operations, design systems and practices, and formulate action plans. To implement strategic change means to shift resources to functional uses that depart from prior allocations. A strategic change, say, that attaches increased importance to improving existing bottlenecks in distribution and to competing for market share, shifts resources into marketing and away from

---

*As he put it, "...only if these facilities and skills were carefully coordinated and integrated could the enterprise achieve the economies of scale and scope that were needed to compete in national and international markets and to continue to grow.... Such organizational capabilities, of course, had to be created, and once established, they had to be maintained. Their maintenance was as great a challenge as their creation, for facilities depreciate and skills atrophy. Moreover, changing technologies and markets constantly make both existing facilities and skills obsolete" (Chandler, A., *Scale and Scope*, Cambridge, MA: Harvard University Press, 1989) p. 594.

manufacturing. A strategic change designed to rekindle the fires of innovation naturally redeploys resources into product development and away from alternative uses.

Recently, older industries have faced technological and competitive challenges requiring large scale redeployments. In braving global competition and technological change, managers in the troubled auto, steel, textile, shoe, and apparel industries, among others, have had to invest prodigious sums in constructing up-to-date facilities, adopting new technologies, and automating manufacturing processes.

In the 1980s, computer-aided manufacturing and robotics revolutionized both the labor-intensive textile industries and the scale-intensive steel and auto industries. Computer-controlled textile machines, not only increase production speeds, but also improve product quality, making yarns stronger and cloth of higher quality. Similarly, steel makers built new plants capable of delivering less costly, yet more sophisticated, and higher-quality steel products. In autos, General Motors' joint venture with Toyota, its purchase of information giant Electronic Data Systems, and extensive investment in setting up Saturn production are aspects of the fundamental transformation GM undertook to meet the challenges posed by the oil crisis, pollution, and Japanese imports.

In newer growth industries such as telecommunications, resource shifts have proved no less significant: Witness AT&T's dramatic divestiture of its operating companies, its extensive layoffs (92,000 since 1986), and its heavy funding of information technologies. IBM managers' delayed reaction to the personal computer market was soon remedied by extensive commitment of research and marketing support in the early 1980s as they recognized the threat to mainframe operations posed by decentralized processing. Witness also the extensive investments that pharmaceutical companies like Merck, Hoffmann-LaRoche, American Home Products, and Warner-Lambert have made in building cutting-edge research laboratories. Since 1986, Warner-Lambert, for instance, has hiked R&D spending from 16 to 19 percent of sales in an attempt to speed up its ability to get drugs from patent to FDA filing. They have also lured top pharmaceutical researchers away from competitors.[8]

Although throwing money at a problem may signal commitment, it remains insufficient to produce strategic change. Where successful, managers have had to dovetail these resource redeployments with parallel changes in their firms' administrative controls, the systems that daily constrain how employees relate to one another in the firm.

Consider industry leader Merck. Besides spending $1 billion annually on R&D and swelling its research staff by more than 40 percent since 1985, Merck also recognized that its centralized structure had become unwieldy, stifling creativity and slowing decision making. Top R&D staff had jumped ship to join rivals Bristol-Myers Squibb, Rhône-Poulenc Rorer, or Sterling Drug. Under Roy Vagelos' leadership, himself the former R&D chief, the research bureaucracy is being dismantled: Decision-making responsibility is being decentralized, different laboratories specialized, and each laboratory organized into project teams responsible for taking products from discovery through marketing. To address equity issues and motivate entrepreneurship, a stock option program was offered to researchers whose work leads to salable products.[9]

Revamping Controls

We often represent firms as organizational charts. Charts encourage us to conceive of firms' structures as fixed in time. Yet this is fallacious. Charts picture only how authority and responsibility are formally alloted in firms. Because they grossly distort the real interactions among employees, however, charts are imperfect tools for conceiving how managers actually control activities.[10]

In fact, structures are only temporary solutions to dynamic problems. Ideally, they evolve to remain in harmony with the evolution of the strategic problem they help to address. As managers revise their strategies in response to changing environmental conditions, so too should they adjust their firms' structures to mirror the strategic change.

Unfortunately, devising continuously evolving structures proves difficult. Because change is disruptive, managers make only episodic adjustments, which means that structures are generally out of synch with the strategies being carried out. Indeed, one could say that firms become lethargic and bureaucratic when the practices, systems, and controls in place take on a life of their own, divorced from the business problems they were designed to address—or, as one observer put it, a bureaucracy is "any company giving less than two-thirds of its energies to its business, and more than one-third of its energies to its organization."[11]

To allow continual evolution, firms' structures must be regenerative—that is, they must loop back on themselves. Each element, like the Hydra of Greek mythology, must be capable of reinventing the firm; each must be autonomous. To combine autonomy with interdependence, therefore, constitutes the structural challenge: By itself autonomy threatens to tear the company apart as individual decisions take the firm in contradictory directions; similarly, on its own, interdependence paralyzes action, like traffic jams at intersections.

Shared values provide one means for resolving the tension. Firms with thick cultures can create commonalities among employees that enable decentralized decision making and at the same time ensure the continual self-renewal of the corporate structure. To meet new circumstances, autonomous employees continually improvise responses; however, these responses cohere through a shared understanding that is propagated by the corporate culture. In a sense, control takes place one step removed: The company does not control the actual decisions employees make; rather, it controls the premises on which employees base their decisions.

The parents among us well recognize the differences in how we might control our children: Some opt to define elaborate rules and regulations governing the lives of our offspring (how to dress, curfews, types of friends); others strive to inculcate world views and, having done so, allow children to make their own decisions like adults.

In a way, managers are akin to parental figures. They can elect to treat employees like children, a style that our traditional bureaucratic structures encourage, or they can treat employees more like adults, granting them the autonomy to reinvent their jobs, departments, and divisions as they confront problems and ad-lib solutions. To achieve the latter is to recognize structures as temporary improvised responses to existing environmental and strategic conditions.

Imagine being asked to create a temporary organization capable of delivering daily up to 700 tons of mail and serving a daily ration of 1.5 million hot meals 6000 miles away from headquarters—all this in 6 months. This is what General Gus Pagonis, Desert Storm's logistician, was asked to do to support the 450,000-strong army assigned to liberate Kuwait from the clutches of Iraq in the fall of 1990. To achieve the objective, the general relied on "centralized command/decentralized execution"—the familiar military structure through which big decisions are made at the top and all operating decisions are delegated to lower-level specialists.

Much like General Pagonis, corporate managers rely on three important administrative tools to reconfigure how work gets done: (1) They manipulate the kind and extent of employees' job specializations and how activities are grouped; (2) they create committees and task forces through which they reshape the number and intensity of personal contacts people have across specialized groups; and (3) they determine the extent to which decisions should be more or less centralized and the choice of which employees to involve.

Boosting employee specialization captures efficiency gains from the division of labor. Ever since the industrial revolution, evolving technologies have forced both people and firms increasingly to specialize: People, because human limitations imply that we can only embrace a limited amount of the rapidly expanding stock of knowledge; and firms, because competition requires ever higher sophistication and efficiency.

But hiring more specialists creates the familiar problem of how to get people to converse. Specialists each have their own languages, attitudes, and world views that make it possible to talk past one another, or not to talk at all. Specialization therefore leads to questions about grouping:

Should experts be gathered into departments of like-minded peers whose activities are standardized? Or should specialists be assigned to generalist teams, where solutions to problems are improvised?

Standardization encourages efficiency and ensures quality at every step in making and distributing a product. To capture the benefits of standardization, managers often reinforce the familiar departmental structures that populate our manufacturing industries. In contrast, managers who recognize a greater need for improvisation and innovation prod their firms to adopt more divisionalized structures organized around project teams—the kind more prevalent among firms competing in dynamic markets such as consumer goods and service industries.[12]

In turn, groupings affect who talks to whom: Firms whose specialized personnel are compartmentalized rely heavily on their bosses to coordinate activities among departments. Communication goes up through the ranks, and personal contact throughout the firm is often limited, occurring principally among like-minded specialists. In contrast, divisional structures force interactions among complementary experts working in teams, thereby minimizing the degree of coordination through common bosses up the hierarchy.

Finally, managers can reorient employees' interactions by opting for a greater or lesser centralization of decisions. Delegating authority down the hierarchy increases the speed with which firms act.[13] However, without extensive monitoring, delegation can reduce the consistency of the decisions made across departments or divisions.

Take the 50,000-member logistics group that General Pagonis managed during the war against Iraq. With such a large organization to run, the general could easily have been overwhelmed with information. To minimize overload, Pagonis required that the 100 or so daily requests for action he received be written on 3 by 5 index cards to which he could respond directly by scrawling in green ink. To coordinate his top 40 officers, the general ran a daily 30-minute meeting, with oral reports limited to 2 minutes each, a rule enforced with an oven timer. A squad of 15 men (the "Ghostbusters") was constantly out among the troups to flag and fix any logistical problems they identified.[14] These improvised administrative controls worked to mitigate the costs of strict specialization down through the centralized hierarchy.

Or take Compaq Computers. Since its founding in 1982, the PC manufacturer relied on a centralized functional structure, with units like marketing, manufacturing, and development. Decision making in such a structure is slow. In 1991, however, growing competition from other IBM-PC clone manufacturers, not only depressed the companies' revenues, but put the company in the red to the tune of some $70 million. Strategic change was commandeered, and a new structure was adopted. The choice: a more decentralized structure consisting of autonomous, cross-functional teams staffed by engineers and marketers.[15]

From Firms into Networks

As managers come to recognize their firms as temporary structures, they are designing revolutionary structures that more closely resemble a network of autonomous satellite companies coordinated through exchange relationships than a bureaucracy. In *The New Industrial Divide*, Michael Piore and Charles Sabel described the relative merits of network constellations of firms providing complementary skills. The production of apparel, for instance, involves just such a loose coordination among specialized textile, coat, dress, shirt, button, trim, and accessories manufacturers. Its strength lies in the flexibility of the network and its ability to quickly innovate and easily adapt to changing fashions that make some types of fabric trim popular one season and less so the next.[17]

Author Stan Davis recently recognized the network firm as "the institution of our time: an open system, a dissipative structure so richly coherent that it is in constant flux, poised for reordering, capable of endless transformation."[18] Because individual units in the network structures of these firms are specialized, they are efficient. Should a unit prove inefficient, managers can easily lop it off without extensive damage to the overall company. The firm-as-network structure also maximizes motivation by decentralizing operational decision making, inciting individual autonomy, and inviting self-control.

By being both temporary and market based, network firms achieve the advantages of encouraging continuous change and stimulating efficiency. They stand one step beyond related diversifiers in relying on self-contained specialized units. But they also overcome the weaknesses of the conglomerate structure by facilitating the flow of resources (financial, human, and informational) across business units. As such, networks constitute the building blocks of a new structure toward which firms tend as they address the revolutionary technological and institutional forces shaping strategic change.

New Recipes

Conventional wisdom has it that a balance develops between environmental conditions and firms' internal structures. As environments grow more turbulent, more dynamic, and more competitive, astute managers hire more specialists, develop more lateral linkages among them, and decentralize decisions down the hierarchy. In the terms of systems theorist Ross Ashby, managers respond to rising variety in their environments by increasing the internal variety of their firms.[19]

Table 10.1 summarizes how key environmental pressures are affecting the structuring of firms. Economic downturns reduce demand for firms' products, diminish revenues, and so place pressure on managers to slash

Table 10.1. Environmental Change and Structure

Environmental trigger	Pressure to improve:	Capabilities	Controls
Efficiency	Timing and Productivity	Automate Just-in-Time	Centralize Specialize
Customer Responsiveness	Quality and Service	Customize Differentiate	Networking De-layering
Technological Change	Innovation and Speed	Build Skills Invest in R&D	Flatten Pyramid Decentralize

costs. Not surprisingly, belt tightening has resulted in many industries, with extensive layoffs in line activities, cuts in administrative support, and a stress on increasing efficiency. To improve coordination, many managers have mistakenly centralized decision making and constrained resource utilization, thereby maintaining more rigid hierarchical control— a structural outcome, in many instances, that has served only to demotivate employees and further frustrate productivity.

At the same time, globalization and competition are forcing many managers to look for productivity gains that might come from automating production processes. Because automation alters the mix of specialties needed to deliver products and services, layoffs have become necessary in countless industries, presenting problems for many large firms, especially those whose internal cultures traditionally emphasized loyalty, rewarded seniority, and promised lifetime security. IBM and AT&T instantly come to mind: Both are struggling with staff reductions and decentralizations as ways of coping with the simultaneous pressures on their operations to be *both* cost effective and innovative.

Within industries, when rival firms achieve technological parity in efficiency, competition revolves around product quality and corporate image. But achieving quality depends heavily on managers' ability to tap the problem-solving abilities of line employees. That has meant a renewed focus on employee involvement. In recent years, managers have sought to mobilize employees by decentralizing key decisions: Quality circles, for instance, constitute a valuable structural innovation when competition makes speed of response critical to market performance. Quality-management programs offered managers a bottom-up means for quickly gathering information and accelerating operational problem solving.

At the same time, globalization has heightened internal tensions between divisional managers who want to respond quickly to local needs and corporate managers who push for uniform responses and global integration. Many managers whose companies operate in multination markets have tried to shape a global mind set among employees. To achieve this, they encourage network-like exchanges among subsidiaries, with complex flows of parts, products, resources, people, and information binding the organization into a whole.[20]

Finally, by eroding the capabilities of established firms, technological developments pressure managers to invest heavily in rebuilding plants, in funding research, in decentralizing decision making, and in building stronger lateral contacts between departments. To generate commitment to innovation, those managers increasingly emphasized the importance of employee autonomy in idea generation. They look for ways to support the entrepreneurial efforts of lower-echelon employees.[21]

Besides altering the basic capabilities that managers try to recreate, these environmental forces are also influencing the kinds of controls firms rely on. Visionary firms today are responding to these revolutionary conditions through corresponding business-, corporate-, and collective-level changes in their structural controls.

Recasting Business Structures

Within industries, firms are: (1) collapsing the time between product development and marketing, (2) strengthening their differentiation; and (3) customizing their offerings. Each strategic change nudges firms in different, frequently contradictory, structural directions. (See Table 10.2)

Accelerating Time to Market. The pressure to remain innovative in increasingly turbulent and competitive environments forces managers to shift resources into R&D in order to remain competitive; to place greater stress on lateral linkages in their firms' control structures; and to stress repeatedly the merits of intrapreneurship throughout the firm. Rather than develop a stream of incremental innovations, managers in revolutionary eras try to produce radical innovations that threaten their own

Table 10.2. Changing Business-unit Structures

If business strategy is to:	Pressure is to:
Innovate	Decentralize Decisions
	Encourage Networks
Differentiate	Centralize Decisions
	Develop Specialists
Customize	Make Team Decisions
	Remove Management Layers

competitive positions built up from prior innovations. In rapidly changing environments, only by cannibalizing their own products can firms retain their first-mover strategic positions. By announcing and committing to large R&D investments, managers preempt rivals who read into their pronouncements the existence of "sleeping patents" that would prove difficult to overcome.[22]

On occasion it has proved advantageous for pioneering firms to delay cannibalizing their own products with an innovation: By waiting for a challenger to innovate, firms could continue to earn the returns associated with their existing products, confident in their ability to respond quickly when rivals brought out their new products.[23] Even then, however, a firm's status as an innovator, even if it acts as a second mover, depends heavily on a strategic commitment across all levels of structure, defined by heavy R&D investments to build up capability, lateral integration to enhance control, and a commitment to innovativeness conveyed in recurring communications from top managers and reinforced throughout the corporate culture.

As business units grow more concerned with encouraging innovation, managers are decentralizing decision making and encouraging more lateral contact between departments.[24] One popular book coined the word *intrapreneurship* to describe pioneering firms whose internal structures encourage bootlegging time from routine activities to devote to risky ventures, and whose corporate cultures inspired champions to sponsor new ideas.[25]

To ride quickly down the experience curve, however, also requires an integrative, intrapreneurial environment in which employees "own" the technologies and products on which they work. Firms with highly segmented structures inhibit the flow of information across functions, thereby limiting managers' ability to capture experience gains. R&D laboratories are notoriously prone to insularity, making it difficult for feedback to migrate from consumers to product designers, to process engineers.[26]

Managers raise barriers to imitation by obscuring their capabilities from competitors. The more complex the combination of technologies involved in making a product, the less rivals are able to identify the critical skills they need to compete. Insofar as firms' internal cultures develop from their own unique histories, they act as structural barriers to imitation: Rivals have trouble reproducing the deep-seated internal features that led pioneers to innovate.[27]

Researchers report that strategic followers often are subsidiaries and divisions of large established firms with existing businesses in related areas, firms such as Fairchild and Texas Instruments.[28] A study of 129 start-up ventures found that imitators had widely diversified parent firms, spent less on marketing their products than rivals, and had lower product quality and customer service than did first movers.[29] What appears to drive the structuring of firms that choose to be followers, then, is an ability to learn quickly from pioneers and an ability to achieve experience gains quickly.

The pressure to keep up with R&D-intensive innovators in producing radical innovations at a breath-taking pace encourages committed imitators to invest heavily in culling competitive information through all available means, be they strategic hiring of leading firms' employees, or other forms of institutional espionage.[30] Early warning signs of radical innovations enable imitators to adopt new industry standards quickly and make it possible to learn rapidly as soon as the innovations become available.

For quick imitation, followers need efficient external information gathering. By cultivating competitor intelligence, constantly scanning environments, and rapidly responding to opportunity, imitators have often successfully capitalized on the early investments made by pioneers in R&D, buyer education, and personnel training. In semiconductors, for instance, Fairchild benefited from the early efforts of Shockley Transistors, the firm started by transistor pioneer William Shockley, which was dissolved and whose employees then joined Fairchild.[31] In banking, the training programs of money center banks serve to diffuse accounting standards and product innovations. Empirical studies of innovation diffusion suggest that imitators gain access to detailed information on products and manufacturing processes within only 1 year of development through the interpersonal and exchange networks that exist within technological communities.

Because imitators rely on other firms to pioneer, they invest little in basic research, and so dwell more heavily on product development in related technologies. By focusing on price as a means of competing with first movers, they strive to acquire experience gains quickly. Competitive intelligence enables them to avoid the technological mistakes made by pioneers and to incorporate into their product designs early feedback from consumers. Not surprisingly, perhaps, imitators have tended to develop stuctures that are dominated by sales departments, to be constrained by their status as product divisions of larger parents, and to show more inertial tendencies than first movers.

Improving Differentiation. The pressure on firms to differentiate themselves through either price or quality has brought many managers to stress tighter control over operations. To achieve price parity and enhance product quality, efficiency and productivity loom high as sources of competitive advantage. Thus, many managers are investing heavily in automating production and having cutting-edge plant and equipment.

Technological development in manufacturing, however, has steadily made scale economies less salient as a source of advantage. Controlling cost has therefore meant: (1) pruning administrative ratios and centralizing decisions; (2) investing in computer-aided design and manufacturing, robotics, and flexible production; and (3) developing just-in-time relationships with suppliers—inspired by the Japanese—to reduce inventories and stock-outs.

Internally, cost efficiency means operating lean, centralized, and differentiated operations in which specialization improves productivity, control is from the top, product quality is decentralized to employees, financial functions dominate, and managers work out strict cooperative agreements with suppliers. Firms tend to develop relatively rigid department lines, with widespread standardization of activities and extensive cooperation within departments, but significant rivalry and mistrust across departments.

Globalization, technological change, and competition also push cost leaders to improve their operations. Whereas standardization was key to competitiveness in volume production, new technologies provide increasingly cost-effective means of tailor-making mass-produced products. In the machine-tool industry, for instance, early automatic mechanical machines consisted of cumbersome cams and gears. The invention of numerical controls by U.S. toolmakers in the 1960s automated the process, enabling higher precision cutting. By 1975, the advent of microprocessors ushered in computerized numerical control, reducing setup times and increasing production flexibility—further revolutionizing tool making. Once automation, computerized production, and roboticization were complete, however, firms achieved parity in efficiency and found themselves competing on peripheral factors of production: the costs of labor and transportation, and organizational efficiency. In the machine tool industry, maintaining cost leadership provided non-U.S. firms with a distinct competitive advantage that helps explain why U.S. firms that once dominated the $30-billion industry now control less than 10 percent of the global market.

As conditions continue to favor variety over standardization, cost leaders are pushed not only to improve productivity, decrease overhead, and increase administrative efficiency, but also to enhance quality. The popular Baldridge Awards encourage attention to questions of quality in cost-competitive environments. So managers become advocates of extensive training to increase employees' versatility and willingness to play multiple roles in plants; and more readily subcontract support operations that prove noncompetitive when provided in-house. The lean and mean firms that result recognize that consumers look for "value": They recognize the trade-off of price and quality, and look to provide both.

Customizing for Markets. The pressure to customize products and services to client needs puts pressure on managers to decentralize decisions. As a result, many firms encourage employees to form cross-functional networks rather than rely on their bosses and to make important decisions in more autonomous teams. Improving a firm's ability to customize product offerings means involving middle managers and employees heavily in decision making.

Where niche players rely solely on their ability to tailor-make products, they find their cost structures higher than those of large mass customizers.[32] Competition pushes niche players further along the customization and service dimensions and requires them to become product designers in their own right—no longer content to provide craft-like product execution and service, but capable of personalizing products to consumers' tastes in ways that the cost leaders, despite their ability to mass-customize, cannot.

A firm such as Steinway, the famous New York–based maker of concert pianos, recently has had to contemplate strategic change in order to compete with aggressive global competitors like Yamaha. A historical strategy of custom-making pianos for demanding buyers made them resistant to standardizing parts and processes. Labor-intensive operations give the firm a high cost burden and a relatively narrow niche in high-price, high-quality pianos. While Yamaha mass-produces lower priced instruments, its gains enable funding more sophisticated manufacturing processes for higher quality products, threatening Steinway's niche. Responding to market conditions means rethinking the company's singular position in the industry and contemplating producing for more than one niche. That will mean raising the firm's craft-based controls in favor of a more fuctionalized structure.

Rebuilding Corporate Structures

Not only are environments driving companies to make changes in their business structures, they also force managers to reconfigure firms' portfolios of businesses. In turn, portfolio modifications mean reshaping companies' administrative controls through core consolidations and delayering.

Consolidating Core Capabilities.   Market opportunities invite managers to capitalize on their strengths and resources by diversifying into more related products and industries. With an established expertise in the production of leisure vehicles, for instance, auto manufacturers readily extend their activities into related markets and products such as light trucks and recreational vehicles; book publishers branch into information services; television networks set up cable operations; forest products firms take up real estate development. Related diversification broadens a firm's corporate portfolio while maintaining its center of gravity, the anchor that focuses managers' strategic commitments and attention.[33]

Structurally, the search for operating synergy encourages managers to group seemingly related activities under distinct product or market umbrellas. Various empirical studies, among which the most comprehensive has been Richard Rumelt's, have demonstrated a direct relationship between strategy and structure. By comparing the strategies and structures of *Fortune* 500 firms over a 20-year span, Rumelt showed that firms pursuing single-business strategies relied heavily on functional structures, while firms chasing after synergy quickly adopted divisional structures, through which they decentralized decision making to divisions and diminished the role of corporate staff in operating decisions.[34]

The resulting divisional structures are not problem-free: Many suffer from excessive autonomy. In their zeal to decentralize operating decisions, managers often fail to identify viable sources of synergy across divisions, leading to costly duplication and inefficiency.[35]

Take Waterford Crystal, the famous Irish maker of fine tableware. In 1986, the ailing company sought a related diversification by acquiring the Wedgewood china company for $360 million. The intention was clear: to integrate the two operations, streamline production, and use the products' overlapping customer base to strengthen the market positions of both brands. However, fusion soon proved problematic because of wide differences between the crystal and china divisions in terms of target markets (Waterford being more heavily dependent on the United States; Wedgewood, Britain), history, and profitability. Some 4 years later, perhaps erroneously, the company abandoned integration and opted for a holding company structure for its two businesses.[36]

Environmental pressures on related diversifiers push them to tie divisions more closely into clusters of shared activities. Three types of clusters commonly result: (1) product clusters, (2) market clusters, and (3) technology clusters. The need to increase the flow of feedback across divisions and to consumers drives managers towards multipoint structures that place units in matrix relationships. The two-dimensional matrix typically appears in rapidly changing environments and forces interaction between managers in both product and market divisions. More complex still, a three-dimensional matrix represents recognition of the need to shape an active dialogue across the firm that forces three-way interactions by market, product, and technology managers around all key decisions.

Even conglomerates are looking to capitalize on intangible sources of synergy. To exploit them, many holding companies are enlarging corporate staffs and centralizing advisory functions to facilitate the transfer of know-how across divisions. Throughout the 1980s, many financial conglomerates actually metamorphosed into synergistic clusters through a combination of acquisitions and divestitures.[37] By purchasing General Foods and Kraft, for instance, Philip Morris solidified its strategy of transferring marketing savvy across conglomerated divisions. Gulf &

Western, once the quintessential financial conglomerate, shifted to a sector structure in the 1980s, expanded its corporate staff, and encouraged them to intrude into divisional managers' operating decisions.

De-Layering. Growth presents managers with the opportunity to hire more people. The result is often a tendency to add layer upon layer of managers and to build taller pyramids of controls to manage the complexity. In turn, hierarchies create natural career progressions for employees, and promotions become the logical way to motivate productivity.

In recent years, we have grown acutely aware that bureaucracy only further exacerbates complexity and demotivates employees. Pyramidal structures slow down decision making, making innovation difficult. Hierarchies intimidate people to conform and distort information processing. Departments resist cooperating and worry more about protecting their "turf" than about corporate goals. As successful bureaucrats corner resources, they build bloated empires that grow impervious to change.

These reasons are prompting many executives to pursue gains from de-layering their firms. By removing strata from their organizations, managers hope to improve internal coordination and the speed with which they respond to market developments, to increase the level of involvement in decision making among employees, and thereby to ameliorate productivity.

Take GE. In the 10 years since becoming chairman, Jack Welch has reshaped the world's tenth-largest industrial corporation: He eliminated over 100,000 jobs (about 25 percent of the work force) through a combination of layoffs, attrition, and divestitures. He also launched a war on bureaucracy, seeking to double GE's productivity from its lowly 2.5 percent level. The consensus opinion was that, under Welch's predecessor, the much-admired institutional statesman Reginald Jones, GE's bureaucracy had become outsized, collecting vast amounts of detailed information and producing detailed daily reports on hundreds of thousands of items. As one observer put it, "the bureaucracy routinely emasculated top executives by overwhelming them with useless information and enslaved middle managers with the need to gather it."[38] And it resisted change.

To overcome the entrenched internal focus of GE, Welch favors face-to-face meetings. He regularly attends management seminars at GE's Crotonville campus. He communicates directly to all GE employees worldwide through an internal satellite communication system. He also launched Work-out, a systematic program that brings together salaried employees in groups in each of GE's 14 business units to agree on lists of unnecessary meetings, reports, approvals, and tasks that they then pledge to eliminate.

Such a structural transformation is not without risk. De-layering makes promotions more scarce, so people have to be motivated through lateral movement. Where the firm once rewarded seniority, pay is increasingly tied to measurable performance outcomes. Where power was hierarchical and decision making centralized, employees are now more autonomous, and specialists are expected to act as general managers with bottom-line responsibilities. The emphasis shifts from external control to self-control, with employees taking on both responsibility and accountability for efficiency, innovation, and corporate image. Ultimately, de-layering must be coupled with a concerted effort to focus attention on costs. Benefits result from two psychological outcomes:

First, creating cost centers provides firms with a barometer of staff performance; second, it instills in staff groups much-needed self-confidence about their own contributions to line organizations.

The large forest products company Weyerhauser began such a program in 1985. Each of 14 cost centers (such as legal and information services) calculates its expenses, and, at competitive rates, "shadow bills" its internal clients for services rendered. In turn, line managers serviced by staff units have the option of going out to external suppliers. The result: Competition has forced efficiency and innovation into Weyerhauser's cost centers, transforming captive bureaucrats into aggressive entrepreneurs.[39]

Creating Collective Structures

The progressive disintegration of large bureaucracies has also encouraged managers to link up with one another more closely within business communities. The proliferation of network ties affects how they perceive environments, and so how firms compete. In a way, these communities resemble the ecological habitats within which plants and animals coexist: As I argued in Chaps. 3 and 4, they condition how managers define themselves, interpret their competitors, and thereby influence rates of innovation in particular industries, as well as firms' abilities to compete on a global scale.

Eastman Kodak recently announced a trans-Atlantic alliance with Sanofi S.A., a French pharmaceutical firm. The alliance is intended to help Kodak's Sterling Drug unit develop a critical mass in sales and new product development that can enable it to counter the merged Bristol-

Myers-Squibb group and Merck. In return for access to Sanofi products now under development or licensed to American companies such as Abbott Labs and Du Pont, Sterling will provide Sanofi with distribution through its 800-person sales force in the United States.

Bellcore, the largest R&D consortium in the United States, was spawned by the breakup of AT&T in 1984. It constitutes the research arm of the seven Baby Bells. Weighted down by a structure of committttees and a rule that every decision had to be unanimous, the consortium failed to deliver cutting-edge products. Projects were often over budget, products overdesigned, timetables overextended. With a new CEO in place, since early 1991 Bellcore has begun speeding up decision making, prioritizing research programs, and streamlining the bureaucracy in order to respond to fast-moving technologies and adapt to the competitive environment of its parent companies. Like individual firms, then, network structures themselves face radical change and need structures that can simultaneously produce efficiency, entrepreneurship, and equity for member firms.[40]

Among nations Japan, through its Ministry of Trade (MITI), has for many years been most active in helping companies structure cooperative research with rivals, openly acting as the leading sponsor of Japanese industries, defining broad technological domains, and prodding companies to invest in joint research consortia. Indeed, it has become increasingly apparent that the Japanese business community as a whole is structured as a collusive network linking business firms and government regulators. By mutual agreement and through exchange of information, personnel, and favors, firms are actively involved, not only in allocating research funds, but in setting prices and safeguarding joint interests. Not surprisingly, foreign competitors have found it daunting to overcome these structural barriers and successfully challenge Japanese firms on their domestic turf.[41]

In the United States, the military has fueled a considerable amount of technological research with potential commercial application. In its good years, the Pentagon's Defense Advanced Research Projects (DARPA) funnelled most of its $1.2-billion budget to promote aggressively U.S. electronics and semiconductor research. Unfortunately, recent support for Sematech, the semiconductor consortium working on new chip-making techniques and for companies working on high-definition television (HDTV), ran smack up against the Bush administration's opposition to the idea of targeting particular industries[42]—this despite the pleas of many executives from computer makers, software houses, chip producers, and telecommunications companies who urge that the United States adopt a high-tech industrial policy to do battle against Japan.[43]

In contrast, the appeals by executives of European firms have not fallen on deaf ears.* European nations straining to integrate their national economies have aggressively sponsored various cooperative R&D mega-projects. *Eureka,* for instance, is a $10-billion program, begun in 1985, that funds 1600 European companies committed to developing semiconductor technologies. *Esprit* is another program sponsored by the European community to bolster competitiveness in computers and information technology. Some 450 projects have been sponsored to date at a projected cost of $5 billion by 1993. Other highly visible programs such as *Race* and *Brite* have budgeted another $1.3 billion to be spent by 1992 on technology development in telecommunications and aeronautics.

No program has been more successful, perhaps, than the manufacturing consortium, dubbed Airbus Industries, formed by Britain, France, Spain, Belgium, and West Germany to produce commercial airplanes. In 10 years, Airbus has taken over 23 percent of the world market, passing McDonnell Douglas to take the number 2 slot behind the United States' Boeing Co. Although its U.S. critics charge that the consortium has benefited unfairly from generous government subsidies, it demonstrates the changing character of competition on a global scale, which calls for collective strategies, not only among firms, but also among nation-states as they vie to develop a global advantage in vital industries.

Though far from concerted, a collective effort is under way to build a computer highway in the United States. It parallels at the national level the efforts many firms are individually making to integrate the diverse computers, software packages, and databases on which they rely in sales, finance, distribution, and manufacturing. Under founder Robert Kahn's leadership, the Corporation for National Research Initiatives, a nonprofit company started in 1986, has quietly built a coalition of large firms, government agencies, and universities to take part in the research necessary to create a nationwide network of computers providing open and instant access to electronic libraries, at an estimated cost of $200 billion.[44] In contrast to the United States, Japan and other nations have taken the high road, encouraging through their nationalized phone systems the kind of aggressive investment in digital switches and optical fiber that will prove necessary to actualize such informational superhighways.[45] Time will tell which form of collective structure will prove more effective.

The current battle over a standard for HDTV illustrates how firms join

---

*A recent competition sponsored by the U.S. Commerce Department picked 20 American companies with sales of more than $1 billion for federal trade assistance in developing the Japanese market, among them Dana Corporation, EDS, and Timken. This suggests a possible opening in Washington's willingness to help U.S. firms compete in industries in which foreign competitors receive direct or indirect support from their governments (Farnsworth, Clyde, "20 Companies Get U.S. Help with Japan," *New York Times:* 29 March 1991, D1, D2.).

into network structures as they try to develop competitive positions in new technologies. As in airlines, computers, and telecommunications, the issue increasingly pits, not only firms, but entire nations against each other: Firms from the United States, Japan, and Europe have each proposed different standards. Adoption of a standard will provide some firms with a competitive advantage, and so favor the countries from which these firms originate. In the struggle for positioning in the large global market for HDTV, Zenith's managers, for instance, have aggressively pursued a multitiered strategy designed to: (1) obtain support by the U.S. government for Zenith's standard; (2) forge domestic alliances with suppliers to develop component parts; and (3) develop foreign alliances with firms and government officials to prepare for rapid distribution as soon as regulations provide broadcast spectrum, permitting production and distribution of HDTVs.

The decision by Zenith's top managers to sell off the firm's profitable computer division to France's Honeywell-Bull in 1989 gambled the firm's future on the success of its efforts in HDTV. By the fall of 1990, however, with its stock price at an all-time low and with both American and Japanese competitors proposing a digital standard that Zenith has yet to develop fully, Zenith faced takeover threats from Nycor, the maker of Fedders air conditioners, and the possibility of significant distraction from the task at hand.[46] A broad alliance with South Korea's Goldstar gave some financial and manufacturing muscle to Zenith's drive towards HDTV, but left the software side begging.[47] In contrast, Japan's leading electronics makers, Sony, Matsushita, NEC, and Toshiba, all introduced consumer HDTV products that included televisions and videocassette recorders in November 1990—a strategy clearly geared to building a first-mover advantage for the Japanese standard. Already Sony and Matsushita are busy converting their purchases of Columbia Pictures and Universal Studios into video software that can exploit HDTV's best features.[48]

The race toward an HDTV standard further accelerated when dramatic technological breakthroughs by Zenith and General Instruments suggested the feasibility of an all-digital system that would make European and Japanese systems obsolete. Rivalry escalated again when Zenith announced a joint venture with AT&T that would compete, not only with the digital system developed by General Instruments, but with one produced by another consortium of NBC, Thomson S.A. of France, North American Philips, NBC, and the David Sarnoff Research Center in Princeton, N.J.[49] In the background, three Japanese companies, Fujitsu, Sony, and Hitachi, joined forces with U.S.-based Texas Instruments to develop the microchips that will prove necessary to any digital HDTV system.[50]

Clearly, firms and governments are increasingly confronting how to structure interfirm networks to support the collective strategies through which many globalizing industries tend. How centralized should the interfirm network be? Which functions should be consolidated and which ones should be immune from antitrust considerations? These questions are likely to receive much attention in the turbulent global environment of the year 2000.

The Architecture of Simplicity

In time, all corporate structures become ineffective: Firms outgrow the systems and procedures that were designed to meet earlier market conditions. Bureaucracy is no exception. The costs of managing many of our tall hierarchies now far outstrip the benefits we gain from them. Not surprisingly, many prominent leaders are altering our conceptions of how firms should run, and of what managers should do to cope with the revolutionary circumstances they now face.

The productivity loss occasioned by structures mired in procedural humdrum is incalculable. It costs us heavily in terms of corporate efficiency, customer satisfaction, tax revenues, and global competitiveness. As enlightened managers contemplate strategic change, they increasingly recognize the artificial limitations placed on them by continued adherence to anachronistic ideas about how to govern, supervise, manage, administer, and motivate. They call into question a canon of beliefs that regards management as the caretaker of ever more standardized operating procedures.

In radically changing environments, then, the structural tools that managers rely on call for them to build interfirm networks; prune bureaucracy; decentralize decisions; improve two-way communication up, down, and laterally; reunite personal and work lives; encourage participation; and expose sheltered units to competition. They constitute the building blocks of a new corporate form, one more attuned to a revolutionary context that requires managers to resolve the contradictions inherent in demands that firms be simultaneously efficient, entrepreneurial, equitable, and ethical.

As both firms and nations prepare to compete more aggressively for the consumer markets of the year 2000, collective structures are heavily featured in efforts to strengthen the capabilities of firms, industries, and nations. Developing these interfirm networks requires a shared awareness of the benefits to be gained from cooperative action among firms and key institutions such as schools, universities, and agencies of government.

In Conclusion:
Creating the Future

*It is often the failure who is the pioneer in
new lands, new undertakings, and new forms
of expression.*

ERIC HOFFER

In 1980 *Business Week* devoted an entire issue to "The Reindustrializa-
tion of America." Reporters brought forth alarming statistics that pur-
ported to show the declining competitiveness of the United States against
Japan and West Germany; its advanced bureaucratic sclerosis visible in its
failure to capitalize on new technologies; the inability of firms to overcome the narcissism of young workers; and the adversarial stance of
organized labor. In its pages, a plethora of executives, academics, and
leaders urged that we build a stronger partnership among business, labor,
and government to respond to the growing challenges posed by heightened global interdependence.

To no avail. Throughout the 1980s, corporate America expended
much of its spare resources in a speculative frenzy. Junk bonds, LBOs,
and asset swaps dominated discussions in the executive suite and fueled
managerial initiatives. Spurred by threatening raiders eager to capitalize
on years of management excess, executives hired aggressive financiers to
defend them, making virtual demigods of Wall Street's wizards.

As managers played corporate roulette with America's assets, they grew
increasingly distant from the operating cores of their firms, neglecting

228

the foundations on which they had built their corporate empires. To think strategically came to mean boosting firms' stock prices, at whatever cost. Logically, many managers cut R&D funding, dampening the likelihood that future innovations would come from U.S. firms. They turned to acquiring other, seemingly more profitable or faster-growing firms to make up for their inability to grow from within. They actively lobbied government for protected status from foreign competition instead of tightening belts and modernizing plants. They invested in slick advertising to make up for declining product quality.

In fact, most of these decisions were never strategically motivated. In a sense, managers' obsession with quick financial gain produced an artificial bubble of rising prices for corporate assets. When the bubble burst at decade's end, few corporate initiatives had actually strengthened firms' global competitiveness. In the glare of the 1990s, it became blatantly apparent in industry after industry that the competitiveness of many fat, sheltered, and complacent firms had declined to an all-time low during the gung-ho years of the casino society, leaving them vulnerable to frontal and flank attacks by aggressive global rivals.

Today the strategic challenge for our firms lies in returning to the operating roots from which they derive their competitiveness. After widespread neglect of firms' financial and human assets, managers are charged with remodeling their firms' basic capabilities, controls, and cultures and thereby helping to rebuild the national infrastructure. Achieving vigor will require aggressive redeployments of capital and people to improve timing and differentiation at the business level, to create synergy at the corporate level, and to mobilize shared interests with rivals and institutional support at the collective level.

Environmental conditions have called attention to some basic failings of our most prized institution, bureaucracy.[1] Rapid technological change and the globalization of industries have sharpened our awareness of bureaucracy's fundamental limitations. Most of our firms rely on specialization and hierarchy to manage complexity, thereby inducing alienation in people who work in those settings. We know well the injurious effects of alienation on corporate efficiency and innovation. Add to that a structural tendency toward inequity in the distribution of rewards and a technocratic reluctance to address moral issues in making decisions, and you have a solid indictment of bureaucracy. A key challenge for managers exploring strategic change, then, is to seek out better ways of enhancing the performance of firms and institutions.

Yet before we can execute change, we must first conceive it, and therein lies the critical problem: To ask, even to demand, of firms that they participate in strategic change cannot be enough. Firms belong to wider institutional settings and business communities that inhibit their ability to call on new conceptions of organizing or to experiment with new styles of leadership. Most managers and employees derive their social understandings from institutions such as business schools, professions, and unions that propagate anachronistic views of how to organize. We train MBA students, for instance, to have hierarchical views of authority and responsibility and to hold top management in heroic regard. We teach them to scorn operations and to hold out for the more alluring, promotion-filled line jobs. We shower our best graduates with power and glory when they take jobs in investment banking or in consulting, and nod with scarcely disguised scorn when they take staff jobs in personnel departments. After all, who can argue with six-figure starting salaries? With uncapped lifetime earnings? With jobs in which the size of your bonus establishes your ranking in the corporate pecking order?

We need nothing less than radical change in our *mental models of management* if we are to reorient our firms' effectiveness as institutions and to enhance their ability to attend simultaneously to questions of efficiency, entrepreneurship, equity, and ethics—the four Es of corporate performance. Change of this sort requires leaders with both vision and skill: the vision to recognize the revolutionary transformation required in our conception of the corporation as a tool for achieving societal goals, and the skill to mobilize employees and other stakeholders behind their efforts. Such leaders are not a dime a dozen.

To inspire rather than dictate, to mobilize rather than rule, to persuade rather than command, mean a fundamental reshaping of firms' internal cultures and controls. Decentralization and self-management warrant our attention as ways to generate strategic change because they tend also to enhance corporate productivity and the quality of peoples' work lives. Involving employees in significant decision making increases the flexibility and speed with which we can respond to competitive challenges. It also builds into our firms an ability to innovate that should prove essential to their survival in the globalized industries of the future. Networking with competitors brings together people with specialized skills to address problems, the resolution of which surpasses the abilities of any single firm. Such strategic reorientations require that we pay careful attention not only to the microcultures of our firms, but also to the macrocultures of the industries and communities in which our firms thrive.

Prescriptions like these apply to all firms competing in the globalizing environment of the late twentieth century. Because they derive from underlying regularities of management, they also describe the enduring dynamics experienced by all institutions that are coping with radical disruptions in their environments. From such strategic changes should rise a new, more active firm, one with managers and employees jointly committed to the task of competing in the turbulent global arena.[2]

Toward the Activist Firm

Many large companies today, including some of our most treasured firms, look less like the sleek and efficient engines of textbook capitalism and more like the public bureaucracies of socialism. Faced with disparate objectives and serving multiple constituents, they have become slow, inefficient, inward-looking, and inert. To increase their competitiveness and institutional effectiveness, their managers are conceiving and executing fundamental reorientations.

To negotiate a passage through these strategic turning points, managers of firms and institutions are charged with the task of selecting the ends they intend to fulfill, the strategies they will rely on to fulfill these ends, the means by which to accomplish them, and the standard against which to evaluate their performance.

What Vision?

As the 1980s taught us, the necessary strategic changes firms must make challenge managers, not only to improve competitiveness and profitability, but also to provide meaningful work; to enhance the lot of minorities in the workplace while maintaining employment; to redress social injustice while innovating to create valuable products and services; and to increase living standards in both home and host countries while protecting the ecological environment. In short, firms must act, not only as economic agents, but as institutions.

Because multiple parties are affected by strategic changes in corporate trajectories, lives are disrupted. As firms' capabilities are recast, managers design new corporate controls to implement them. They transform job categories, displace workers, disrupt careers, challenge established patterns of interaction, and try to shape new cultural assumptions. Clearly, not everyone's interests are served. Whose interests should weigh more heavily? Those of active traders concerned about firms' short-run financial performance? Those of investors interested in dividends and the stability of future earnings? Those of employees concerned about their jobs, careers, and wages? Or those of public interest groups clamoring for attention to firms' social responsibilities?

The pressure to act as institutional caretakers means that managers face constant tension: They participate in a strained tug-of-war between the diverse objectives of their different stakeholders. The danger is twofold: On the one hand, managers may overemphasize one group's preferences over another's, thereby misrepresenting corporate objectives and necessarily alienating many stakeholders. On the other hand, the struggle to address all concerns equally can paralyze corporate decision making, forcing managers to make inadequate responses to all environmental challenges. Neither alternative is appealing.

Simultaneously, the diversity of audiences and objectives often makes the difference between success and failure of a strategic change quite small. Much as promoters use word-of-mouth to generate advance ticket sales for Broadway-bound musicals, the success of a strategic change requires generating praise from key corporate audiences, few of which have sufficient information to assess fully the merits of a strategic change. So, increasingly, the key battle is over interpretations: What do managers intend to achieve; whose pet projects or businesses will prevail; how long will it take; who will gain or lose; whose jobs, pay, perks, careers, and expectations will be affected; what will be the impact on customers, on shareholders, on the stock's price? Since all involve forecasting uncertain outcomes of implementing strategic change, all are clouded by misunderstandings, manipulated by coalitions, and distorted by self-interest. And corporate performance is essentially a matter of *appearances*.

So strategic change increasingly involves the manipulation of information. Armed with actions that are invariably inadequate to all stakeholders' queries, the ultimate success of senior executives depends on their ability to produce, for both internal and external observers, a consistent and credible interpretation of both the environment and of the company's strategy. This is no simple public relations task. To completely master stakeholders' interpretations requires an understanding of how strategic changes affect, not only bottom-line accounting results, but also regulators, the trade press, the business media and, for publicly traded firms, the stock market.

What Strategies?

Globalization and competition are influencing the kinds of strategic changes managers make at the business, corporate, and collective levels. Within business units, managers are being pushed to pursue a more aggressive stance to compete with assertive rivals. In an increasingly entrepreneurial world, environmental challenges erode barriers separating firms from their competitors. They demand that managers become more aggressive.

In turn, aggressiveness means a riskier deployment of resources to align corporate capabilities with the requirements of the marketplace. Shifting competitive conditions are forcing managers to make strategic moves designed to increase the speed with which their firms act, to deepen their firms' differentiation, or to narrow their firms' scope.

At the corporate level, the pressure is unilaterally toward increased relatedness across business portfolios. In an environment characterized by ever more rapidly changing technologies and competitive incursions by aggressive rivals, top managers today are carefully scrutinizing the sources of synergy across their businesses and looking for ways of tapping the latent sources of competitive advantage related diversifications present. More than ever, being competitive at the corporate level involves tapping the secret reservoir of efficiencies that lies hidden in the vast array of products and businesses many large firms have brought under their corporate portfolios.

Simultaneously, rising complexity makes solitary action difficult. Increasingly, then, managers are contemplating strategic changes that require coordinating with, targeting, or outright alliance with direct competitors. These collective strategies already have proven themselves highly important in enabling firms to meet environmental challenges. They are a vital means by which managers are altering their firms' trajectories and overcoming resistance to change. In the rapidly changing environment of the 1990s, as financially driven mergers and acquisitions wane and as global companies find themselves locked in mortal combat, these collective strategies are clearly gaining in importance.

So the competitive landscape is getting more clustered. As managers recognize their reciprocity with other firms and interest groups in many product groups where firms once competed in isolation, they now compete as allies in business communities—as clusters of firms and institutions that jointly produce products and services. These business communities constitute filters that link corporate action to societal outcomes. They form recognizable contexts for the growing competition between nations and firms in the development, production, and distribution of goods and services. As citizens of these business communities, firms and managers must play a vital role in bringing about social change by encouraging, for instance, responsible decision making about pollution, energy conservation, education, health, and the public good.

What Means?

As GE, IBM, AT&T, and many others are demonstrating actively, executing these strategic changes involves shaping a new corporate form, one with a streamlined, more decentralized internal structure that can support simultaneous and often contradictory stakeholder pressures for increased efficiency, entrepreneurship, equity, and ethics.

Implementation concerns require that senior managers not fall victim to bureaucratic principles that encourage them to dictate rather than to mobilize, to repress rather than to inspire, to control rather than to lead. Successfully guiding firms through strategic turning points asks of executives that they embrace a view of strategic change as a deep-seated transformation of their firms, one that entails involvement, inclusion, participation, and commitment from the entire corporate population.

Firms with boards and top teams subservient to their CEOs are more likely to succumb to inertial forces that favor the status quo. The more top teams dominate the board through insider appointments, the more likely they are to screen out information that might compel strategic change. Healthy boards and heterogeneous top teams bring breadth and diversity to firms, compelling managers to confront events, opinions, and possibilities they otherwise might choose to bypass.

Visionary leaders are paying close attention to how the cultural underpinnings of their firms have been affected by changing market conditions. As nations increasingly interpenetrate and as firms globalize, the cultural bonds that once tied employees closely to one another are weakening. Corporate cultures are becoming more dilute and incoherent, less able to provide firms with the internal glue that once shaped common interpretations of environments, strategies, and events. Simultaneously, environments have placed added pressure on managers to make their firms' cultures, not only more efficient and entrepreneurial, but also more equitable and ethical. Enlightened leaders, therefore, are relying more than ever on cultural symbols as a beacon around which to engage employees and other stakeholders rather than as a vehicle for exerting control and inducing conformity.

To cope with changing environments, managers negotiating turning points are engaging in a deep restructuring of their firms' cost structures, capabilities, staffs, and decision-making processes. Exposure to the global arena has weakened the bonds of corporate culture and reaffirmed the importance of finding means to regenerate employee commitment and involvement. In recent years, visionary firms have increased their experimentation with restructuring their operations in ways that can produce cost savings, while pruning cumbersome bureaucracies and encouraging more entrepreneurial networking among employees.

Decentralization also looms higher on managers' priorities. By granting more autonomy to employees and units, more self-control over their own performance, managers are revamping their internal structures, making them more like loosely coupled networks of specialized profit centers—each more entrepreneurial and efficient, and the totality more flexible. These network structures are a revolutionary new form of organization, one that requires new management practices and controls different from those applied in our anachronistic bureaucracies.

For one thing, this new form means that firms whose leaders encourage employees to take initiatives must recognize that failure is inevitable when risks are involved. So, not only do they tolerate failure, they demand it. For another, executives admit that success requires fairness: Employees resist contributing to tasks for which they are poorly rewarded. Finally, exposure to market forces, and wide-ranging and open communication more closely bind employees, enabling a culture to emerge that reunites the personal and work lives of employees. Productivity invariably increases in such a firm, as does its effectiveness as an institution.

Building the Active Society

Global as our industries have become, they continue to operate in a fragmented political system of nation-states. In international exchanges, individual countries vie to defend the parochial interests of their people. In recent years, countries such as Japan, Germany, Singapore, South Korea, and Taiwan have showed an exemplary capacity to mobilize their populations around societal projects designed to enhance the competitiveness of their domestic industries in the global marketplace. In so doing, they have shown how collaborations between business, government, and unions can help build for their nations a competitive advantage. The United States lags in applying the lessons learned. Since the early Reagan years, we have paid lip service to laissez-faire principles that make us skeptical of governmental guidance and suspicious of cooperative relationships.

In contrast, with consummate skill, Japan has shown how government can collaborate with private-sector firms to achieve societal objectives. In the postwar era, Japanese bureaucrats have regularly targeted industry after industry, whether consumer electronics, robots, machine tools, or semiconductors. Support policies have included tax incentives that compel citizens to save and provide business with cheap capital to invest; protective walls that prevent foreign intrusion and aggressive domestic competition; and R&D subsidies that encourage innovation. The point, then, is not the targeting of specific industries. Instead, it is the generic backing that various institutional actors provide to business communities—particularly government through its tax policies, educational subsidies, and regulations.

After all, even in the most perfectly competitive settings, firms do not compete single-handedly. They inhabit institutional environments that facilitate, push, or inhibit development. To build high-performing firms, therefore, requires that we question our design of the institutional context within which businesses compete, and explore different ways of structuring these corporate environments. Can U.S. institutions keep up with global developments? Can they themselves carry out the much needed radical changes that can contribute to rebuilding the decaying infrastructure?

Invigorating Schools

Many U.S. institutions have faltered badly in the postwar era, none more prominently than those responsible for building the nation's human capital. Critics charge that public schools fail to equip the lowest-common-denominator student with basic skills like reading, writing, and arithmetic. Colleges are chastised for graduating too many liberal arts majors with no applied skills. Graduate schools of business are accused of producing specialists versed at managing by the numbers, but lacking any fundamental insight into the basic operating cores of their firms.

Like all institutions, schools, too, must rise to the challenge of strategic change. Listen to the objectives outlined by U.S. President George Bush in his State of the Union address of January 31, 1990:

> By the year 2000, every child must start school ready to learn. The United States must increase the high school graduation rate to no less than 90%. In critical subjects, at the fourth, eighth, and 12th grades, we must assess our students' performance. U.S. students must be the first in the world in math and science achievement. Every American adult must be a skilled, literate worker and citizen. Every school must offer the kind of disciplined environment that makes it possible for our kids to learn.

As those familiar with the U.S. public school system attest, to meet these ambitious objectives requires strategic change at the federal, state, city, and school levels. At every level, inertia prevails, reinforced by a web of regulations and ingrained practices that impede change. For instance, the amount of federal aid provided to many schools is proportional to the school's dropout rate, a seemingly logical allocation. However, such a reward system creates a built-in disincentive to reduce dropout rates since doing so would reduce funding. State boards of education also dictate what teachers teach and from what texts, divorcing educators from any entrepreneurial potential their jobs might have. In most public school systems, pay is controlled centrally and is mainly based on seniority, making excellence difficult to reward.

Various entrepreneurial schools and states throughout the United States have begun experimenting with various programs designed to deregulate and revitalize education. Most studies indicate that more effective schools tend to have: (1) strong principals who provide leadership in instructional matters, (2) teachers with high expectations of student achievement, (3) a strong emphasis on learning basic skills, (4) an ability to maintain good order and discipline, (5) regular evaluation of students, and (6) a large allotment of time to study.[3] An analysis by the RAND think tank concluded that successful urban high schools in particular tended sharply to define goals for students. These schools also were more inclined to solve their own problems and to take initiatives, and considered themselves more accountable to local communities than to higher authorities.[4]

Critics point out how our educational system is run, in fact, like turn-of-the-century factories: They are centrally managed, inclined to efficiency and regulation, and rely on teachers trained in repetitive pedagogical techniques, rigid scheduling, and standardized texts and tests. Clearly, they suggest, a revolution is at hand, one that parallels the ongoing transformation of American industry into less rigid, more decentralized structures.[5] Schools might benefit from an internal organization that can deliver, like private-sector firms, a bit more efficiency, entrepreneurship, equity, and ethics.

To tackle efficiency, for instance, some states and cities are trying to dismantle the regulatory web that now centralizes both responsibility and accountability and circumscribes their ability to improvise solutions. They involve more stakeholders in the governance of their schools: administrators, union leaders, parents, teachers, students, and business firms from the community. They also pay higher salaries to attract more competent teachers and administrators, and promote after-school programs to accelerate learning.

Competition is another way to discipline schools and build equity among teachers. In recent years, several states in the United States have inaugurated a market-like system for inducing school performance: Minnesota, Nebraska, Iowa, Arkansas, and Ohio now offer parental choice, and students can attend any public school in the state. To further fuel performance, eight states now allocate financial incentives to teachers and schools for improving test scores and graduation rates. Tests themselves are being reevaluated to assess students on such qualities as creativity and teamwork.[6] A proposal to introduce national student testing is now under consideration.[7]

Indeed, the school reform program that President Bush presented to Congress in April 1991 explicitly calls for "...a revolution in American education." The key points of the plan involve: (1) promoting freedom of choice among public and private schools; (2) close but decentralized monitoring of student progress in grades 4, 8, and 12 in five core subject areas; (3) a pay-for-performance system to reward differentially better teachers; (4) voluntary nationwide examinations in English, math, science, history, and geography; and (5) skills standards provided by business and labor.[8]

In the United States' leading graduate schools of business, strategic change is also in the offing. Competition for students has grown to a fever pitch in the last few years, doubtless exacerbated by the popular *Business Week* and *U.S. News & World Report* annual issues that rate the best American business schools. Traditional surveys had polled only deans of business schools under the assumption that they would be the best informed about educational quality. Since 1988, however, the magazine has chosen instead to poll the schools' clients, namely graduates and recruiters. The resulting rankings suggested that many customers felt shortchanged by the emphasis that leading institutions have placed on research rather than on teaching, on specialties such as finance rather than on general management, and on structure-oriented problem formulation rather than on people-based implementation. In many of these schools, strategic changes are under way as deans vie for first place in redressing

238

In Conclusion: Creating the Future

eir MBA programs to prepare students for managerial careers in the topsy-turvy environment of the year 2000.[9]

At 17th-ranked New York University's Leonard N. Stern School of Business, for instance, a review committee had this to say:

> Although emphasizing faculty research has taken us a long way over the past two decades, moving the Stern School into the top tier of the nation's business schools cannot be achieved merely by increasing the faculty's list of publication; it requires, we believe, a commitment to the mission of achieving consistent excellence across the full range of our activities, and a reward system consistent with that commitment.[10]

One outcome of increased competition for students and closer monitoring of performance has been a concerted effort to meet better the needs of business schools' diverse constituents. At Stern, this has meant consolidating the school's activities in a newly built, state-of-the-art management center, reducing the school's student-faculty ratio, and revising its curriculum to do a better job of addressing students' concerns.

Similarly aggressive reforms have been implemented or are being contemplated by other business schools around the country to enhance their competitiveness. For instance, after ranking a lowly 11th in the *Business Week* survey of 1988, the University of Chicago's Graduate School of Business launched an internal study that came to some sobering conclusions: For one, Chicago does not sufficiently emphasize either the interpersonal skills needed to manage people, nor the skills needed in everyday problem solving. Courses lacked practical applications or a focus on leadership or on management techniques. One result has been a rethinking of Chicago's curriculum offerings and the hiring of consultants to devise seminars in "soft" skills such as negotiation tactics and team building.[11] At the University of Texas at Austin's business school, students voted to pay $200 more a year in fees to finance computer purchases and administrative positions that might help raise the ranking among the nation's leading business schools.[12]

Ethical considerations loom large in educational reform. For instance, all eight Ivy League schools (Brown, Columbia, Cornell, Dartmouth, Harvard, Princeton, Penn, and Yale) now face charges of price fixing in setting tuition increases and in assigning students financial aid.[13] After scrutinizing research grants, the federal government has also accused 250 campuses of submitting bills for expenses related only remotely, if at all, to research activities. Audits of 19 universities and medical centers are now in the works. As a result, many of these institutions are carefully probing their internal cultures and structures to screen out unethical practices. Already Stanford University, the California Institute of Technology, and the Harvard Medical School have each returned to the government $500,000 in illegitimate research costs.[14] So far, Stanford appears to have paid the heaviest price for its ethical transgressions: Its president has resigned and the accounting firm Arthur Andersen is reviewing the university's budgets as far back as 1983.[15]

Shaking Up Unions and the Professions

Accustomed to resisting managerial initiatives, unions have historically inhibited efforts at executing strategic change, even when faced with extinction. Eastern Airlines was driven into bankruptcy by its striking unions, a result that can hardly have been attractive to any one of the parties to the conflict. Striking unions also forced established firms such as Greyhound Lines into bankruptcy reorganizations from which they are unlikely to emerge unscathed.

Declining unionization rates compel unions to rethink their function and implement strategic changes of their own. Whereas in slack environments unions could once act as corporate disciplinarians, preventing managerial excess, now the global market subjects firms to strict control. Where the corporate surplus was once easily appropriated by managers, multiple stakeholders, regulators, and external interest groups now actively monitor managers' actions, and insist on relative fairness in managers' dealings with employees. Where safety was once a prerogative of management, government regulations, insurance plans, and a litigious society now protect workers from the vagaries of work. No wonder the 1980s were characterized by so-called concession bargaining in most sectors of the economy: Having successfully championed workers for decades, unions by then had become virtually devoid of constituents.

Moreover, whereas the owners of capital were once a class distinct from the workers, employee stock ownership plans now grant ownership rights to employees in over 20,000 firms of all sizes. If employees are themselves owners, then they already have legitimate authority over the actions taken by nonowning managers. What role, then, for unions?

Leading unions such as the United Auto Workers now struggle with precisely that question. The answer is that unions might play a more useful role, not as managerial adversaries, but as productivity coordinators—a role more closely resembling that of an ombudsman than a negotiator.[16] As such, they would shoulder equal responsibility with management for coping with environmental challenges, formulating strategies, and devising viable means for executing them. Clearly, this approach requires a profound strategic change in union leaders' self-concepts, in union structures, and in union cultures. It is occuring in many organizations committed to blurring the line between workers and managers.[17]

In the development of General Motors' long-anticipated Saturn model, for instance, the UAW pointed the way by joining hands almost from the very beginning with GM managers. The GM-UAW agreement hammered out in 1985 has little in common with the standard contract that emphasized grievance procedures, work rules, and safety nets in case of layoffs. Instead, a partnership of management and labor makes decisions about who will work, benefit, or lose in the Saturn plant. All decisions require a consensus. So UAW members participate in selecting Saturn's suppliers, ad agency, and dealers. All the plant's employees are salaried, not paid hourly wages, and eat in the same company cafeterias. Pay increases are contingent on meeting productivity targets. Staffing for all blue- and white-collar jobs had to be approved by a Saturn panel drawn from both union and management ranks. The panel's selections were based, not only on technical skill, but on the kinds of interpersonal skills required for work done in teams.[18]

If, in the past, unions have constrained our ability to respond to changing environments, today they increasingly recognize the need to execute fundamental reorientations that can make them active partners in the running of firms. Take Corning. In partnership with the American Flint Glass Workers union, the company opted for a team-based production system in the mid-1980s that would give line workers more responsibility for operating decisions. The progressive union recognized the new role it would be called on to play in helping Corning remain competitive in the global marketplace.[19]

More drastically, in 1989 Republic Engineered Steels became one of the few U.S. companies that are solely owned by the employees who work there. Workers, through their union, hold the same number of board positions as managers, and share in all decision making. Faced with a weak economy and necessary modernization investments, both managers and workers actively collaborated to produce cost savings that could help avoid massive layoffs among the company's 4000 workers. The hardest task: abandoning the traditional adversarial relationship that had so long characterized the interactions between managers, supervisors, and workers.[20]

In a sense, unions as organizations now compete directly with other stakeholder associations in representing workers. They have two choices: change or vanish. Forward-thinking unions are choosing to collaborate with managers in creative ways and to implement strategic change.

So are other professionals. Take accountants, for instance. As scandal after scandal has washed down on the financial community, the role of accountants and auditors has never been more subject to scrutiny. Cross-national comparisons suggest that auditors in the United States have been less than independent in corporate reviews, and have allowed firms too easily to build momentum in undesirable directions. After all, whose agents are accountants: the managers who hired them, firms' shareholders, or the wider public?[21] Should accountants incorporate into their role, in addition to its dominant technical focus, a view of themselves as active, critical elements of society?[22]

Reformists propose that auditors share information with regulating and prosecuting authorities in order to act as legitimate checks on managers' initiatives. As one observer points out, "under current professional rules of the American Institute of Certified Public Accountants and the Securiites and Exchange Commission, when auditors detect serious improprieties that management refuses to correct, the most they can do is resign from the audit and make sure the client informs regulators of the reason for the split." However, U.S. auditors have no obligation to act as whistle blowers nor to help regulators investigate.[23]

In contrast, England's Banking Act of 1987 created a three-way coordination between auditors, clients, and regulators that invests auditors with the responsibility for reporting incriminating information about clients. Since then, auditors and regulators have cooperated on various troubled banks, without loss of client support.

Indeed, it was the Bank of England that instructed the accounting firm Price Waterhouse to investigate its client, the Bank of Credit Commerce International, an effort that led to its multinational indictment for fraud. The ongoing investigation revealed that in April 1990, despite having expressed mounting concern to the bank over "false or deceitful" transactions, the accounting firm signed less than 2 weeks later BCCI's annual report for 1989, making no mention either of false or deceitful transactions, or of other concerns.

Similar three-way interactions between professionals, a regulator, and a client may make sense beyond the confines of the auditing community, by providing a check on corporate excess. Moreover, just as financial audits provide information about managers' expenditures, so it may make sense to supply stakeholders with climate surveys that audit how well the firm has managed its employees, reduced environmental pollution, or safeguarded consumer safety.

Emancipating the Bureaucrats

Cost overruns, inefficiency, and the capture of government agencies by the businesses that they were designed to regulate attracted considerable attention in Japan, the United Kingdom, France, and the United States throughout the 1980s. Government-managed businesses proved disappointing in their inability to innovate and create new products, and slow to react to evolving technologies.

Much as schools began experimenting with strategic changes that introduced market discipline as a way to enhance their performance, so in recent years have city, state, and federal governments tried to subject regulatory agencies to competitive pressure. Around the world, computer companies made dramatic inroads on state telephone monopolies throughout the 1980s, challenging Japan's Nippon Telephone and Telegraph, France's PTT, and West Germany's Bundespost. By the late

1980s, these countries had all chosen to privatize their phone services, either partially or completely. The collapse of the Soviet empire has resuscitated extensive dialogue about privatization. In countries like Poland, where central planning long stifled growth, governments are unloading plants and companies. Czechoslovakia sold off its auto plants Skoda and BAZ to Volkswagen, and auctioned close to 100,000 small state businesses in 1991. In Latin America a similar trend is taking place: Mexico, Brazil, Argentina, Chile, and Venezuela have taken private a host of mining, airline, steel making, and telephone companies.[24]

Detailed studies comparing government services supplied through private firms and those provided by public agencies conclude that private supply tends to be more efficient than public provision. A comparison of public and private trash collection in the United States, Canada, Switzerland, and Japan concluded than in 11 of 14 cases private collection was more efficient.[25] Researchers report similar results for street cleaning, ship maintenance, law enforcement, fire protection, prisons, school bus operation, railroad track repair, fire departments, and housing construction.

In fact, privatization may not even be necessary. Since the critical variable affecting efficiency is competition, most services will be more efficiently delivered by both public and private firms *as long as consumers can turn to other suppliers.*[26] The U.S. Post Office, although a public agency, is among the more efficient because of its rivalry with U.P.S., Federal Express, and Emery Air.

Exposing public agencies to market forces also extends to private-sector firms that have themselves become too bureaucratic: Staff departments in many large companies have shown a tendency similar to that of public agencies toward developing cost overruns and inefficiency when they operate exclusively for a parent firm. To improve efficiency, many large firms have opted to open captive departments to outside competition by requiring service acquirers to get rival bids before contracting in-house and by pushing those departments to offer their services externally as well.

To introduce captive agencies and departments to market dynamics is to call for radical strategic change within government institutions. As for schools and unions, external competition can provide discipline where hierarchical control systems have not.

Counterbalancing the Media

Reporters clearly contribute to shaping how events are interpreted by firms' outside observers. Far from being neutral, the record suggests that the press play an outsized role in swinging public perceptions to extremes, either dampening or magnifying events far beyond their real effects. The pressure to communicate quickly in print and television often induces reporters to present stories with limited investigative content, which leaves them prone to bias in presentation and interpretation.

In recent years, the press' role in biasing perceptions has grown more significant, resulting in pressure for firms to confer greater attention and resources upon public relations, investor relations, and government relations. Most large firms hire internal staffs, PR agencies, and lobbyists to mediate their relationships with key stakeholders and improve their self-presentations in the media.

The media's influence on public perceptions was perhaps most clearly demonstrated during the 1982 Tylenol poisonings. Johnson & Johnson, the manufacturer of Tylenol, has since been lauded for its skillful handling of the media: They took care to capitalize on their position as the victims of a crime; by acting quickly to remove all inventory from store shelves, they also demonstrated concern for the consumer and affirmed their social responsibility. They took on the media as partners in communicating with the public.[27] In contrast, Exxon's managers proved far less skillful in managing their ties to the media in the wake of the Valdez oil spill of 1989.

In general, managers appear to be of two sorts: Those who favor spending heavily to build cozy relationships with reporters and analysts, with an eye to coopting them; and those who distance themselves from public relations, avoiding contact and maintaining a veil of secrecy over their firms' actions.

Neither is to the good.

Whether during crises or in revolutionary periods, as events swirl around them, publics demand assistance in interpreting the goings on. Managers who hold the press at arm's-length only encourage suspicious explorations by investigative reporters and so invite one-sided presentations in the press. At the same time, managers who pander to the press also bias reporters' views and invite slanted presentations.

During uncertain eras, we can only approximate objectivity by searching for consensually validated information. That means finding ways to build more *balanced* attention to issues and events. Both managers and reporters would benefit from viewing their relationships as a balancing of interpretations about events with indeterminate causes and unpredictable consequences. Publics benefit from more rather than less information, and from balanced accounts rather than sensationalism.

Positions, Please... Action!

For years notions of Darwinian evolution have guided our thinking about how change takes place in organisms and individuals and, by implication, in firms and societies. We have assumed that most change is gradual and incremental, that individuals and firms evolve slowly to keep things in equilibrium.

In contrast, various scientists have pointed to the revolutionary periods that appear to punctuate the timeline of organisms, individuals, firms, and societies. They remind us of the dramatic disappearance of the dinosaurs as a metaphor for understanding how, throughout time, dramatic change in life conditions have marked the historical record.[28] Individuals, too, often go through radical life changes during which they shed old self-concepts, jobs, careers, and identities, as do whole societies— witness the dizzying succession of modern empires since Ming China in the Middle Ages.[29]

We are in the midst of such a revolution. Whether in the economic, social, political, or cultural realms, chaos reigns. In this turbulent era, our firms and institutions today increasingly resemble the dinosaurs of old, struggling for survival. Unlike those dinosaurs, however, they have a choice: They are at a strategic turning point.

The principal choice facing managers is between traditional incremental adjustments designed to move their firms slowly toward increased competitiveness, and radical changes designed to alter their fundamental postures. This book has argued the case for a radical realignment of the strategic postures that grant firms their competitiveness on the global stage. In turn, it has suggested how implementing strategic change requires a wholesale recasting of firms' internal features that involves dismantling, in particular, the bureaucratic structures that generate inertia.

In the swirling vortex of changing technologies and political systems in the late twentieth century, business firms are responsible for pumping the life-giving blood of products, services, employment, and trade into the international economy. We can only hope that our leaders and managers will rise to the challenge of re-creating the goals, strategies, and means on which our firms and institutions rely. To maintain the status quo is to condone the prerevolutionary system that produced inefficient bureaucracies, coaxed flagrant inequities, dampened innovation, and induced moral turpitude within firms. It would be disingenuous of us at best— downright suicidal at worst.

Bibliography: Selected Readings on Strategic Change

Altheide, David L. and Johnson, J.M. (1980) *Bureaucratic Propaganda*. Boston, MA: Allyn & Bacon.

Beer, Michael, Russell A. Eisenstat, and Bert Spector (1990) *The Critical Path to Corporate Renewal*. Cambridge MA: Harvard Business School Press.

Bennis, Warren and Bernard Nanus (1985) *Leaders: The Strategies for Taking Charge*. NY: Harper & Row.

Bartlett, Christopher A. and Sumantra Ghoshal (1989) *Managing across Borders*. Boston, MA: Harvard Business School Press.

Blasi, Joseph R. and Douglas L. Kruse (1991) *The New Owners: The Mass Emergence of Employee Ownership in Public Companies and What it Means to American Business*. New York: Harper Business.

Bowsher, Jack E. (1989) *Educating America*. NY: John Wiley & Sons.

Burns, James McGregor (1979) *Leadership*. NY: Harper & Row.

Cameron, K., R.I. Sutton, and D.A. Whetten (eds.) (1988) *Readings on Organizational Decline: Frameworks, Research, and Prescriptions*. Cambridge, MA: Ballinger.

Carlton, Dennis W. and Jeffrey M. Perloff (1990) *Modern Industrial Organization*. Glenview, IL: Scott, Foresman.

Carroll, Glenn (ed.) (1988) *Ecological Models of Organizations*. Boston, MA: Ballinger.

Chandler, Alfred (1962) *Strategy and Structure*. Garden City, NY: Anchor Books.

Chandler, Alfred (1977) *The Visible Hand*. Cambridge, MA: Harvard University Press.

Chandler, Alfred (1989) *Scale and Scope*. Cambridge, MA: Harvard University Press.

Crystal, Graef S. *In Search of Excess: The Overcompensation of the American Executive*. New York: W.W. Norton, 1991.

Davis, Stanley M. (1987) *Future Perfect*. Reading, MA: Addison-Wesley.

Deal, Terrence E. and Alan A. Kennedy (1982) *Corporate Cultures: The Rites and Rituals of Corporate Life.* Reading, MA: Addison-Wesley.

Diebold, John (1990) *The Innovators: The Discoveries, Inventions, and Breakthroughs of Our Time.* NY: New American Library/Plume.

Doeringer, Peter, and Michael Piore (1971) *Internal Labor Markets and Manpower Analysis.* Lexington, MA: D.C. Heath.

Dosi, Giovanni (1984) *Technical Change and Industrial Transformation.* London: MacMillan.

Drucker, Peter (1985) *Innovation and Entrepreneurship.* NY: Harper & Row.

Drucker, Peter (1989) *The New Realities.* NY: Harper & Row.

Etzioni, Amitai (1984) *Capital Corruption: The New Attack on American Democracy.* San Diego, CA: Harcourt, Brace, Jovanovich.

Etzioni, Amitai (1988) *The Moral Dimension.* NY: Free Press.

Etzioni, Amitai (1968) *The Active Society.* NY: Free Press.

Fombrun, Charles J., Noel M. Tichy, and Mary Anne Devanna (1984) *Strategic Human Resource Management.* NY: John Wiley & Sons.

Freeman, Edward (1984) *Strategic Management: A Stakeholder Approach.* Boston: Pitman.

Freeman, Richard B. and James L. Medoff (1984) *What Do Unions Do?* NY: Basic Books.

Frost, Peter J. et al. (eds.) (1985) *Organizational Culture.* Beverly Hills, CA: Sage Publications.

Galbraith, Jay (1977) *Organization Design.* Reading, MA: Addison-Wesley.

Galbraith, Jay and Robert Kazanjian (1986) *Strategy Implementation.* St. Paul, MN: West Publishing Co.

Gilder, George F. (1989) *Microcosm: The Quantum Revolution in Economics and Technology.* NY: Simon & Schuster.

Gilpin, Robert (1987) *The Political Economy of International Relations.* Princeton, NJ: Princeton University Press.

Grinyer, Peter and David Mayes (1989) *Sharpbenders: Secrets of Unleashing Corporate Potential.* Oxford: Basil Blackwell.

Halberstam, David (1986) *The Reckoning.* NY: William Morrow.

Harrison, Bennett and Harry Bluestone (1990) *The Great U-Turn.* NY: Basic Books.

Hayes, Robert. H. & Steven C. Wheelwright (1984) *Restoring our Competitive Edge: Competing through Manufacturing.* NY: John Wiley & Sons.

Hinings, C. Robert, Royston Greenwood, Stewart Ranson, and Kieron Walsh (1989) *The Dynamics of Strategic Change.* Oxford, UK: Basil Blackwell.

Hofer, Charles W. and Dan Schendel (1978) *Strategy Formulation: Analytical Concepts.* St. Paul, MN: West Publishing.

Hrebiniak, Lawrence and William Joyce (1985) *Implementing Strategy.* NY: MacMillan.

Huff, Ann (1988) *Mapping Strategic Thought.* NY: John Wiley & Sons.

Janis, Irving (1973) *Victims of Groupthink.* Boston: Houghton, Mifflin.

Jelinek, Mariann and Claudia Schoonhoven (1990) *The Innovation Marathon.* Oxford: Basil Blackwell

Johnson, Gerry (1987) *Strategic Change and the Management Process.* Oxford: Basic Blackwell.

Kanter, Rosabeth M. (1989) *When Giants Learn to Dance.* NY: Touchstone.

Kanter, Rosabeth M. (1983) *Change Masters.* NY: Simon & Schuster.

Kash, Don E. (1989) *Perpetual Innovation: The New World of Competition.* NY: Basic Books.

Keller, Maryann (1989) *Rude Awakening.* NY: William Morrow.

Kennedy, Paul (1987) *The Rise and Fall of the Great Powers.* NY: Random House.

Kidder, Tracy (1981) *The Soul of the New Machine.* Boston: Little Brown.

Kimberly, John R., Robert H. Miles, and Associates (1980) *The Organizational Life Cycle.* San Francisco: Jossey-Bass.

Kotter, John (1988) *The Leadership Factor.* NY: Free Press.

Lawler, Edward E. III (1986) *High Involvement Management.* San Francisco: Jossey-Bass.

Lawrence, Paul and Davis Dyer (1983) *Renewing American Industry.* NY: Free Press.

Lindblom, Charles E. (1990) *Inquiry and Change: The Troubled Attempt to Understand and Shape Society.* New Haven, CT: Yale University Press.

Lydenberg, S.D., A.T. Marlin, and S.O. Strub (1986) *Rating America's Corporate Conscience.* Reading, MA: Addison-Wesley.

Magaziner, Ira and Mark Patinkin (1989) *The Silent War: Inside the Global Business Battles Shaping America's Future.* NY: Random House.

March, James and Johan Olsen (1989) *Rediscovering Institutions: The Organizational Basis of Politics.* NY: Free Press.

Mensch, Gerhard O. (1979) *Stalemate in Technology: Innovations Overcome the Depression.* Cambridge, MA: Ballinger.

Meyer, John and W. Richard Scott (1983) *Organizational Environments: Ritual and Rationality.* Beverly Hills, CA: Sage Press.

Meyer, Marshall W. and Associates (1978) *Environments and Organizations.* San Francisco: Jossey-Bass.

Miles, Raymond and Charles Snow (1978) *Organizational Strategy, Structure, and Process.* NY: McGraw-Hill.

Miles, Robert H. with Kim Cameron (1982) *Coffin Nails and Corporate Strategy.* Englewood Cliffs, NJ: Prentice-Hall.

Miller, Danny and Peter Friesen (1980) *Organizations: A Quantum View.* Englewood Cliffs, NJ: Prentice-Hall.

Miller, Danny (1990) *The Icarus Paradox: How Exceptional Companies Bring About Their Own Downfall.* NY: Harper Business.

Mintz, Beth and Michael Schwartz (1985) *The Power Structure of American Business.* Chicago: University of Chicago Press.

Mintzberg, Henry (1979) *The Structuring of Organizations.* Englewood Cliffs, NJ: Prentice-Hall.

Nelson, Richard and Sidney Winter (1982). *The Evolutionary Theory of Economic Change.* Cambridge, MA: Harvard University Press.

Ohmae, Kenichi (1985) *Triad Power: The Coming Shape of Global Competition.* NY: Free Press.

Ohmae, Kenichi (1990) *The Borderless World: Power and Strategy in the Interlinked World Economy.* NY: Harper Business.

Olson, Mancur (1982) *The Rise and Decline of Nations: Economic Growth, Stagflation, and Social Rigidities.* New Haven, CT: Yale University Press.

Ouchi, William (1980) *Theory Z: How American Business Can Meet the Japanese Challenge.* Reading, MA: Addison-Wesley.

Pascale, Richard T. (1990) *Managing on the Edge.* NY: Simon & Schuster.

Perrow, Charles (1984) *Normal Accidents: Living with High Risk Technologies.* NY: Basic Books.

Peters, Thomas J. and Robert H. Waterman, Jr. (1982) *In Search of Excellence: Lessons from America's Best-Run Companies.* NY: Harper & Row.

Pettigrew, Andrew (1988) *The Management of Strategic Change.* Oxford, England: Basil Blackwell.

Pfeffer, Jeffrey, and Gerald R. Salancik (1978) *The External Control of Organizations: A Resource Dependence Perspective.* NY: Harper & Row.

Phillips, Kevin (1990) *The Politics of Rich and Poor.* NY: Random House.

Pinchot, Gifford III (1985) *Intrapreneuring.* NY: Harper & Row.

Piore, Michael and Charles Sabel (1984) *The Second Industrial Divide: Possibilities for Prosperity.* NY: Basic Books.

Porter, Michael E. (1980) *Competitive Strategy: Techniques for Analyzing Industries and Competitors.* NY: Free Press.

Porter, Michael E. (1985) *Competitive Advantage.* NY: Free Press.

Porter, Michael E. (1988) *Competition in Global Industries.* Cambridge, MA: Harvard Business School Press.

Porter, Michael E. (1990) *The Competitive Advantage of Nations.* NY: Free Press.

Reich, Robert B. (1983) *The Next American Frontier.* NY: Times Books.

Reich, Robert B. (1991) *The Work of Nations.* NY: Alfred Knopf.

Reid, Peter (1990) *Well Made in America.* NY: McGraw-Hill.

Rock, Milton L. and Robert H. Rock (1990) *Corporate Restructuring.* NY: McGraw-Hill.

Rumelt, Richard P.P. (1974) *Strategy, Structure, and Economic Performance.* Boston: Harvard Business School Press.

Sahal, Devendra (1981) *Patterns of Technological Innovation.* Reading, MA: Addison-Wesley.

Schein, Edgar H. (1985) *Organizational Culture and Leadership.* San Francisco: Jossey-Bass.

Scherer, Fred M. (1980) *Industrial Market Structure and Economic Performance* (2nd ed.). Boston: Houghton Mifflin.

Schlesinger, Leonard A., D. Dyer, T.N. Clough, and D. Landau (1987) *Chronicles of Corporate Change: Management Lessons from AT&T and Its Offspring.* Lexington, MA: Lexington Books.

Schon, Donald (1971) *Beyond the Stable State.* NY: Random House.

Shrivastava, Paul (1987) *Bhopal: Anatomy of a Crisis.* Cambridge, MA: Ballinger.

Sonnenfeld, Jeffrey (1988) *A Hero's Farewell.* NY: Oxford University Press.

Teece, David J. (1987) *The Competitive Challenge.* Cambridge, MA: Ballinger.

Thompson, James D. (1967) *Organizations in Action.* NY: McGraw Hill.

Thurow, Lester (1980) *The Zero-Sum Society.* NY: Simon & Schuster.

Tichy, Noel M. (1983) *Managing Strategic Change.* NY: John Wiley & Sons.

Tichy, Noel M. and Mary Anne Devanna (1986). *The Transformational Leader.* NY: John Wiley & Sons.

Tirole, Jean (1988) *The Theory of Industrial Organization.* Cambridge, MA: MIT Press

Toffler, Alvin (1980) *The Third Wave.* NY: Bantam Books.

Tunstall, W. Brooke (1985) *Disconnecting Parties.* NY: McGraw-Hill.

Ulrich, Dave and Dale Lake (1990) *Organizational Capability: Competing from the Inside Out.* NY: John Wiley & Sons.

Useem, Michael (1984) *The Inner Circle: Large Corporations and the Rise of Business Political Activity in the U.S. and U.K.* NY: Oxford University Press.

Walter, Ingo (1988) *Global Competition in Financial Services.* Boston, MA: Ballinger.

Weick, Karl E. (1979) *The Social Psychology of Organizing.* Reading, MA: Addison-Wesley.

Weitzman, Martin (1984) *The Share Economy: Conquering Stagflation.* Cambridge, MA: Harvard University Press.

Weston, J. Fred, Kwang S. Chung, and Susan E. Hoag (1990) *Mergers, Restructuring, and Corporate Control.* Englewood Cliffs, NJ: Prentice-Hall.

Wilson, James Q. (1989) *Bureaucracy: What Government Agencies Do and Why They Do It.* NY: Basic Books.

Zucker, Lynn (ed.) (1988) *Institutional Patterns in Organizations: Culture and Environment.* Boston, MA: Ballinger.

Notes

Introduction

1. Edward Freeman in *Strategic Management: A Stakeholder Approach* (Boston: Pitman, 1984).

2. Charles Perrow in *Normal Accidents: Living with High Risk Technologies* (NY: Basic Books, 1984) discusses how rising complexity increases the probability that an unpredictable interaction of elements will be observed, increasing the likelihood of accidents as we deal with ever more sophisticated technologies.

3. Bennis, Warren, "Changing Organizations," *Journal of Applied Behavioral Science*, 1966, *2*: 247–263.

Chapter 1

1. Tunstall, B. *Disconnecting Parties* (NY: McGraw-Hill, 1985) and Schlesinger, Dyer, Clough, and Landau. Chronicles of Corporate Change: Lessons from AT&T and Its Offspring (Lexington, MA: Lexington Books, 1987).

2. Tichy, N.M. and Ram Charan, "Speed, Simplicity, Self-Confidence," *Harvard Business Review*, 1989, *89*: 116.

3. Based on John Akers' memo to IBM employees, and also "The New IBM: Is it New Enough?" *Business Week*: 16 December 1991, 112–118.

4. The review by Gould, S.J. "Punctuated Equilibrium in Fact and Theory," *Journal of Social Biological Structure*, 1989, *12*: 117–136.

5. Gersick, C.J.G. "Revolutionary Change Theories: A Multilevel Exploration of the Punctuated Equilibrium Paradigm," *Academy of Management Review*, *16*: 1991, 10–36. Also Miller and Friesen (1980).

6. For a review of studies of strategic change around such a framework, see Ginsberg, A. "Measuring and Modelling Changes in Strategy: Theoretical Foundations and Empirical Directions," *Strategic Management Journal*, 1988, *9*: 559–575.

7. Charles McCoy provides an overview of the changes made in "Combat Banking: A Slashing Pursuit of Retail Trade Brings BankAmerica Back," *Wall*

Street Journal, 1: 2 October 1989. BankAmerica Chairman Clausen provides his own assessment in "Strategic Issues in Managing Change," *California Management Review,* 1990, *32:* 98–105.

8. "Whirlpool goes off on a World Tour," *Business Week:* 3 June 1991, 99–100.

9. Hedberg, Nystrom, and Starbuck (1976).

10. For an application of ecological theory to organizations, see Astley, W.G. and C.J. Fombrun "Organizational Communities: An Ecological Perspective." In *Research in the Sociology of Organizations.* Greenwich, CT: JAI Press, 1987.

11. Perry, Nancy J. "The Arms Makers' Next Battle," *Fortune:* 27 August 1990, 84–88.

12. Broad, William J. "How the $8 Billion Space Station Became a $120 Billion Showpiece," *New York Times:* 10 June 1990, 1,30.

13. Greiner, L.E and A. Bhambri "New CEO Intervention and Dynamics of Deliberate Strategic Change," *Strategic Management Journal,* 1989, *10:* 67–86.

14. Galbraith, J. and Kazanjian, R. *Strategy Implementation* (St. Paul, MN: West Publishing Co., 1986).

15. Deutsch, Claudia. "An Overly Ambitious Scott Paper is Stretched Thin," *New York Times:* 24 March 1991, 8.

16. "Haute Couture that's Not so Haute," *Business Week:* 22 April 1991, 108.

17. "H&R Block Expands its Tax Base," *Business Week:* 22 April 1991, 52.

18. Table in *New York Times:* 15 April 1991, D10.

19. "Honeywell is finally Tasting the Sweet Life," *Business Week:* 3 June 1991, 34.

20. Pfeffer, J. and Salanak, G.R. in *The External Control of Organizations: A Resource Dependence Perspective* (NY: Harper and Row, 1978) and Etzioni, A., *The Moral Dimension* (NY: The Free Press, 1988) for discussions of how firms can buffer themselves from competitive processes.

21. "Something Special in the Air: Hitchhiking VIPs," *Business Week:* 8 July 1991, 33.

22. For instance, see the commentary by D. Depke, "IBM and Apple: Can Two Loners Learn to Say 'Teamwork'?" *Business Week:* 22 July 1991, 25.

23. Clegg, S. "Organization and Control," *Administrative Science Quarterly,* 1981, *26:* 545–562.

24. Fombrun, C.J. "Structural Dynamics within and between Organizations," *Administrative Science Quarterly,* 1986, *31:* 403–421.

25. "Corning's Class Act," *Business Week:* 13 May 1991, 68–76.

26. Peters, T. and Waterman, R. *In Search of Excellence: Lessons from America's Best-Run Companies* (NY: Harper and Row, 1982) highlight the symbolic role top managers play in promulgating cultural values and thereby driving productivity.

27. Tichy, N. and Devanna, M. in *The Transformational Leader* (NY: Wiley, 1986), draw on the work of Burns (1979) to contrast "transactional" and "transformational" forms of corporate leadership.

28. Tichy, N., in *Managing Strategic Change* (NY: Wiley, 1983) proposed that managing change involves untangling a rope made up of distinct technical, political, and cultural strands.

Chapter 2

1. E. Freeman discussed stakeholder models of strategic management in *Strategic Management: A Stakeholder Approach* (Boston: Pitman, 1984) and Thurow (1980) described paralysis in national decision making due to interest group politics in *The Zero-Sum Society* (NY: Simon & Schuster).

2. Jones, A., "Newly Profitable, Post Plans to Share with its Unions," *New York Times*; 14 June 1991, B3.

3. Reich (1991) and Porter, M., *The Competitive Advantage of Nations* (NY: Free Press, 1990).

4. S. Strange in *States and Markets* (London: Pinter, 1989) discusses the complex mesh of politics and markets.

5. Gilder (1989) assesses the revolution brought on by miniaturization. Piore and Sabel, in *The Second Industrial Divide: Possibilities for Prosperity* (NY: Basic Books, 1984), conclude that technological change has placed us on the threshold of a second industrial revolution.

6. Huber, P., *The Geodesic Network: 1987 Report on Competition in the Telephone Industry* (U.S.: Department of Justice, 1987), for an analysis of the transformation of the telecommunications industry.

7. For instance, see "The Baby Bells Learn a Nasty New Word: Competition," *Business Week:* 25 March 1991, 96–101.

8. As described in *International Direct Investment: Global Trends and the U.S. Role.* U.S. Dept of Commerce, International Trade Administration, 1988, pp. 8–9.

9. Walter, I., *Global Competition in Financial Services* (Boston: Ballinger, 1988).

10. Clyde Farnsworth, "Free-Trade Accord is Enticing Canadian Companies to U.S.," *New York Times:* 9 August 1991, 1, D4.

11. *New York Times:* 27 November, 1990, A3.

12. Magaziner, I. and Patinkin, M. *The Silent War: Inside the Global Business Battles Shaping America's Future* (NY: Random House, 1989).

13. "The Mexico Pact: Worth the Price?" *Business Week:* 27 May 1991, 32–36.

14. F. Protzman, "Greetings from Fortress Germany," *New York Times:* 18 August 1991, F1, F6.

15. *New York Times:* 2 July 1989, 2.

16. An excellent overview of the region is provided in "Asia: The Next Era of Growth," *Business Week:* 11 November 1991, 56–68.

17. As reported in Phillips, K., *The Politics of Rich and Poor* (New York: Random House).

18. For a discussion of developments in the financial services industry, see Walter, I., *Global Competition in Financial Services* (Boston: Ballinger, 1988).

19. For a detailed analysis of the S&L crisis, see White, L. *The S&L Debacle.* NY: Oxford University Press, 1991. The analysis highlights the unintended behavioral consequences of various regulatory acts passed by Congress.

20. Bluestone, B. and B. Harrison *The DeIndustrialization of America.* NY: Basic Books, 1982.

21. In *New York Times:* 22 November 1990, D4.

22. James Sterngold, "Nomura's President Resigns," *New York Times:* 24 June 1991, D1.

23. "Other Brokers in Japan are Linked to Scandal," *New York Times:* 23 June 1991, 8.

24. Steve Iohr, "World Class Fraud: How BCCI Pulled it Off," *New York Times:* 12 August 1991, A1-D4.

25. J. Fuerbringer, "Salomon Brothers Admits Violations at Treasury Sales," *New York Times:* 10 August 1991, A1. Also K. Eichenwald, "Wall Street Sees a Serious Threat to Salomon Brothers," *New York Times:* 16 August, 1991, A1. K. Eichenwald, "Salomon's 2 Top Officers to Resign Amid Scandal," *New York Times:* 17 August 1991, A1.

26. Phillips, K. *op. cit.* discusses the unbalanced effect that the Reagan administration's tax reforms and government programs had on the distribution of incomes during the 1980s.

27. See Harrison, B. and Bluestone H., *op. cit.*

28. Political scientist Susan Strange first described the inner workings of the casino society in *Casino Capitalism.* London: Oxford, Blackwell, 1986.

29. Robert Pear, "In Bush Presidency, the Regulators Ride Again," *New York Times:* 28 April 1991, 5.

30. These data are from Milliken, F.J., J.E. Dutton, and J.M. Beyer "Understanding Organizational Adaptation to Change: The Case of Work-Family Issues," *Human Resource Planning, 13:* 1990, 91–107.

31. "Taking Baby Steps Toward a Daddy Track," *Business Week:* 15 April 1991, 90–92.

32. Lawson, C. "Like Growing Number of Companies, IBM is Building Child-Care Centers," *New York Times:* 12 December 1990, A20.

33. John Holusha, "Packaging and Public Image: McDonald's Fills a Big Order," *New York Times:* 2 November 1990, 1,D5.

34. Keith Schneider, "Chemical Plants Buy Out Neighbors as Safety Zone," *New York Times:* 28 November 1990, 1, B8.

35. Shrivastava, P. Bhopal: Anatomy of a Crisis (Cambridge, MA: Ballinger, 1987) for an overview of the organizational dimensions of industrial accidents.

36. Environmental data were drawn from discussions in Walter H. Corson *The Global Ecology Handbook* (Boston: Beacon Press, 1990).

37. These data were drawn from a report by the United Nations Center on Transnational Corporations (1988: 228ff) *Transnational Corporations in World Development,* ST/CTC/89. NY: United Nations.

38. Corson, *op.cit.,* p. 68.

39. R. Edward Freeman and Daniel R. Gilbert, *Corporate Strategy and the Search for Ethics* (Englewood Cliffs, NJ: Prentice Hall, 1988) for a discussion of the ethical foundations of strategic planning.

Chapter 3

1. For an entertaining account of Xerox's failure to capitalize on PARC innovations, see the popular book by Douglas K. Smith and Robert C. Alexander, *Fumbling the Future* (NY: William Morrow, 1988).

2. Lawrence P. and Dyer D., in *Renewing American Industry* (NY: Free Press, 1983), pp. 55–85, present a comparative analysis of the forces operating industries that prevent their adaptation.

3. Tushman, M.L. and E. Romanelli, "Organizational Evolution: A Metamorphosis Model of Convergence and Reorientation." In L.L. Cummings and B.M. Staw (eds.), *Research in Organizational Behavior*, Vol. 7: 171–222 (Greenwich, CT: JAI Press, 1985).

4. Fombrun, C., Tichy, N., and Devanna, M., in *Strategic Human Resource Management* (NY: Wiley, 1984), analyze how human resource systems can facilitate or hinder strategy implementation. Galbraith, J., in *Organization Design* (Reading, MA: Addison-Wesley, 1977) provides a classic review of the role played by structure in implementing change.

5. John Diebold in *The Innovators: The Discoveries, Inventions, and Breakthroughs of Our Time* (NY: New American Library/Plume, 1990), describes the rise of Xerox.

6. "At Xerox, They're Shouting 'Once More into the Breach,' " *Business Week:* 23 July 1990, 62–66.

7. In Duhaime, B., "The Bureaucracy Busters," *Fortune: 123: 17* June 1991, 36–50.

8. Weitzel, W. and E. Jonsson, "Reversing the Downward Spiral: Lessons from W.T. Grant and Sears Roebuck," *Academy of Management Executive*, 1991, 5(3): 7–22.

9. "Flight Plans for a Much Altered Future," *Business Week:* 27 May 1991: 74–75.

10. For instance, see Tunstall, B. in *Disconnecting Parties* (NY: McGraw-Hill, 1985) and Schlesinger et al. in *Chronicles of Corporate Change: Management Lessons from AT&T and Its Offspring* (Lexington, MA: Lexington Books, 1987). Also Kanter, R.M., "Championing Change: An Interview with Bell Atlantic's CEO Raymond Smith," *Harvard Business Review:* January–February 1991: 119–130.

11. Dosi, G., "Technological Paradigms and Technological Trajectories: A Suggested Interpretation of the Determinants of Technical Change" *Research Policy*, 1982, *11:* 147–162. See also Tushman, M.L. and P. Anderson "Technological Discontinuities and Organizational Environment," *Administrative Science Quarterly*, 1986, *31:* 439–465. Sahal, D., in *Patterns of Technological Innovation* (Reading, MA: Addison-Wesley, 1981), documents improvement technologies in a wide variety of settings.

12. D., Schon in *Beyond the Stable State* (NY: Random House, 1971) first described how these loosely linked businesses form into constellations.

13. Freeman, J. and S.R. Barley, "The Strategic Analysis of Interorganizational Relations in Biotechnology." In R. Loveridge and M. Pitt (eds.), *Strategic Management of Technological Innovation* (NY: Wiley, 1989).

14. For a descriptive study of how firms involved in telecommunications fuse into business communities, see Astley, W.G. and C.J. Fombrun, "Technological Innovation and Industrial Structure: The Case of Telecommunications." In R. Lamb (ed.), *Research in Strategic Management*, 1983, Vol. 1: 2–5–229.

15. As concluded in a report by the Office of Technology Assessment, *U.S. Textile and Apparel Industry: A Revolution in Progress*, U.S. Department of Commerce, National Technical Information Service, Special Report #PB87-19676, Washington, D.C., April 1987.

16. Starbuck, W.H. and B.L.T. Hedberg, "Saving an Organization from a Stagnating Environment." In Hans B. Thorelli (ed.), *Strategy + Structure = Performance:* 249–258. (Bloomington, IN: Indiana University Press, 1977).

17. Tichy, N., *Managing Strategic Change* (NY: Wiley, 1983).

18. Cameron K., R. Sutton, and D. Whetten (eds.), *Readings on Organizational Decline: Frameworks, Research, and Prescriptions* (Cambridge, MA: Ballinger, 1988).

19. Hambrick, D.C. and R.A. D'Aveni, "Large Corporate Failures as Downward Spirals," *Administrative Science Quarterly:* 1988, *33:* 1–23.

20. See Miller and Friesen (1984) and Nelson, R. and S. Winter in *The Evolutionary Theory of Economic Change* (Cambridge, MA: Harvard University Press, 1982).

21. An excellent review of Chase's decline in the 1980s is provided by Peter Grant and Robert McNatt, "Squandered Decade: How a Corporate Culture & A CEO's Reticence in the '80s Imperil Chase's Future," *Crain's New York Business:* 17 June 1991: 23–31.

22. Kelly, D. and T.L. Amburgey, "Organizational Inertia and Momentum: A Dynamic Model of Strategic Change," *Academy of Management Journal,* 1991, *34:* 591–612.

23. Matthew Wald, "Steinway Changing Amid Tradition," *New York Times,* 28 March 1991: D1,D8.

24. See Scherer F., in *Industrial Market Structure and Economic Performance* (2nd ed.) (Boston: Houston Mifflin, 1980).

25. Sahal, D., *Patterns of Technological Innovation* (Reading, MA: Addison-Wesley, 1981) for a pathbreaking analysis of how radical innovations are impacting industry dynamics. For a study that relates these discontinuities to organizational features, see Tushman, M.L. and P. Anderson, "Technological Discontinuities and Organizational Environments," *Administrative Science Quarterly,* 1986, *31:* 439–465.

26. The best conceptual discussion of strategic groups was by Caves, R.E. and M.E. Porter "From Entry Barriers to Mobility Barriers," *Quarterly Journal of Economics,* 1979, *91:* 421–434. Numerous empirical studies have been conducted since then, debating the impermeability of these mobility barriers. See Cool, K. and D. Schendel "Performance Differences among Strategic Group Members," *Strategic Management Journal,* 1988, *9:* 207–224.

27. Scherer *op. cit.*

28. Journalist David Halberstam's discussion in *The Reckoning* (NY: William Morrow, 1986) is among the more entertaining accounts.

29. Porter, M., Competitive Strategy: Techniques for Analyzing Industries and Competitors (NY: Free Press, 1980).

30. See Saxenian, A., "Regional Networks and the Resurgence of Silicon Valley," *California Management Review,* 1990, *33:* 89–112.

31. "Mighty Mitsubishi is on the Move," *Business Week:* 24 September 1990: 98–107.

32. Alan Blinder makes a similar argument in "A Japanese Buddy System that could benefit U.S. Business," *Business Week:* 14 October 1991, 32.

33. Various recent authors have discussed Japanese trade practices, among the most vocal, perhaps, the former U.S. trade representative Clyde Prestowitz in *Trading Places* (NY: Basic Books, 1988).

34. For a useful conceptual review of institutional constraints on change, see P. DiMaggio and W. Powell "The Iron Cage Revisited: Institutional Isomorphism and Collective Rationality in Organizational Fields," *American Sociological Review*, 1983, *48:* 147–160.

35. For Japan, see "Hidden Japan," *Business Week:* 26 August 1991, 34–38. For Germany, the experience of retailer Toys 'R' Us is described in F. Protzman, "Greetings from Fortress Germany,"*New York Times:* 18 August 1991: F1–F6.

36. Mintz and Schwartz (1985: 30), point to ratings agencies as key institutions influencing market prices for firms' securities.

37. A more recent analysis of how the financial markets drive a short-term managerial orientation is provided by Michael Jacobs, *Short-Term America: The Causes and Cures of Our Business Myopia* (Boston, MA: Harvard Business School, 1991).

38. See *Forbes*, November 7, 1990.

39. The longitudinal study of Miles and Cameron (1980: 442) demonstrates how differently firms adapted to a threatening environment in the tobacco industry.

40. Roy, W.G., "The Process of Bureaucratization in the U.S. Department and the Vesting of Economic Interests, 1886–1905," *Administrative Science Quarterly*, 1981, *26:* 419–433.

41. Jacobs, D., "Corporate Economic Power and the State: A Longitudinal Assessment of Two Explanations," *American Journal of Sociology*, 1988, *93:* 852–881.

42. Carlton, D. and J. Perloff, *Modern Industrial Organization* (Glenview, IL: Scott, Foresman, 1990) p. 831.

43. David Altheide and J.M. Johnson analyze how propaganda infiltrates schools, in *Bureaucratic Propaganda* (Boston: Allyn and Bacon, 1980).

44. Reich, Robert B., *The Next American Frontier* (NY: Alfred Knopf, 1983).

45. A stronger indictment of managerialism is provided by William G. Scott, "Organizational Revolution: An End to Managerial Orthodoxy," *Administration and Society*, 1985, *17:* 149–170. He criticizes schools for promoting a philosophy that trivializes workers and widens the gap between managers and other people.

46. Doeringer, P. and M. Piore *Internal Labor Markets and Manpower Analysis* (Lexington, MA: D.C. Heath, 1971).

47. Cohen, R., "News's Owners Speak Softly but Take a Hard Line," *New York Times:* 1 November 1990, B2.

48. Hoerr, J., "What Should Unions Do?" *Harvard Business Review:* May–June 1991, 30–45.

49. "How Can We Be Laid Off If We Own the Company?" *Business Week:* 9 September 1991, 66.

50. See Fombrun C., N. Tichy, and M. Devanna, *op. cit.*

51. "Pressure on Professionals," *Business Week:* 23 July 1990, 24–25.

52. Burgelman, R., "A Process Model of Internal Corporate Venturing in the Diversified Major Firm," *Administrative Science Quarterly*, 1983, *28:* 223–224.

Chapter 4

1. Quint, M. and J.C. Freed, "Bank Losses Worst in 50 Years, But No Danger to System is Seen," *New York Times:* 17 February 1991, 1,35.

2. For a useful summary of the psychological processes that bias decision-making in organizations, see Kiesler, S. and L. Sproull "Managerial Response to Changing Environments: Perspectives on Problem Sensing from Social Cognition," *Administrative Science Quarterly:* 1982, *27:* 548–570.

3. "Rethinking the Computer," *Business Week:* 26 November 1990, 116–124.

4. Shwartz, Peter, "Accepting the Risk in Forecasting," *New York Times:* 2 September 1990, Forum 13.

5. Individuals draw on simple heuristics to make decisions: See Tversky, A. and D. Kahneman, "Availability: A heuristic for Judging Frequency and Probability," *Cognitive Psychology,* 1973, *5:* 207–232. Janis's (1973) work on group decisions demonstrated how peer pressure can shape conformity and distort problem solving.

6. Rhonda Reger's article in Huff, A., *Mapping Strategic Thought* (NY: John Wiley & Sons, 1988).

7. Billings, R.S., T.W. Milburn, and M.L. Schaalman "A Model of Crisis Perception: A Theoretical and Empirical Analysis," *Administrative Science Quarterly,* 1980, *25:* 300–316. Also, Staw, B. and J. Ross "Commitment to a Policy Decision: A Multi-Theoretical Perspective," *Administrative Science Quarterly,* 1978, *23:* 40–64.

8. Fombrun, C.J. and E.J. Zajac, "Structural and Perceptual Influences on Intraindustry Stratification," *Academy of Management Journal,* 1987, *30:* 33–50.

9. For an insightful summary of different causal fallacies that plague forecasts in general, and the illusory correlation between sunspots and other events, see Pant, N. and W. Starbuck, "Innocents in the Forest: Forecasting and Research Methods," *Journal of Management,* 1990 Special Issue.

10. Tversky and Khaneman (1973), op. cit.

11. Ned Bowman's article showed how managers in the farm products industry ascribed years of high profitability to themselves and years of poor profitability to the weather for damaging crops and yields. See "Strategy and the Weather," *Sloan Management Review, 17:* 1976, 49–62.

12. Salancik, G.R. and J.R. Meindl, "Corporate Attributions as Strategic Illusions of Management Control," *Administrative Science Quarterly,* 1984, *29:* 238–254.

13. Staw, B., L. Sandelands, and J. Dutton, "Threat-Rigidity Effects in Organizational Behavior: A Multilevel Analysis," *Administrative Science Quarterly,* 1981, *26:* 501–524.

14. Finkelstein, S. and D.C. Hambrick, "Top-Management-Team Tenure and Organizational Outcomes: The Moderating Role of Managerial Discretion," *Administrative Science Quarterly,* 1990, *35:* 484–503.

15. For more detail, see Ross, J. and B. Staw, "Expo 86: An Escalation Prototype," *Administrative Science Quarterly,* 1986, *31:* 274–297.

16. The original use of the expression "strategic issue" was by H.I. Ansoff in "Managing Strategic Surprise by Response to Weak Signals," *California Management Review,* 1975, *28*(2): 21–33.

17. Dutton, J.E. and R.B. Duncan, "The Creation of Momentum for Change through the Process of Strategic Issue Diagnosis," *Strategic Management Journal*, 1987, *8:* 279–295.

18. Fombrun, C.J. and M. Shanley, "Of Pageants and Horse Races: The Causes and Consequences of Corporate Reputations," New York University, Working Paper, 1991.

19. Thomas, J.B. and R.R. McDaniel, Jr., "Interpreting Strategic Issues: Effects of Strategy and the Information-Processing Structure of Top Management Teams," *Academy of Management Journal*, 1990, *33:* 286–306.

20. Dearborn, D.C. and H.A. Simon, "Selective Perception: A Note on the Departmental Identifications of Executives," *Sociometry*, 1958, *21:* 140–144.

21. Bantel, K. and S. Jackson, "Top Management and Innovations in Banking: Does the Composition of the Top Team Make a Difference?" *Strategic Management Journal*, 1989, *10:* 107–124. Also Gupta, A.K. and V. Govindarajan, "Business Unit Strategy, Managerial Characteristics, and Business Unit Effectiveness at Strategy Implementation," *Academy of Management Journal*, 1984, *27:* 25–41.

22. Eisenhardt, K.M. and C.B. Schoonhoven, "Organizational Growth: Linking Founding Team, Strategy, Environment and Growth Among U.S. Semiconductor Ventures (1978–1988)," *Administrative Science Quarterly*, 1990, *35:* 504–529.

23. Hambrick, D.C. "Environment, Strategy, and Power within Top Management Teams," *Administrative Science Quarterly*, 1981, *26:* 253–276.

24. Nulty, P., "Recycling Becomes A Big Business," *Fortune:* 13 August 1990, 82–86.

25. Thomas and McDaniel (1990), *op. cit.*

26. For additional information, see Meyer, A.D., "Adapting to Environmental Jolts," *Administrative Science Quarterly*, 1982, *27:* 515–537.

27. Milliken, F., "Perceiving and Interpreting Environmental Change: An Examination of College Administrators' Interpretation of Changing Demographics," *Academy of Management Journal*, 1990, *33:* 42–63.

28. Daft, R.L., J. Sormunen, and D. Parks, "Chief Executive Scanning, Environmental Characteristics and Company Performance: An Empirical Study," *Strategic Management Journal*, 1988, *9:* 123–139.

29. D.K. Sinha, "The Contribution of Formal Planning to Decisions," *Strategic Management Journal*, 1990, *11:* 479–492.

30. Odom, R.Y. and W.R. Boxx, "Environment, Planning Processes, and Organizational Performance of Churches," *Strategic Management Journal*, 1988, *9:* 197–205.

31. The study was reported in Mezias, S., "An Institutional Model of Accounting Practice: Financial Reporting at the Fortune 200," *Administrative Science Quarterly*, 1990, *35:* 431–457. The theory has been well articulated by institutionalists, Zucker, L. (ed.), *Institutional Patterns in Organizations: Culture and Environment* (Boston: Ballinger, 1988).

32. Pant and Starbuck (1990), *op. cit.*

33. Reger (1988), *op. cit.*

34. The hierarchy was described in research by Porac, J., H. Thomas, and C. Baden-Fuller, "Competitive Groups as Cognitive Communities: The Case of

Scottish Knitwear Manufacturers," *Journal of Management Studies,* 1989, *26:* 397–416.

35. Porac, J. and H. Thomas, "Taxonomic Mental Models in Competitor Definition," *Academy of Management Review,* 1990, *15:* 224–240.

36. The theoretical articulation of industrial economics viewed through the lenses of game theory is well summarized by Tirole, J., *The Theory of Industrial Organization* (Cambridge, MA: MIT Press, 1988).

37. Scherer, F., *Industrial Market Structure and Economic Performance* (2nd ed.) (Boston, MA: Houghton Mifflin, 1980).

38. See Ashenfelter, O., "How Auctions Work for Wine and Art," *Journal of Economic Perspectives,* 1989, *3:* 23–36.

39. See Chandler, A., *Strategy and Structure* (Garden City, NY: Anchor, 1962).

40. See Duhaime and Schwenk (1985).

41. See Prahalad, C.K. and R.A. Bettis, "The Dominant Logic: A New Linkage between Diversity and Performance," *Strategic Management Journal,* 1986, *7:* 485–502.

42. See Grant, R.M., "On 'Dominant Logic,' Relatedness and the Link between Diversity and Performance," *Strategic Management Journal,* 1988, *9:* 639–642.

43. See Hrebiniak, L. and Snow, "Strategy, Distinctive Competence, and Organizational Performance," *Administrative Science Quarterly,* 1980, *25:* 307–335.

44. Hicks, Jonathan, "Tire Company's Uphill Struggle," *New York Times:* 13 June 1989.

45. Walsh, J.P., "Top Management Turnover Following Mergers and Acquisitions," *Strategic Management Journal,* 1988, *9:* 173–183.

46. Article by Marlene Fiol in Huff (1988), *op. cit.*

47. Fombrun and Zajac (1987), *op. cit.*

48. Ratcliff, R.E., "Banks and Corporate Lending: An Analysis of the Impact of the Internal Structure of the Capitalist Class on the Lending Behavior of Banks," *American Sociological Review,* 1980, *45:* 553–570.

49. Mizruchi, M.S., "Similarity of Political Behavior among Large American Corporations," *American Journal of Sociology,* 1989, 401–424. Also see Galaskiewicz, J., *Social Organization of an Urban Grants Economy* (Orlando, FL: Academic Press, 1985).

Chapter 5

1. *Inc.* magazine interviewed Harvard's Alfred Chandler in its issue of July 1985: **54**.

2. Mensch, G., *Stalemate in Technology: Innovations Overcome the Depression* (Cambridge, MA: Ballinger, 1979).

3. Gilder, G., *Microcosm* (NY: Simon & Schuster, 1989).

4. Tushman, M.L. and P. Anderson "Technological Discontinuities and Organizational Environments," *Administrative Science Quarterly,* 1986, *31:* 439–

465. Also Anderson, P. and M.L. Tushman "Technological Discontinuities and Dominant Designs: A Cyclical Model of Technological Change," *Administrative Science Quarterly*, 1990, *35:* 604–633.

5. Tirole, J., *The Theory of Industrial Organization* (Cambridge, MA: MIT Press, 1988) and Porter, M., *Competitive Strategy: Techniques for Analyzing Industries and Competitors* (NY: Free Press, 1980).

6. For a contrast between these different mechanisms for building advantage, see Lieberman, M.B. and C.B. Montgomery "First-Mover Advantages," *Strategic Management Journal*, 1988, *9:* 41–58.

7. *Business Week:* 19 March 1990, 118–122.

8. *Business Week:* 20 August 1990, 68.

9. Cf. "Sharp's Long-Range Gamble on its Innovation Machine," *Business Week:* 29 April 1991, 84–85.

10. "Doing unto Compaq as it did unto IBM," *Business Week:* 19 November 1990, 130–137.

11. "Design Patents: How the Courts help the Copycats," *Business Week:* 5 November 1990, 105.

12. Chandler, A., *Strategy and Structure* (Garden City, NY: Anchor Books, 1962); *The Visible Hand* (Cambridge, MA: Harvard University Press, 1977); and *Scale and Scope* (Cambridge, MA: Harvard University Press, 1989).

13. Lieberman, M.B. "The Learning Curve, Diffusion, and Competitive Strategy," *Strategic Management Journal*, 1987, *8:* 441–452.

14. "The Rival Japan Respects," *Business Week:* 13 November 1989, 108–121.

15. Barney, J. "Types of Competition and the Theory of Strategy: Towards an Integrative Framework," *Academy of Management Review*, 1986, *11:* 791–800, also Lippman, S. and R. Rumelt "Uncertain Imitability: An Analysis of Interfirm Differences in Efficiency under Competition," *Bell Journal of Economics*, 1982, *13:* 418–438, and Reed, R. and R.J. DeFillippi "Causal Ambiguity, Barriers to Imitation, and Sustainable Competitive Advantage," *Academy of Management Review*, 1990, *15:* 88–102.

16. "The Pharmaceuticals Industry: Sending R&D Abroad," *Multinational Business:* 1989, No. 1, 10–15.

17. Mansfield, E. "R&D and Innovation: Some Empirical Findings," in Zvi Griliches (ed.), *R&D, Patents, and Productivity* (Chicago: University of Chicago Press, 1984).

18. "Doing unto Compaq as it Did Unto IBM," *Business Week:* 12 November 1990, 130–137.

19. Article by Brittain and Freeman in Kimberly, Miles, and Associates, *The Organizational Life Cycle* (San Francisco: Jossey-Bass, 1980).

20. Lambkin, M. "Order of Entry and Performance in New Markets," *Strategic Management Journal*, 1988, *9:* 127–140.

21. Brittain and Freeman in Kimberly, Miles, and Associates (1980), *op. cit.*

22. Mansfield (1984), *op. cit.*

23. Richard Caves and Michael Porter suggested how reputations might stratify industries into strategic groups in "From Entry Barriers to Mobility Barriers," *Quarterly Journal of Economics*, 1977, *91:* 421–434. A large literature also has developed in economics that regards reputations as a reflection of the

investments firms make in advertising to stabilize sales and signal product quality, cf. Tirole, J., *The Theory of Industrial Organization* (Cambridge, MA: MIT Press, 1988) for a thorough review.

24. Mintzberg, H., "Generic Strategies: Toward a Comprehensive Framework," *Advances in Strategic Management*, 1988, *5:* 1–67. Also Porter, M., *Competitive Advantage* (NY: Free Press, 1985).

25. "Itching to Get Onto the Factory Floor," *Business Week:* 14 October 1991, 64–66.

26. For a discussion of how new technologies are reducing the economic order quantity and enabling firms both to control costs and customize products, see the article by M. Jelinek and J. Goldhar, *Columbia Journal of World Business*, Fall 1983.

27. "Smart Factories: America's Turn?" *Business Week:* 8 May 1989, 142–150.

28. "War, Recession, Gas Hikes... GM's Turnaround Will Have to Wait," *Business Week:* 4 February 1991, 94–96.

29. For instance, see Mintzberg (1988), *op. cit.*

30. Lev, Michael. "Taco Bell Finds Price of Success (59¢)," *New York Times*, 17 December 1990, D1,D9.

31. "Shaking Up Detroit," *Business Week:* 14 August 1989, 74–80.

32. "The Push for Quality," *Business Week:* 6 August 1987, 130–136; "It's Time for a Tune-Up at GM," *Business Week:* 9 July 1987; "Winning Back the Work that Got Away," *Business Week*, Special Issue, *Innovation*, 148.

33. Feder, B., "Kodak Plans to Cut 3000 from Payroll," *New York Times:* 13 August 1991, D1, D8.

34. "3M Run Scared? Forget About It," *Business Week:* 16 September 1991, 59–62.

35. Walter H. Corson, *The Global Ecology Handbook* (Boston: Beacon Press, 1990), p. 205.

36. Goldsmith, E. and N. Hildyard, *The Earth Report: The Essential Guide to Global Ecological Issues* (Los Angeles: Price Stern Sloan, 1988) p. 229.

37. Mintzberg (1988) *op. cit.*, p. 22.

38. Hayes, R. and S. Wheelwright, *Restoring Our Competitive Edge: Competing through Manufacturing* (NY: Wiley, 1984).

39. Gilpin, R., *The Political Economy of International Relations* (Princeton, NJ: Princeton Univeristy Press, 1987).

40. Lawrence, P. and D. Dyer, in *Renewing American Industry* (NY: Free Press, 1983), diagnose the decline and failure of several industries as a consequence of failed adaptation to changes in the information and resource environments of firms.

41. Sanger, D., "U.S. Suppliers get a Toyota Lecture," *New York Times:* 1 November 1990, D1.

42. Womack, J.P., D. Jones, and D. Roos, "How Lean Production Can Change the World," *New York Times Magazine:* 23 September 1990, 20–38.

43. "A New Era for Auto Quality," *Business Week:* 22 October 1990, 82–96.

44. "The Rival Japan Respects," *Business Week:* 13 November 1989, 108–121.

45. "King Customer," *Business Week:* 12 March 1990, 89.

46. "Value Marketing: Quality, Service, and Fair Pricing are the Keys to Selling in the 90s," *Business Week:* 11 November 1991, 132–140.

47. A survey of shareholders confirmed that many want companies to direct more resources to cleaning up plants, stopping environmental pollution, and making safer products. See Epstein, M., "What Shareholders Really Want," *New York Times:* 28 April 1991, B11.

48. Holusha, J., "Ed Woolard Walks Du Pont's Tightrope," *New York Times:* 14 October, 1990, Section 3, 1, 6.

49. Pfeffer, J. and G. Salancik, in *The External Control of Organizations: A Resource Dependence Perspective* (NY: Harper and Row, 1978) discuss how firms are dependent on external groups that constrain their activities and effectively control their strategic decisions.

50. "The Greening of Detroit," *Business Week:* 8 April 1991, 54–60.

51. Holusha, J. "Hutchinson No Longer Holds its Nose," *New York Times:* 3 February 1991, Section 3, 1, 6.

52. Lydenberg, S.D., A.T. Marlin, and S.O. Strub *Rating America's Corporate Conscience* (Reading, MA: Addison-Wesley, 1986); also Ryan, Swanson, Buchholz (1987).

53. *New York Times:* 2 November 1990, 1, D5.

54. *New York Times:* 8 December 1990, 50.

55. *New York Times:* 27 November 1990, C1, C13.

56. *New York Times:* 14 December 1990, A6.

57. Porter, M., Competitive Strategy: *Techniques for Analyzing Industries and Competitors* (NY: Free Press, 1980).

58. "The Real Thing is Getting Real Aggressive," *Business Week:* 26 November 1990, 94–104.

59. As Mintzberg (1988), *op. cit.*, p. 28, points out.

60. For instance, see the in-depth study of the publishing industry by Coser, L.., C. Kadushin, and W. Powell, *Books: The Culture and Commerce of Publishing* (NY: Basic Books, 1986).

61. "The Fourth Network," *Business Week:* 17 September 1990, 114–121.

62. Matthew Wald, "Steinway Changing Amid Tradition," *New York Times:* 28 March 1991, D1, D8.

63. Quint, M., "Chemical is Proving the Rumors Wrong," *New York Times:* 22 April 1990, B12. See also Kleinfield, N.R., "A Soldier's Tale from the Middle Market," *New York Times:* 21 October 1990, Section 3, 1, 6.

64. Stanley Davis' provocative monograph, *Future Perfect* (Reading, MA: Addison-Wesley, 1990).

65. "Stalking the New Consumer," *Business Week:* August 18, 1989, 58.

66. "Dogfight: United and American Battle for Global Supremacy," *Business Week:* 21 January 1991, 56–62.

67. Holusha, J., "Factory Tradition, Fashion Imperative, and Foreign Competition," *New York Times:* 9 September 1990, F4.

68. Cf. *Business Week:* 9 July 1990, 46–50.

69. Wudunn, S., "McDonnell's Rich Taiwanese Backer," *New York Times:* 2 December 1991, D1–D3.

70. Lippman and Rumelt (1982), *op. cit.*

71. Cool, K. and D. Schendel, "Performance Differences Among Strategic Group Members," *Strategic Management Journal, 9:* 1988, 207–223.

72. Lewis, P. and H. Thomas, "The Linkage between Strategy, Strategic Gorups, and Performance in the U.K. Retail Grocery Industry," *Strategic Management Journal, 11:* 1990, 385–398.

73. Fombrun, C.J. and E.J. Zajac, "Structural and Perceptual Influences on Intraindustry Stratification," *Academy of Management Journal, 30:* 1987, 33–50.

74. For a much more extensive discussion of how the investment banks have benefited from deregulation, see Eccles, R. and D. Crane, *Doing Deals: Investment Banks at Work* (Cambridge, MA: Harvard Business School Press, 1988) pp. 91–118.

Chapter 6

1. Hicks, J.P., "The Wall Streeter Who Runs TLC Beatrice," *New York Times:* 9 June 1991, 5.

2. For a similar breakdown of corporate strategies into portfolio and financial restructurings, see the article by Ned Bowman and Harbir Singh in Rock, M. and R. Rock, *Corporate Restructuring* (NY: McGraw-Hill, 1990).

3. Carlton, D. and J. Perloff, *Modern Industrial Organization* (Glenview, IL: Scott, Foresman, 1990) pp. 162–165; Chandler, A., *The Visible Hand* (Cambridge, MA: Harvard University Press, 1977); and Scherer, F., *Industrial Market Structure and Economic Performance* (2nd ed.) (Boston: Houghton Mifflin, 1980).

4. For an impassioned defense of restructurings, see Jensen, M. "Eclipse of the Public Corporation," *Harvard Business Review:* September-October 1989.

5. See Miles and Cameron (1982).

6. "This Steel Sale Seems Far from Stainless," *Business Week:* 2 April 1990, 36.

7. Maupin, R.J., C.M. Bidwell, and A.K. Ortegren, "An Empirical Investigation of the Characteristics of Publicly Quoted Corporations with Change to Closely Held Ownership through Management Buyouts. *Journal of Business Finance and Accounting,* 1984, *11:* 435–450. Also Maupin, R.J., "Financial and Stock Market Variables as Predictors of Management Buyouts," *Strategic Management Journal,* 1987, *8:* 319–327.

8. Stefan Wally develops this theme at length in his doctoral dissertation, *Corporate Flexibility, Governance, and the Institutional Entrepreneur: The Diffusion of Leveraged Buyouts.* New York University, Stern School of Business, 1991.

9. Jensen (1989), *op. cit.,* p. 72.

10. Singh, H., "Management Buyouts: Distinguishing Characteristics and Operating Changes Prior to Public Offering," *Strategic Management Journal,* 1990, *11:* 111–130.

11. Eichenwald, "Bankruptcy Court a Threat to Buyout Profits of the 80's," *New York Times:* 3 January 1991, D1–2.

12. "KKR is Doing Just Fine—without LBOs," *Business Week:* 30 July 1990, 56–61.

13. "Reynolds Draws a Bead on the Marlboro Man," *Business Week:* 24 December 1990, 47–48.

14. The historical analyses by Chandler, A., *Strategy and Structure* (Garden City, NY: Anchor Books, 1962) and *Scale and Scope* (Cambridge, MA: Harvard University Press, 1989).

15. Fromson, B.D., "Life after Debt: How LBOs Do It," *Fortune: 13:* March 1989, 91–98.

16. "The Best and Worst Deals of the '80s," *Business Week:* 15 January 1990, 52–62.

17. Ramanujam, V. and P. Varadarajan, "Research on Corporate Diversification: A Synthesis," *Strategic Management Journal*, 1989, *10:* 523–551.

18. Sobel, R., *The Rise and Fall of the Conglomerate Kings* (NY: Stein and Day, 1984).

19. Sobel (1984).

20. Dundas, K.N.M. and P.R. Richardson, "Implementing the Unrelated Product Strategy," *Strategic Management Journal*, 1982, *3:* 287–301.

21. Sobel (1984), *op. cit.*, p. 139.

22. Rumelt, R., *Strategy Structure, and Economic Performance* (Boston: Harvard Business School Press, 1974).

23. Shelton, L., "Strategic Business Fits and Corporate Acquisition: Empirical Evidence," *Strategic Management Journal*, 1988, *9:* 279–287.

24. Cf. Shapiro, Eben "AT&T Buying Maker in Stock Deal Worth $7.4 Billion," *New York Times:* 7 May 1991, 1, D6.

25. Ramanujam and Varadarajan (1989), *op. cit.* for a comprehensive review of cross-national studies of diversification.

26. Williams, J.R., B.L. Paez, and L. Sanders, "Conglomerates Revisited," *Strategic Management Journal*, 1988, *9:* 403–414.

27. In Porter, M., *Competitive Advantage* (NY: Free Press, 1985).

28. Chaterjee, S., "Types of Synergy and Economic Value: The Impact of Acquisitions on Merging and Rival Firms," *Strategic Management Journal*, 1986, *7:* 119–139.

29. Harrop, Froma, "The Classic Conglomerate Wades into the 90's," *New York Times:* 4 February 1990, 5.

30. Grant, R.M., "On 'Dominant Logic,' Relatedness and the Link between Diversity and Performance," *Strategic Management Journal*, 1988, *9:* 639–642.

31. Prahalad, C.K. and R.A. Bettis, "The Dominant Logic: A New Linkage between Diversity and Performance," *Strategic Management Journal*, 1986, *7:* 485–502.

32. Ginsberg, A., "Connecting Diversification to Performance: A Sociocognitive Approach," *Academy of Management Review*, 1990, *15:* 514–535.

33. Greenhouse, Steven, "A Luxury Fight to the Finish," *The New York Times Magazine:* 17 December 1989, 38–54. Also "Meet Monsieur Luxury," *Business Week:* 30 July 1990, 48–52.

34. "It's a New Day for ITT's Rand Araskog," *Business Week:* 2 July 1990, 50–51.

35. The interview with Jack Welch conducted by Noel Tichy and Ram Charan "Speed, Simplicity, Self-Confidence," *Harvard Business Review:* September-October 1989, 112–120.

36. "Armand Hammer Wouldn't Recognize This Oxy," *Business Week:* 28 January 1991, 58.

37. A. Pollack, "BankAmerica in $4 Billion Deal to Acquire Rival Security Pacific," *New York Times:* 13 August 1991, 1, D6.

38. "Emery Is One Heavy Load for Consolidated Freightways," *Business Week:* 26 March 1990, 62–64.

39. "Marriage Becomes Bristol-Myers Squibb," *Business Week:* 3 December 1990, 138–139.

40. "Kodak May Wish It Never Went to the Drugstore," *Business Week:* 4 December 1989, 72–73.

41. "Troubles of a Model Merger," *Business Week:* 18 November 1991, 114–115.

42. Jemison, D.B. and S.B. Sitkin, "Corporate Acquisitions: A Process Perspective," *Academy of Management Review*, 1986, *11:* 145–163.

43. Yip, G.S., "Diversification Entry: Internal Development versus Acquisition," *Strategic Management Journal*, 1982, *3:* 331–345.

44. Carmody, D., "Beating Time Warner at Its Own Game," *New York Times:* 8 April 1990, Section 3, 1, 6.

45. The popular book by Clifford Pinchot III, *Intrapreneuring* (NY: Harper & Row, 1985) discusses this concept at length.

46. Pitts, R.A., "Strategies and Structures for Diversification," *Academy of Management Journal*, 1977, *20:* 197–208.

47. See "Why SONY Is Plugging into Columbia," *Business Week:* 16 October 1989, 56–58. Also "Media Collossus," *Business Week:* 25 March 1991, 64–74.

48. Hill, C.W.L. and S.A. Snell, "External Control, Corporate Strategy, and Firm Performance in Research Intensive Industries," *Strategic Management Journal*, 1989, *9:* 577–590.

49. Biggadike, R., "The Risky Business of Diversification," *Harvard Business Review*, 1979, *57:* 103–111.

50. Amihud, Y. and B. Lev, "Risk Reduction as a Managerial Motive for Conglomerate Mergers," *Bell Journal of Economics:* 1981, 605–617.

51. Burgelman, R., "Corporate Entrepreneurship and Strategic Management: Insights from a Process Study," *Management Science*, 1983, *29:* 1349–1364.

52. Maidique, M.A., "Entrepreneurs, Champions, and Technological Innovation," *Sloan Management Review*, Winter 1980, 59–76.

53. "TI Bets Most of Its Marbles on Chips," *Business Week:* 29 January 1990, 73–74.

54. "Psst! The Trustbusters Are Back in Town," *Business Week:* 25 June 1990, 64–67.

55. The data are from various issues of *Mergers & Acquisitions*. The growing international character of these mergers is discussed in "The Process of Transnationalization and Transnational Mergers," *United Nations Centre on*

Transnational Corporations, ST/CTC/SER.A/8, United Nations, NY, February 1989.

56. "The New, Improved Unilever Aims to Clean Up in the U.S.," *Business Week:* 27 November 1989, 102–106.

Chapter 7

1. *Business Week:* 25 September 1989, 222.

2. *Business Week:* 23 October 1989, 62.

3. A. Pollack, "Progress Reported in Talks on an IBM-Apple Venture," *New York Times:* 14 June 1991, D1, D3, also D. Depke, "IBM and Apple: Can Two Loners Learn to Say Teamwork?" *Business Week:* 22 July 1991, 25; and "IBM-Apple Could be Fearsome," *Business Week:* 7 October 1991, 28–30.

4. Dollinger, M., "The Evolution of Collective Strategies in Fragmented Industries," *Academy of Management Review,* 1990, *15:* 266–285.

5. Piore, M. and C. Sabel, *The Second Industrial Divide: Possibilities for Prosperity* (NY: Basic Books, 1984) pp. 213–216. Also Schon, D., Beyond the *Steady State* (NY: Random House, 1971).

6. For a discussion of how business communities originate and the effect they have on competitive dynamics, see Astley, W.G. and C.J. Fombrun, "Organization Communities: An Ecological Perspective," in S. Bacharach and N. DiTomaso (eds.), *Research in the Sociology of Organizations* (Greenwich, CT: JAI Press, 1987).

7. "Psst! The Trustbusters are Back in Town," *Business Week:* 25 June 1990, 64–65.

8. Carlton, D. and J. Perloff, *Modern Industrial Organization* (Glenview, IL: Scott, Foresman, 1990).

9. For an elegant contrast between economic and social theories of competition, see Granovetter, M., "Economic Action and Social Structure: The Problem of Embeddedness," *American Journal of Sociology,* 1985, *91:* 481–510.

10. Amitai Etzioni, in *The Moral Dimension* (NY: Free Press, 1988) builds an elaborate theory in an attempt to incorporate the impact of the social context on firms.

11. Useem, M., *The Inner Circle: Large Corporations and the Rise of Business Political Activity in the U.S. and U.K.* (NY: Oxford University Press, 1984).

12. McCaffrey, D.P., "Corporate Resources and Regulatory Pressures: Toward Explaining a Discrepancy," *Administrative Science Quarterly,* 1982, *27:* 398–419.

13. Porter, M., *The Competitive Advantage of Nations* (NY: Free Press, 1990).

14. Pennings, J., "Strategically Interdependent Organizations," in P. Nystrom and W. Starbuck (eds.), *Handbook of Organization Design* (NY: Oxford University Press, 1981), p. 433–455.

15. An unpublished study by John Dutton, Richard Freedman, and Subbanarasimha at New York University's Stern School of Business, 1987.

16. Sanger, D., "Hot New Scandal in Tokyo: A Case of Industrial Spying," *New York Times:* 20 July 1991, D1, 35.

17. Deutsch, Claudia. "007 It's Not. But Intelligence is In," *New York Times:* 23 December 1990, 24. Also "Should the CIA Start Spying for Corporate America?" *Business Week:* 14 October 1991, 96–100.

18. Baty, G.B., W.M. Evan, and T.W. Rothermer, "Personnel Flows as Interorganizational Relations," *Administrative Science Quarterly*, 1971, *16:* 430–443.

19. Useem (1984) *op. cit.*

20. Etzioni (1988) *op. cit.*

21. Fombrun, C.J. and E. Abrahamson "Producing Cognitive Environments: The Macro-Culture of Business Communities," Working Paper, New York University, Stern School of Business, 1990.

22. Sterling, C.H. and T.R. Haight, *The Mass Media: Aspen Institute Guide to Communication Industry Trends* (NY: Praeger, 1978) pp. 120–129.

23. For a well documented study of corporate contributions to political campaigns and their possible effects on legislators, see Etzioni, A., *Capital Corruption: The New Attack on American Democracy* (San Diego: Harcourt, Brace, and Jovanovich, 1984).

24. Clawson, D., A. Neustadl, and J. Bearden, "The Logic of Business Unity: Corporate Contributions in the 1980 Election," *American Sociological Review*, 1986, *51:* 797–811.

25. Berke, Richard, "Pragmatism Guides Political Gifts, a Study Shows," *New York Times:* 16 September 1990, 26.

26. Useem (1984) *op. cit.*, p. 83.

27. Kuhn, Susan, "How Business Helps Schools," *Fortune:* Special Issue on Education, 1990, 91–106.

28. Doeringer P. and M. Piore, *Internal Labor Markets and Manpower Analysis* (Lexington, MA: D.C. Heath, 1971).

29. Dreyfuss, Joel, "The Three R's on the Shop Floor," *Fortune:* Special Issue on Education, 1990, 86–89.

30. "Charity Doesn't Begin at Home Anymore," *Business Week:* 25 February 1991, 91.

31. There is a large literature on interlocks. For reviews, see Mintz B. and M. Schwartz, *The Power Structure of American Business* (Chicago, IL: University of Chicago Press, 1985), and Useem (1984) *op. cit.*

32. One of the earliest studies to point out the centrality of financial institutions was Levine, J., "The Sphere of Influence," *American Sociological Review*, 1972, *34:* 14–27.

33. Ratcliff, R.E., "Banks and Corporate Lending: An Analysis of the Impact of the Internal Structure of the Capitalist Class on the Lending Behavior of Banks," *American Sociological Review*, 1980, *45:* 553–570.

34. Lang, J.R. and D.E. Lockhart, "Increased Environmental Uncertainty and Changes in Board Linkage Patterns," *Academy of Management Journal*, 1990, *33:* 106–128.

35. Levine (1972), *op. cit.*, and Mintz and Schwartz (1987).

36. Ratcliff (1980, *op. cit.*

37. Mizruchi, M., "Similarity of Political Behavior among Large American Corporations," *American Journal of Sociology*, 1989, *94:* 401–424. Also Galas-

kiewicz, J. and R.S. Burt, "Interorganization Contagion in Corporate Philanthrophy," *Administrative Science Quarterly*, 1991, *36:* 88–105.

38. Useem (1984), *op. cit.*

39. Altheide, D. and J.M. Johnson, *Bureaucratic Propaganda* (Boston: Allyn and Bacon, 1980).

40. Salancik and Meindl (1984) *op. cit.*, p. 253.

41. Green, M. and R. Massie (eds.), *The Big Business Reader: Essays on Corporate America* (NY: Pilgrim Press, 1980).

42. Pfeffer J. and G. Salancik, *The External Control of Organizations: A Resource Dependence Perspective* (NY: Harper & Row, 1978).

43. Miles, R. with K. Cameron, *Coffin Nails and Corporate Strategy* (Englewood Cliffs, NJ: Prentice-Hall, 1982).

44. "Asia: A New Front in the War on Smoking," *Business Week:* 25 February 1991, 66.

45. C. Fombrun and M. Shanley "What's in a Name? Reputation-Building and Corporate Strategy," *Academy of Management Journal*, 1990, *33* 233–258.

46. For example, see Freeman, E., *Strategic Management: A Stakeholder Approach* (Boston: Pitman, 1984).

47. Cf. Pfeffer and Salancik (1978) *op. cit.*

48. Kogut, B., "Joint Ventures: Theoretical and Empirical Perspectives," *Strategic Management Journal*, 1988, *9:* 319–332.

49. Hennart, J.F., "A Transaction Costs Theory of Equity Joint Ventures," *Strategic Management Journal*, 1988, *9:* 361–374.

50. Berke, Richard, "Networks Quietly Abandon Competition and Unite to Survey Voters," *New York Times:* 7 November 1990, B1.

51. In Porter, M., *Competitive Advantage* (NY: Free Press, 1985).

52. "Will Uncle Sam be Dragged Kicking and Screaming into the Lab?" *Business Week:* 15 July 1991, 128–129. Cf. also Prestowitz, C., *Trading Places* (NY: Basic Books, 1988).

53. "Genetech is Climbing Down from its High Horse," *Business Week:* 11 February 1991, 79.

54. Hannan, M. and J. Freeman, "Structural Inertia and Organizational Change," *American Sociological Review*, 1984 *49:* 149–164.

55. Gerlach, L.P. and G.B. Palmer, "Adaptation through Evolving Interdependence," In P.C. Nystrom and W.H. Starbuck (eds.), *Handbook of Organization Design*, Vol. 1 (NY: Oxford University Press, 1981) pp. 323–381.

56. Berg, S. and P. Friedman, "Joint Ventures in American Industry: An Overview," *Mergers and Acquisitions*, 1978, *13:* 28–41.

57. Fombrun, C.J. and A. Kumaraswamy, (1990) "Strategic Alliances in Corporate Communities: The Evolution of Telecommunications 1980–1988," forthcoming in *Japan and World Business*, 1990, *3:* 15–32.

58. Friedman, P., S.V. Berg, and J. Duncan, "External vs. Internal Knowledge Acquisition: JV Activity and R&D Intensity," *Journal of Economics and Business*, 1979, *31:* 103–110.

59. Fombrun and Kumaraswamy (1990), *op. cit.*

60. Hoskisson, R.E. and M.A. Hitt, "Strategic Control Systems and Relative R&D Investment in Large Multiproduct Firms," *Strategic Management Journal*,

1988, *9:* 605–621. Also Bettis, R.A., "Performance Differences in Related and Unrelated Diversified Firms," *Strategic Management Journal,* 1981, *2:* 379–393.

61. Barton, S.L. and P.J. Gordon, "Corporate Strategy and Capital Structure," *Strategic Management Journal,* 1988, *9:* 623–632.

62. Rumelt, R., *Strategy, Structure, and Economic Performance* (Boston: Harvard Business School Press, 1974).

63. Conner, K.R., "Strategies for Product Cannibalism," *Strategic Management Journal,* 1988, *9:* 9–26.

64. Shan, W., "An Empirical Analysis of Organizational Strategies by Entrepreneurial High-Technology Firms," *Strategic Management Journal,* 1990, *11:* 129–140.

65. "The Silicon Valley Orchestra is Playing in Tune," *Business Week:* 25 March 1991, 32. Also, Markoff, John, "Group Seen Nearing PC Accord," *New York Times:* 9 February 1991, L29, 31.

66. Marsh, B. "Merchants Mobilize to Battle Wal-Mart in a Small Community," *Wall Street Journal: 5 June 1991, 1, A4.*

Chapter 8

1. "Compaq's New Boss Doesn't Even Have Time to Wince," *Business Week:* 11 November 1991, 41.

2. These figures include long-term compensation from stock options. See *Business Week,* Special Issue, "The Corporate Elite," January 1990. Also "The Flap over Executive Pay," *Business Week:* 6 May 1991, 90–96. And "How Much CEO's Really Make," *Fortune:* 17 June 1991, 72–80.

3. "CEO Disease," *Business Week:* 1 April 1991, 52–60.

4. Tosi, H.L. and L.R. Gomez-Mejia, "The Decoupling of CEO Pay and Performance: An Agency Theory Perspective," *Administrative Science Quarterly,* 1989, *34:* 169–189.

5. Wade, James, Charles O'Reilly III, and Ike Chandratat, "Golden Parachutes: CEOs and the Exercise of Social Influence," *Administrative Science Quarterly,* 1990, *35:* 587–603.

6. Mintzberg, H., *The Nature of Managerial Work* (Boston: MIT Press, 1973).

7. "Where 1990s-Style Management is Already Hard at Work," *Business Week:* 23 October 1989, 92–100.

8. For an integration of the conceptual and empirical work on the impact of employee participation on individual productivity and satisfaction, see Locke, E.A. and D. Schweiger, "Participation in Decision-Making: One More Look," in B. Staw (ed.), *Research in Organizational Behavior,* Vol. 1 (Greenwich, CT: JAI Press, 1979) pp. 265–339.

9. A review of the research on autocratic and participative leadership is provided by House, R.J. and M.L. Baetz, "Leadership: Some Empirical Generalizations and New Research Directions," in B. Staw (ed.), *Research in Organizational Behavior,* Vol. 1 (Greenwich, CT: JAI Press, 1979) pp. 341–423.

10. Bennis, W. and B. Nanus, *Leaders: The Strategies for Taking Charge* (NY: Harper and Row, 1985), p. 4.

11. Kirkpatrick, S.A. and E.A. Locke, "Leadership: Do Traits Matter?" *Academy of Management Executive*, 1991, 5(2): 48–60.

12. Cf. the original argument of Goffman, E., in *The Presentation of Self in Everyday Life* (NY: Doubleday, 1959). See also Westley, F. and H. Mintzberg, "Visionary Leadership and Strategic Management," *Strategic Management Journal*, 1989, *10:* 17–32.

13. Burns, J.M., *Leadership* (NY: Harper and Row, 1979).

14. Tichy, N., *Managing Strategic Change* (NY: Wiley, 1983).

15. Kotter, J., *The Leadership Factor* (NY: Free Press, 1988).

16. The study by Norburn, D., "The Chief Executive: A Breed Apart," *Strategic Management Journal*, 1989, *10:* 1–15.

17. Sonnenfeld, J., *A Hero's Farewell* (NY: Oxford University Press, 1988).

18. Cf. Bennis and Nanus (1985) *op. cit.*, p. 226.

19. Markoff, J. "IBM's Chief Criticizes Staff Again," *New York Times*. 19 June 1991, D1, D5.

20. "At Lucky-Goldstar, the Koos loosen the Reins," *Business Week:* 18 February 1991, 72–73.

21. Quoted in Quickel, S., "Welch on Welch," *Financial World:* 3 April 1990, 62.

22. Cf. Beer, M., R. Eisenstat, and B. Spector, *The Critical Path to Corporate Renewal* (Cambridge, MA: Harvard Business School Press, 1990).

23. Cf. Shrivastava, P., *Bhopal: Anatomy of a Crisis* (Cambridge, MA: Ballinger, 1987); Mitroff and Killman (1984). Kreps, A., "Sociological Inquiry and Disaster Research," *Annual Review of Sociology*, 1984, *10:* 309–330.

24. Guth, W.D. and I.C. MacMillan, "Strategy Implementation vs. Middle Management Self-Interest," *Strategic Management Journal*, 1986, *7:* 313–327.

25. Burgelman, R.A., "A Process Model of Internal Corporate Venturing in the Diversified Major Firm," *Administrative Science Quarterly*, 1983, *28:* 223–244.

26. In Wooldridge, B. and S.W. Floyd, "Strategic Process Effects on Consensus," *Strategic Management Journal*, 1989, *10:* 295—302.

27. Westley, F., "Middle Managers and Strategy: Microdynamics of Inclusion," *Strategic Management Journal*, 1990. *11:* 337–352.

28. "The Mess at Pru-Bache," *Business Week:* 4 March 1991, 66–72.

29. "The Inside Battle is About Over at First Boston," *Business Week:* 18 February 1991, 110–111.

30. House and Baetz (1979) *op. cit.*

31. Lawler, E., in *High Involvement Management* (San Francisco: Jossey-Bass, 1986), reviewed these studies.

32. Cotton, J.L., D.A. Vollrath, K. Froggatt, M.L. Lengnick-Hall, and K.R. Jennings, "Employee Participation: Diverse Forms and Different Outcomes," *Academy of Management Review*, 1988, *13:* 8–22.

33. The former were reviewed in Conte, M. and A. Tannenbaum, "Employee-Owned Companies: Is the Difference Measurable," *Monthly Labor Review*, 1978, *101:* 23–29. The latter figures are from Rosen, C., Klein, and K. Young, *Employee Ownership in America* (Lexington, MA: Lexington Books, 1986).

34. For a discussion of the impact of ownership on participation, see Rhodes, S.R. and R.M. Steers,"Conventional vs. Worker-Owned Organizations," *Human Relations*, 1981, *34:* 1013–1035.

35. "Offering Employees Stock Options They Can't Refuse," *Business Week:* 7 October 1991, 34.

36. Lawler (1986), *op. cit.*

37. Whyte, William F., "Models for Building and Changing Organizations," *Human Organization*, 1967, *26:* 22–31.

38. Cf. Kanter, R., *When Giants Learn to Dance* (NY: Touchstone, 1989) pp. 127–133.

39. Ulrich, D., "Tie the Corporate Knot: Gaining Complete Customer Commitment," *Sloan Management Review:* Summer 1989, 19–27.

40. Gupta, A.K. and V. Govindarajan, "Business Unit Strategy, Managerial Characteristics, and Business Unit Effectiveness at Strategy Implementation," *Academy of Management Journal*, 1984, *27:* 25–41.

41. Cf. Govindarajan, V., "Implementing Competitive Strategies at the Business Unit Level: Implications of Matching Managers to Strategies," *Strategic Management Journal*, 1989, *10:* 251–269.

42. Fuerbringer, J., "Suddenly, an Outsider Becomes Mr. Inside," *New York Times:* 19 August 1991, D1, D5.

43. Maidique, M.A. and R.H. Hayes, "The Art of High-Technology Management," *Sloan Management Review:* Winter 1984, 17–31.

44. Burgelman (1983) *op. cit.*; Pinchot, G., *Intrapreneuring* (NY: Harper and Row, 1985); and Peters, T.J. and R.H. Waterman, *In Search of Excellence: Lessons from America's Best-Run Companies* (NY: Harper and Row, 1982).

45. Cohen, R., "In Unforgiving Haste, A Shift atop Bantam," *New York Times:* 25 June 1991, D1, D5.

46. Ramirez, A., "New Chief for Philip-Morris," *New York Times:* 28 March 1991, D1. Also "From Chuck Wagon to Trail Boss of Marlboro Country," *Business Week:* 15 April 1991, 60–66.

47. "The Failed Vision," *Business Week:* 19 March 1990, 106–113.

48. Ramirez, A., "A President at American Express," *New York Times:* 23 July 1991, D5.

49. Gupta, A.K., "Contingency Linkages between Strategy and General Manager Characteristics: A Conceptual Examination," *Academy of Management Review*, 1984, *9:* 399–412.

50. "Taking Over the Helm of Germany, Inc." *Business Week:* 18 December 1989, 66–67.

51. Fombrun, C.J., "An Interview with Reginald Jones," *Organizational Dynamics*, 1981.

52. "Meet Du Pont's 'In-House Conscience,' " *Business Week:* 24 June 1991, 62–65.

53. Jay Lorsch's *Pawns or Potentates?* (Cambridge, MA: Harvard Business School Press, 1986).

54. Hambrick, D.C. and P.A. Mason, "Upper Echelons: The Organization as a Reflection of Its Top Managers," *Academy of Management Review*, 1984, *9:* 193–206.

55. Bantel, K.A. and S.E. Jackson, "Top Management and Innovations in Banking: Does the Composition of the Top Team Make a Difference?" *Strategic Management Journal*, 1989, *10:* 107–124.

56. Finkelstein, S. and D.C. Hambrick, "Top Management Team Tenure and Organizational Outcomes: The Moderating Role of Managerial Discretion," *Administrative Science Quarterly*, 1990, *35:* 484–503.

57. Dess G.G., "Consensus on Strategy Formulation and Organizational Performance: Competitors in a Fragmented Industry," *Strategic Management Journal*, 1987, *8:* 259–277.

58. Priem, R.L., "Top Management Team Group Factors, Consensus, and Firm Performance," *Strategic Management Journal*, 1990, *11:* 469–478.

59. "Bolting the Boardroom Door at Sears," *Business Week:* 13 May 1991, 86–87.

60. In keeping with theories of how firms are externally controlled, see Pfeffer, J. and G. Salancik, *The External Control of Organizations: A Resource Dependence Perspective* (NY: Harper and Row, 1978).

61. Kesner, I.F. and R.B. Johnson, "An Investigation of the Relationship between Board Composition and Stockholder Suits," *Strategic Management Journal*, 1990, *11:* 327–336.

62. For instance, see "Al Haig: Embattled in the Boardroom," *Business Week:* 17 June 1991, 108–109.

63. Eichenwald, K., "Salomon is Punished by Treasury, Which Partly Relents Hours Later," *New York Times:* 19 August 1991, 1, D4.

64. Tushman, M.L., W.H. Newman, and E. Romanelli, "Convergence and Upheaval: Managing the Unsteady Pace of Organizational Evolution," *California Management Review*, 1986, *29*(1).

65. "Compaq's New Boss Doesn't Even Have Time to Wince," *Business Week:* 11 November 1991, 41.

66. Even the popular press has taken note of the trend away from relying on insiders as CEOs, for example, "CEO Wanted. No Insiders, Please," *Business Week:* 12 August 1991, 44–45.

67. Hicks, J., "Goodyear Bets on an Outsider," *New York Times:* 10 June 1991, D1, D5.

68. Greiner, L.E. and A. Bhambri, "New CEO Intervention and Dynamics of Deliberate Strategic Change," *Strategic Management Journal*, 1989, *10:* 67–86.

69. For instance, see the study by E.J., Zajac "Economic and Behavioral Perspectives on the Structuring of CEO Compensation Contracts: Evidence from CEOs," Northwestern University, J.L. Kellogg Graduate School of Management, Working Paper, 1990.

70. Tosi, H.L. and L. Gomez-Mejia, "The Decoupling of CEO Pay and Performance: An Agency Theory Perspective," *Administrative Science Quarterly*, 1989, *34:* 169–189.

71. Hax, A.C. and N.S. Majluf, *The Strategy Conconept and Process.* (Englewood Cliffs, NJ: Prentice-Hall, 1990).

72. Cf. Hicks (1991), *op. cit.*

73. Finkelstein and Hambrick (1990), *op. cit.*

Chapter 9

1. Hylton, Richard, "Salomon's Remaining Challenges," *New York Times:* 19 August 1991, D1, D4.

2. Lohr, S., "Unraveling the Dealings of a Global Institution," *New York Times:* 30 July 1991, A14.

3. From Clifford's Testimony on BCCI to Congress, see *New York Times:* 12 September 1991, D7.

4. Pfeffer, J., "The Ambiguity of Leadership," *Academy of Management Review,* 1977, *2:* 104–112.

5. Bahrami, H. and S. Evans, "Emerging Organizational Regimes in High Technology Firms: The Bi-Modal Form," *Human Resource Management,* 1989, *28:* 25–50.

6. From Van Maanen, J. and E.H. Schein, "Toward a Theory of Organizational Socialization," in B. Staw (ed.) *Research in Organizational Behavior,* Vol. 1: (San Francisco: JAI Press, 1979) pp. 209–264.

7. For instance, see Ouchi, W., *Theory Z: How American Business Can Meet the Japanese Challenge* (Reading, MA: Addison-Wesley, 1980).

8. Sociologist Erving Goffman first described the unusual features of what he termed "total" institutions, cf. *Asylums* (NY: Doubleday/Anchor, 1961).

9. In Sethi, S.P., N. Namiki, and C.L. Swanson, *The False Promise of the Japanese Miracle* (Boston: Pitman Publishing, 1984) p. 270.

10. England, G.W., "Personal Value Systems of American Managers," *Academy of Management Journal,* 1967, *10:* 53–68. Also, England, G.W., *The Manager and His Values* (Cambridge, MA: Ballinger, 1975).

11. The review of this research by Beyer, J., "Ideologies, Values, and Decision Making in Organizations," in P. Nystrom and W.H. Starbuck (eds.), *Handbook of Organization Design,* Vol. 2 (NY: Oxford University Press, 1981), pp. 166–202.

12. Ronen, S. and O. Shenkar, "Clustering Countries on Attitudinal Dimensions: A Review and Synthesis," *Academy of Management Review,* 1985, *10:* 435–454.

13. Porac, J.F. and H. Thomas, "Taxonomic Mental Models in Competitor Definition," *Academy of Management Review,* 1990, *15:* 224–240.

14. Gregory, K.L., "Native-View Paradigms: Multiple Cultures and Culture Conflicts in Organizations," *Administrative Science Quarterly,* 1983, *28:* 359–376.

15. See the heavily cited article by DiMaggio, P.J. and W.W. Powell, "The Iron Cage Revisited: Institutional Isomorphism and Collective Rationality in Organizational Fields," *American Sociological Review,* 1983, *48:* 147–160.

16. Fombrun, C.J. and E. Abrahamson, "Producing Cognitive Environments: The Macro-Culture of Business Communities," New York University, Stern School of Business, Working Paper, 1990.

17. Berke, Richard, "Congress Votes to Halt Rail Strike Hours After Thousands Walk Off Job," *New York Times:* 18 April 1991, B8.

18. Norris, F., "Such Is War for Salomon," *New York Times:* 19 August 1991, A1, D5.

19. Colin Camerer and Ari Vepsalainen suggested these as underlying dimensions of company cultures, in "The Economic Efficiency Corporate Culture," *Strategic Management Journal*, 1988, *9:* 115–126.

20. For an argument about the efficiency of cultural rules in firms, see Wilkins, A.L. and W.G. Ouchi, "Efficient Cultures: Exploring the Relationshpi between Culture and Organizational Performance," *Administrative Science Quarterly*, 1983, *28:* 468–481.

21. For example, see Fombrun, C.J., "Corporate Culture, Environment, and Strategy," *Human Resource Management*, 1983, *22:* 139–152.

22. Cf. Wilkins and Ouchi (1983), *op. cit.*

23. Cf. Ouchi (1980) *op. cit.*; and Deal T. and Kennedy, A., *Corporate Cultures: The Rites and Rituals of Corporate Life* (Reading, MA: Addison-Wesley, 1982).

24. As Peters and Waterman found in their sample of "excellent" companies. See Peters, T. and R. Waterman, Jr., *In Search of Excellence: Lessons from America's Best-Run Companies* (NY: Harper and Row, 1982).

25. See the chapter by John Van Maanen and Steve Barley (1985) in Frost book.

26. See Fombrun, C., N. Tichy, and M. Devanna, *Strategic Human Resource Management* (NY: Wiley, 1984).

27. Cf. Kidder, T., *The Soul of the New Machine* (Boston: Little Brown, 1981).

28. Berg, N., "Strategic Planning in Conglomerate Companies," *Harvard Business Review, 43:* 1965, 79–92.

29. In Lorsch, J.W. and S.A. Allen III, *Managing Diversity and Interdependence: An Organizational Study of Multidivisional Firms.* (Boston, MA: Division of Research, Graduate School of Business Administration, Harvard University, 1973).

30. Cf. Galbraith, J. and R. Kazanjian, *Strategy Implementation* (St. Paul, MN: West Publishing Co., 1986) p. 70.

31. Shapiro, E., "Will Intramural Squabbling Derail Debt-Ridden Sony?" *New York Times:* 11 August 1991, F5.

32. Wayne, L. "Remaking Kidder in GE's Image," *New York Times:* 29 January 1989, B1, B2.

33. Cf. Kanter, R.M., "The Attack on Pay," *Harvard Business Review:* March-April 1987, 60–67.

34. Weitzman, M., *The Share Economy: Conquering Stagflation* (Cambridge, MA: Harvard University Press, 1984).

35. Lawler, E., in *High Involvement Management* (San Francisco: Jossey-Bass, 1986) reviews incentives for building a sense of ownerhsip and involvement in firms.

36. Kanter, R., *Change Masters* (NY: Simon & Schuster, 1983).

37. Kanter, R., *When Giants Learn to Dance* (NY: Touchstone, 1989).

38. Maidique, M.A., "Entrepreneurs, Champions, and Technological Innovation," *Sloan Management Review*, Winter 1980, 59– 76.

39. Cf. Burgelman "Corporate Entrepreneurship and Strategic Management: Insights from a Process Study," *Management Science*, 1983, *29:* 1349–1364.

40. Cf. Tichy, N.M. and R. Charam, "Speed, Simplicity, Self-Confidence," *Harvard Business Review:* September-October 1989, 112–120.

41. "Big Changes are Galvanizing General Electric," *Business Week:* 18 December 1989, 100–102.
42. Cf. McCann, Joseph, *Sweet Success: How NutraSweet Created a Billion Dollar Business* (NY: Business One/Irwin, 1990).
43. The details of this joint venture were presented in Kanter (1989), *op. cit.*
44. "Merck Needs More Gold from the White Coats," *Business Week:* 18 March 1991, 102–104.
45. Feder, Barnaby, "Helping Corporate America Hew to the Straight and Narrow," *New York Times:* 3 November 1991, F5.
46. Johnston, David, "Congress Gets Sentence Guide on Corporate Crime," *New York Times:* 28 April 1991, 26.

Chapter 10

1. Shapiro, Elen, "The Doughboy Gets a Streamlined Look," *New York Times:* 22 April 1990, B5.
2. *New York Times:* 30 October 1990; also 7 November 1990.
3. "Raging Bull: The Trimmer New Look of Merrill Lynch," *Business Week:* 25 November 1991, 218–221.
4. *New York Times:* 8 November 1990; also 15 April 1991: D10.
5. Eichenwald, K., "Changing the Culture of Spending at Merrill Lynch," *New York Times:* 4 February 1990, 12.
6. Based on the memo of John Akers to IBM employees and John Markoff's article, "The First Draft of IBM's Future," *New York Times:* 6 December 1991, D1-D2. See also "The New IBM," *Business Week:* 16 December 1991, 112–118.
7. "Hewlett Packard Rethinks Itself," *Business Week:* 1 April 1991, 76–79.
8. "Warner-Lambert: Can R&D Take It to the Top Tier," *Business Week:* 24 September 1990, 66–68.
9. "Merck Needs More Gold from the White Coats," *Business Week:* 18 March 1991, 102–104.
10. For a study that showed how networks represent structure better than standard charts, see Tichy, N.M. and C.J. Fombrun, (1979) "Network Analysis in Organizational Setting," *Human Relations*.
11. In Stanley Davis, *Future Perfect* (Reading, MA: Addison-Wesley, 1987), p. 197.
12. Cf. Hrebiniak and Joyce (1985).
13. Mintzberg, H., in *The Structuring of Organizations* (Englewood Cliffs, NJ: Prentice-Hall, 1979), provides an integrative review of research on organization structure.
14. "Half Audie Murphy, Half Jack Welch," *Business Week:* 4 March 1991, 42–43.
15. "Can Rod Canion Stop Compaq's Erosion?" *Business Week:* 4 November 1991, 134–140.
16. For an early discussion of organizations as networks, see Miles, R.E. and C.C.

Snow, "Organizations: New Concepts for New Forms," *California Management Review*, 1986, *28:* 62–73.

17. Piore, M. and C. Sabel, *The Second Industrial Divide: Possibilities for Prosperity* (NY: Basic Books, 1984).

18. Davis, S.M., *Future Perfect* (Reading, MA: Addison-Wesley, 1987).

19. Ashby, W.R., *An Introduction to Cybernetics* (London: Chapman and Hall, 1956).

20. Bartlett, C. and S. Ghoshal's study of transnational firms, *Manging across Borders* (Boston: Harvard Business School Press, 1989).

21. Maidique, M.A., "Entrepreneurs, Champions, and Technological Innovation," *Sloan Management Review:* Winter 1980, 59–76.

22. Gilbert, R. and D. Newberry, "Preemptive Patenting and the Persistence of Monopoly," *American Economic Review*, 1982, *72:* 514–526.

23. Conner, K.R., "Strategies for Product Cannibalism," *Strategic Management Journal*, 1988, *9:* 9–26.

24. Miller, D., "Relating Porter's Business Strategies to Environment and structure: Analysis and Performance Implications," *Academy of Management Journal*, 1988, *31:* 280–308.

25. Cf. Pinchot, G., *Intrapreneuring* (NY: Harper and Row, 1985).

26. For instance, see Allen, T.J. and S. Cohen, "Information Flow in R&D Labs," *Administrative Science Quarterly*, 1969, *14:* 12–19.

27. Lippman, S. and R. Rumelt, "Uncertain Imitability: An Analysis of Interfirm Differences in Efficiency under Competition," *Bell Journal of Economics*, 1982, *13:* 418–438.

28. The article by Jack Brittain and John Freeman in Kimberly J., R. Miles, and Associates, *The Organizational Life Cycle* (San Francisco: Jossey-Bass, 1980).

29. Lambkin, M., "Order of Entry and Performance in New Markets," *Strategic Management Journal*, 1988 *9:* 127–140.

30. Pennings, J., "Strategically Interdependent Organizations," in P. Nystrom and W.H. Starbuck (eds.), *Handbook of Organization Design*, Vol. 1 (NY: Oxford University Press, 1981) pp. 433–455.

31. According to Brittain and Freeman (1980), *op. cit.*

32. Davis, Stanely, *Future Perfect* (Reading, MA: Addison-Wesley, 1987).

33. Jay R. Galbraith, *Organization Design* (Reading, MA: Addison-Wesley, 1983).

34. Rumelt, R., *Strategy, Structure and Economic Performance* (Boston: Harvard Business School Press, 1974).

35. Porter, M., *Competitive Advantage* (NY: Free Press, 1985) pp. 383–384.

36. Stead, D., "A Parting at Waterford Wedgwood," *New York Times:* 14 December 1990, D1, D8.

37. Williams, J.R., B.L. Paez, and L. Sanders, "Conglomerates Revisited," *Strategic Management Journal*, *9:* 1988, 403–414.

38. Sherman, S. "Inside the Mind of Jack Welch," *Fortune:* 27 March 1989, 42.

39. Paré T., "How to Cut the Cost of Headquarters," *Fortune:* 11 September 1989, 189–196.

40. "Pumping up the Baby Bells' R&D Arm," *Business Week:* 5 August 1991, 68–69.

41. "Hidden Japan," *Business Week:* 26 August 1991, 34–38.

42. "If You Control... Computers, You Control the World," *Business Week:* 23 July 1990, 31.

43. "The Future of Silicon Valley," *Business Week:* 5 February 1990, 54–60.

44. Markoff, J., "Creating a Giant Computer Highway," *New York Times:* 2 September 1990, Section 3, pp. 1, 6.

45. "How Do You Build an Information Highway?" *Business Week:* 16 September 1991, 109–112.

46. Andrews, E., "Zenith's Strategy Pressed for Time," *New York Times:* 21 November 1990, D10.

47. Sanger, D., "Goldstar's Stake in Zenith Involves Widespread Links," *New York Times:* 26 March 1991, 1, D10.

48. Sanger, D., "Advanced TV Makes Debut in Japan," *New York Times:* 6 December 1990, D1–2.

49. Fisher, L., "AT&T and Zenith in Venture," *New York Times:* 18 December 1990, D1, D13. Also Andrews, E., "U.S. Makes Gains in Race to Develop Advanced TV," *New York Times:* 21 December 1990, 1, D16. Also Andrews, E., "Six Systems in Search of Approval as HDTV Moves to the Testing Lab," *New York Times:* 18 August 1991, F7.

50. "Advanced TV Collaboration," *New York Times:* 16 August 1991.

In Conclusion

1. Wilson, J., *Bureaucracy* (NY: Basic Books, 1989) for a review of public bureaucracies.

2. Etzioni, A., in The Active Society (NY: Free Press, 1968), provided a useful platform for conceiving how a more mobilized and involved society would act.

3. Wilson (1989), *op. cit.*, p. 23.

4. Hill, P., G. Foster, and T. Gendler, "High Schools with Character: Alternatives to Bureaucracy," RAND Corporation, Fall 1990. The study was favorably renewed in an article by Robert McFadden, "A Report on Urban Schools Urges a Variety of Changes," *New York Times:* 22 October 1990, B3.

5. Fiske, E.B. with S. Reed, *Smart Schools, Smart Kids: Why Do Some Schools Work?* (NY: Simon & Schuster, 1991).

6. Ann Reilly Dowd, "How Washington Can Pitch In," *Fortune:* Special Issue on Education, 1990, 53–62.

7. Clymer, A., "Bush to Propose Broad Changes in U.S. Schools," *New York Times:* 14 April 1991, 1, 22.

8. "Bush Unveils Education Bill Calling for Parental Choice," *New York Times:* 19 April 1991, A1, B7.

9. "The Best B-Schools," *Business Week:* 29 October 1990, 52–66.

10. "First Report of the Professional Programs Review Committee," New York University, Leonard N. Stern School of Business, 15 January 1990.

11. "Chicago's B-School Goes Touchy-Feely," *Business Week:* 27 November 1989, 140.

12. Deutsch, C., "The MBA Rate Race," *New York Times:* Education Issue, 4 November 1990, 50–52.

13. DePalma, A., "Ivy Universities Deny Price-Fixing but Agreed to Avoid it in the Future," *New York Times:* 23 May 1991, 1, B13.

14. Celis, W. III, "All Involved Share Blame for Research Overcharges," *New York Times:* 14 April 1991, L23.

15. Brozan, N., "Stanford President's Decision is Praised," *New York Times:* 31 July 1991, A16.

16. See Peter F. Drucker, *The New Realities* (NY: Harper & Row, 1989), p. 194.

17. Cf. Lawler, E., *High Involvement Management* (San Francisco: Jossey-Bass, 1986).

18. "Here Comes GM's Saturn," *Business Week:* 9 April 1990, 56–62.

19. Hoerr, J. "What Should Unions Do?" *Harvard Business Review:* May-June 1991, 30–45.

20. Kilborn, P., "Scrapping 'Us' versus 'Them,' Industry is Giving Workers a Say and a Stake," *New York Times:* 22 November 1991, A24.

21. Westra, L.S., "Whose Loyal Agent? Towards an Ethic of Accounting," *Journal of Business Ethics,* 1986, *5:* 119–128.

22. Boland, R.J., Jr., "Myth and Technology in the American Accounting Profession," *Journal of Management Studies,* 1982, *19:* 109–127.

23. Cowan, A.L., "Rethinking Obligations of Auditors," *New York Times:* 29 July 1991, D1, D3.

24. "The Global Push to Privatize," *Business Week:* 21 October 1991, 49–56.

25. Wolf, Charles, Jr., *Markets or Governments: Choosing Between Imperfect Alternatives* (Cambridge, MA: MIT Press, 1988). Also Savas, E.S., *Privatization: The Key to Better Government* (Chatham, NJ: Chatham House, 1987).

26. Wilson, James, *Bureaucracy* (NY: Basic Books, 1989) p. 353.

27. Leon, M., "Tylenol Fights Back," *Public Relations Journal:* March 1983, 9–12.

28. The seminal article on punctuated equilibrium was by N. Eldredge and S.J. Gould, "Punctuated Equilibria: An Alternative to Phyletic Gradualism." In T.J. Schopf (ed.), *Models in Paleobiology* (San Francisco: Freeman, Cooper & Co., 1972), pp. 82–115.

29. Kennedy, P., *The Rise and Fall of the Great Powers* (NY: Random House, 1987), for an analysis of the decline of various empires.

Index

About the Author

Charles J. Fombrun is Research Professor of Management at the Leonard N. Stern School of Business at New York University. Before coming to NYU, he taught at Columbia University and The Wharton School. Dr. Fombrun has authored numerous articles that discuss how managers conceive and carry out strategies, and how companies compete, collaborate, and change. His work has been widely published in books and journals, including *Organization Dynamics, Sloan Management Review, Journal of Business Strategy, Administrative Science Quarterly,* and *Academy of Management Journal,* as well as *The New York Times*. He is coauthor of the acclaimed *Strategic Human Resources Management*.